AGAINST DEMOCRACY

AGAINST DEMOCRACY

JASON BRENNAN

WITH A NEW PREFACE BY THE AUTHOR

PRINCETON UNIVERSITY PRESS
Princeton and Oxford

Copyright © 2016 by Princeton University Press

Preface to the paperback edition © 2017 by Princeton University Press

Published by Princeton University Press
41 William Street, Princeton, New Jersey 08540

In the United Kingdom: Princeton University Press
6 Oxford Street, Woodstock, Oxfordshire OX20 1TR

press.princeton.edu

Cover design by Faceout Studio.

All Rights Reserved

Fifth printing, and first paperback printing, 2017

Paper ISBN 978-0-691-17849-3

The Library of Congress has cataloged the cloth edition of this book as follows:

Names: Brennan, Jason, 1979– author.
Title: Against democracy / Jason Brennan.
Description: Princeton : Princeton University Press, [2016] | Includes bibliographical
    references and index.
Identifiers: LCCN 2016001826 | ISBN 9780691162607 (hardcover : acid-free paper)
Subjects: LCSH: Democracy—Philosophy. | Knowledge, Theory of—Political aspects. |
    Expertise—Political aspects.
Classification: LCC JC423 .B7834 2016 | DDC 321.8—dc23
LC record available at http://lccn.loc.gov/2016001826

British Library Cataloging-in-Publication Data is available

This book has been composed in Sabon Next LT Pro and Univers LT Std

Printed on acid-free paper. ∞

Printed in the United States of America

10 9 8 7 6

CONTENTS

PREFACE TO THE 2017 PAPERBACK EDITION

In 2016, democracy had a bad year. By contrast, critics of democracy had a good year. Witness:

- I wrote about nineteen invited op-eds and magazine articles pointing out the flaws in democracy. There wasn't the same kind of interest in 2014 or 2012 when I was writing about this.
- Similarly, I went on public radio to discuss my thesis that some voters should not vote. Listeners called in to say, "I know! What do we do?" I had done the same program on same topic a year before; then, listeners called in to demand, "How dare you?"
- I had multiple media inquiries per day from October through December.
- *Against Democracy* enjoyed widespread media coverage in major outlets in the US, Canada, the United Kingdom, Germany, Ireland, France, Sweden, Norway, Switzerland, the Netherlands, and elsewhere. So far, it's being translated into six languages.

This isn't just a brag sheet, (okay maybe a little). Rather, it's telling. I've been writing books and articles which challenge our most sacred ideas about political participation since 2009. Yet in 2016, people were unusually inclined to listen. They might not agree, but they are now much more willing to consider it.

In the Brexit referendum, "Leave" won by a slim margin. A month before the Brexit vote, the polling form Ipsos Mori discovered that the British public was systematically misinformed about the facts relevant to the decision. For instance, Leave voters believed that EU immigrants comprised 20 percent of the UK's population. Remain voters estimated 10 percent. They were both wrong, though the Leave voters were *more* wrong: The truth is closer to 5 percent. On average, both Leave and Remain voters overestimated by a factor of 40 to 100 how much the United Kingdom pays in Child Benefits to people in other countries. Both vastly underestimated the amount of foreign investment from the European Union and vastly overestimated the amount from China.[1] This doesn't prove, of course, that Remain was the right decision. But it sure looks fishy that the more a person got the relevant facts wrong, the more likely she was to vote Leave.

The United States had its own dance of the dunces. I am skeptical that Donald Trump will turn out to be quite the disaster that my anxiety-ridden colleagues think he'll be. But, nevertheless, Trump's initial support in the primaries came from unusually low-information voters. He won the nomination in part because the Republican primaries split the higher information voters. Once he became the presumptive nominee, the party tribalism I describe in chapters two and three of this book took over; many of the "Never Trump" Republicans held their noses and voted Trump.

The American Left had its own vicious display of misinformed economic populism. Bernie Sanders pushed roughly the same protectionist, anti-immigrant agenda, as Trump. Economist Brad DeLong commented:

> The political truthiness has been flying thick and fast on this subject for decades now. Politicians are taking claims that have a very tenuous connection to economic reality—claims that *feel true*—and running with them, sometimes out of ignorance, sometimes because of cynical calculation.
>
> . . . Trump and Sanders were apocalyptic in their discussions of trade, and then Clinton abandoned the truth, too.[2]

As I discuss in chapter 2, the economic ideas Trump and Sanders pushed do not simply fly against hundreds of years of economic research and mountains of empirical evidence. In addition, those economic ideas that support protectionism and promote antagonism toward immigrants are negatively correlated with political information. On average, high information voters, regardless of their background demographics or their background political affiliation, support free trade and increased immigration.

Some popular press reviewers noted that *Against Democracy* contained no references to Trump or Brexit. When I turned in the final manuscript, Trump was gaining a lead, but he was not yet the nominee. The Brexit referendum had not yet taken place. I did not expect either of these developments.

Against Democracy is not a response to Trump or Brexit, though both illustrate my worries. My criticisms of democracy are based on long-standing, systematic empirical trends. About 65 years ago, we started measuring how much voters know.. The results were depressing then and they are depressing now. For as long as we've been measuring, the mean, model, and median voters have been misinformed or ignorant about basic political information; they have known even less about more advanced social scientific knowledge. Their ignorance and misinformation causes them to support policies and candidates they would not support if they were better-informed. As a result, we get suboptimal and sometimes quite bad political outcomes. Since, as I argue in chapters four and five, democracy and the equal right to vote have no intrinsic value, we should be open to experimenting with other forms of governance. Justice requires "one person, one vote" only if it turns out, empirically, that doing so generates more substantively good outcomes than other forms of government.

I'm a critic of democracy, but I'm also a fan. In, "Democracy and Freedom," forthcoming in the *Oxford Handbook of Freedom*, I argue that as a matter of fact, democracy is positively correlated with a number of important outcomes, and this appears not to be mere correlation, but causation.[3] Democracies do a better job of protecting economic and civil liberties than non-democracies, and democracies tend to be richer than non-democracies. Right now, the best places to live in the world are generally quite democratic. But given that we know democracy has systematic flaws, we should be open to investigating and possibly experimenting with other alternatives.

In *Against Democracy*, I defend experimenting with what most people would regard as the most offensive alternative: epistocracy. Epistocratic forms of government retain most of the normal features of republican representative government. Political power is widespread rather than concentrated in the hands of the few. Powers are separated. There are checks and balances. But, by law, epistocracies do not automatically distribute fundamental political power evenly. Rather, by law, in some way or other, more competent or knowledgeable citizens have slightly more political power than less competent or knowledgeable citizens.

In chapter one, I introduce three models of voter behavior. Hobbits are low-information citizens with low interest and low levels of participation in politics. Hobbits generally have unstable or only weak ideological commitments. In contrast, hooligans are higher-information citizens who have strong commitments to politics and to their political identity. They are beset by cognitive biases, such as confirmation bias or intergroup bias. For them, politics is largely a team sport. (I forgot to acknowledge Drew Stonebraker in the original hardcover; Drew suggested to me that I use the label "hooligan".) Vulcans are an ideal type—perfectly rational, high-information thinkers with no inappropriate loyalty to their beliefs.

I argue in chapter 2 that nearly all citizens fall on the hobbit-hooligan spectrum. The average non-voter in the United States is a hobbit and the average voter is a hooligan. But the problem is that many philosophical theories of democracy presume that citizens will behave like vulcans. Philosophers presume or hope that getting citizens involved in politics will transform them from hobbits into vulcans. But, I argue in chapter 3, our best evidence is that political engagement tends to turn hobbits into hooligans, and tends to make hooligans even worse hooligans. Democracy is the rule of hobbits and hooligans.

So, is epistocracy therefore rule of vulcans? I should make it clear here: no. My point in invoking the idea of vulcans was not say that vulcans should rule, or that epistocracies will successfully empower the vulcans over the hooligans and hobbits. There are probably just too few vulcans out there.

Further, while it's relatively easy to distinguish high-information from low-information voters, it's more difficult to test for cognitive bias on a large scale. That's not to say it can't be done. We could in-deed create a test that both examines how much knowledge a person has, and also tests to see if they interpret data in a biased way. For in-stance, in chapter two I discuss Dan Kahan's studies on cognitive bias. We could use his kinds of questions to distinguish high-information vulcans from high-information hooligans.

Still, my point is less ambitious: realistically, epistocracy would be the rule of hooligans, but it would be a better batch of hooligans than what we get in democracy. Alternatively, one of my epistocratic proposals—what I call government by simulated oracle—uses hooli-gan and hobbit voters to estimate what the vulcans would want.

Many journalists have asked me, since there's little chance any country will implement epistocracy in the short term, what's the practical upshot of this book? What, if anything, can we do now? Bryan Caplan has proposed a national "Voter Achievement Exam." Each year (or maybe before an election) the government offers a vol-untary test which covers basic political information and basic social scientific matters. Citizens who take the exam get a cash prize, pays a thousand dollars for getting 90–100 percent of the questions right, five hundred dollars for getting 80–89 percent right, one hundred dollars for 70–79 percent, and zero dollars for anything less.[4] The gov-ernment could do this in lieu of funding civics education—after all, civics education doesn't work, so cutting it out of the curriculum has no negative consequences. (The reason it doesn't work is explained in chapter two: rational ignorance. Most citizens have no incentive to remember the civics information they learn in school.) This pro-posal doesn't run afoul of the US constitution. As Caplan puts it, it's a "cheap, inoffensive way to make democracy work better."[5]

Another idea: we should change our civic culture. I've been argu-ing since "Polluting the Polls" was published in 2009 that the mantra "Get out the vote! Every vote counts!" is dangerous. Most citizens are not doing us any favor by voting. Asking everyone to vote is like asking everyone to litter.

Against Democracy was published in late August, 2016. I know some symposia are forthcoming, but as of February 2017, when I'm writing this, there haven't been any major peer-reviewed papers criticizing it. Philosophy and political science have notoriously slow turnaround times. Thus, I don't yet know what the major criticisms of the book will be, though I'm sure they're coming.

Still, from the thirty or so public talks I've given so far on this book, I know that what I call the "Demographic Objection to Epistocracy" most troubles audiences. Note that this is not a new objection others have raised since publication, but rather an objection I had already discussed in chapter 8, and once which I often describe to audiences. The Demographic Objection goes as follows:

Most epistocratic systems give more knowledgeable citizens greater political power than less knowledgeable citizens. However, surveys of basic political knowledge routinely find that political knowledge is not shared equally by members of all demographic groups. Some demographic groups, particularly *advantaged* groups, tend to have more political knowledge than other, *disadvantaged* groups. In particular, whites tend to know more than blacks, the rich more than the poor, the employed more than the unemployed, and men more than women.[6] Thus, the epistocratic electorate will tend to be whiter, richer, better employed, and more male than a democratic electorate.

This isn't the complete objection. There are two ways of filling it in. One way says that the mere fact that epistocracy could lead to unequal demographic representation is unfair and unjust, regardless of whether this in turn produces worse outcomes or not. A second, I think more troubling version, holds that because epistocracy could have these demographic disparities, epistocracy will tend to produce substantively bad outcomes, in particular, outcomes that help the advantaged and harm the disadvantaged.

I've have a paper coming out which provides a more thorough and substantive response to the Demographic Objection than what appears in chapter 8. Anyone interested can email me for a copy. Here, I'll just recount a related story:

A student at a prominent university asked me about the Demographic Objection. She wondered, If members of some disadvantaged group vote, won't the government respond to their interests properly? If they fail to vote, won't the government ignore their interests?

I responded with something like this: Imagine I have a magic wand. If I wave it, it will induce, let's say, every black person to vote. But they will all vote for Donald Trump rather than Hillary Clinton, and for Republicans rather than Democrats. In fact, henceforth, it will cause blacks always to vote for the equivalent of Donald Trump, or for candidates who support political policies you dislike, such as reductions in the welfare state, reduced funding for education, and an increase in the war on drugs. Do you want me to wave the magic wand?

She said, No, of course not. So far, every person to whom I've posed that question has also said, No, of course not. This shows that the people asking the question agree with me—it matters *how* one votes, not just *that* one votes. When members of a group vote, if they are misinformed, they might not be helping themselves, but instead shooting themselves in their collective foot. Indeed, the student in question (and others) even agreed that Donald Trump wasn't particularly good for rural white Americans, his main demographic.

What we might call the Naïve Theory of Democracy holds that if you (and people like you) vote, then the government will support your objective interests, regardless of how you vote. According to the Naïve Theory, you could vote to shoot yourself in the face, but because you voted, the government would instead help you. There is little empirical support for the Naïve Theory. In the past six months, I've learned few audience members really believe it.

While Against Democracy focuses on epistocracy as an alternative to democracy, it's certainly not the only alternative. My deeper view is that because democracy is not inherently just, we should look for better functioning alternatives. The philosophers Ben Saunders and Alex Guerrero have defended sortition and lottocracies—systems which distribute power randomly—on the grounds that certain versions of such systems are likely to be smarter and more fair than democracy. The economist Robin Hanson and law and economics professor Michael Abramowicz have argued that we should use specialized betting markets to choose policy. Call their favored form of government "futarchy" or "predictocracy." Betting markets have greater predictive accuracy than polls of experts or of laypeople, and there are ways of using such markets to choose policy. Legal theorist Ilya Somin argues we should have more decentralized government and more "foot-voting." If people could easily move from one polity to another, this would both A) give people a strong incentive to be informed and choose where to live wisely and B) would give government leaders an incentive to produce better policy. I don't officially take a stand here on any of these ideas, but I'm attracted to each of them, especially futarchy.

Democracy is a tool, nothing more. If we can find a better tool, we should feel free to use it. Indeed, as I argue in chapter 6, we have a duty to use it. Justice is justice. Bad decisions are not rendered just simply by political fiat. Political decisions are high stakes. How dare anyone make such decisions incompetently?

NOTES TO THE PREFACE

1. "The Perils of Perception and the EU," Ipsos MORI Website, www.ipsos-mori.com/researchpublications/researcharchive/3742/The-Perils-of-Perception-and-the-EU.aspx.

2. "NAFTA and Other Trade Deals Have Not Gutted American Manufacturing—Period," Vox Website, www.vox.com/the-big-idea/2017/1/24/14363148/trade-deals -nafta-wto-china-job-loss-trump.

3. Jason Brennan, "Democracy and Freedom," in *The Oxford Handbook of Freedom*, ed David Schmidtz. (New York: Oxford University Press, 2017).

4. Bryan Caplan, "A Cheap, Inoffensive Way to Make Democracy Work Better," Library of Economics and Liberty Website, econlog.econlib.org/archives/2013/10/a_cheap_inoffen.html

5. Ibid.

6. See, for example, Delli-Carpini and Keeter 1996, 135–177.

PREFACE AND ACKNOWLEDGMENTS

Ten years ago, I found most philosophical democratic theory perplexing. To me, philosophers and political theorists seemed too impressed with symbolic arguments for democracy. They constructed highly idealized accounts of the democratic process that bore little semblance to real-world democracy. These kinds of ideas seemed entirely unmotivated. Politics isn't a poem, I thought, and under those ideal conditions, we'd want to be anarchists, not democrats.

Later I realized that my dissatisfaction with philosophical democratic theory was a reason to work in the field rather than one to avoid it. At the very least, democratic theory needs someone to play devil's advocate. Although I'm happy to play that role, in true devilish fashion I now doubt whether I'm defending the devil, and philosophers and political theorists are defending the angels.

Many of my colleagues entertain a somewhat romantic view of politics: politics brings us together, educates and civilizes us, and makes us civic friends. I see politics as doing the opposite: it pulls us apart, stultifies and corrupts us, and makes us civic enemies.

Against Democracy is in a sense the third part in a trilogy of books, including 2011's *The Ethics of Voting* and 2014's *Compulsory Voting: For and Against*. While *Against Democracy* takes up themes from the other two, it defends the most ambitious claims. My half of *Compulsory Voting* argues that compulsory voting is unjustified. *The Ethics of Voting* maintains that the best ways to exercise civic virtue occur outside politics, and that most citizens have a moral obligation to refrain from voting, even if they have a right to vote. This work goes further. For that reason, if the reasoning here fails, that doesn't mean the arguments in the other books do. Here I'll contend that if the facts turn out the right way, some people ought not have the right to vote, or ought to have weaker voting rights than others.

I thank my editor at Princeton University Press, Rob Tempio, for suggesting I take up what became one of the major themes of this book: politics is bad for us, and most of us should, for the sake of our characters, minimize our involvement. (This may or may not be something Rob agrees with.) I thank Geoffrey Brennan for suggesting I pursue the second major theme: in light of widespread voter incompetence, epistocracy is superior to democracy. A few years ago, after reading *The Ethics of Voting*, Geoff asked me, "If voters are that bad, why should we put up with democracy at all?" My attempt to answer that question led to a series of articles and ultimately the present work. (Again, Geoff probably does not agree, but he thought I should explore the argument.)

Most of the material here is new, but it draws significantly on, and in some cases incorporates large parts of, my previously published material, including the following articles and anthology chapters: "The Right to a Competent Electorate," *Philosophical Quarterly* 61 (2011): 700–724; "Political Liberty: Who Needs It?" *Social Philosophy and Policy* 29 (2012): 1–27; "Epistocracy and Public Reason," in *Democracy in the Twenty-First Century*, eds. Ann Cudd and Sally Scholz (Berlin: Springer, 2013), 191–204; and "How Smart Is Democracy? You Can't Answer That A Priori," *Critical Review* 26 (2014): 4–30.

It's important to note one deliberative omission: one of the popular arguments for democracy and against epistocracy is that epistocracy is supposedly incompatible with public reason liberalism. I decided against taking on that claim here for two reasons. First, I'm deeply skeptical of the public reason project, but I didn't want to devote half a book to debating it. Second, as I've already argued (Brennan 2013), epistocracy and public reason liberalism are in fact compatible. Since public reason liberals haven't yet responded to that contention, I didn't have anything new to add here.

Thanks to audiences at La Sierra University, the University of Buffalo, Cal State at Sacramento, the Public Choice Society, Wellesley

College, Duke University, the American Political Science Association, Charles Sturt University, the Center for Applied Philosophy and Public Ethics, Australian National University, Georgia State University, James Madison University, the Wharton School of Business, Hamden-Sydney College, the University of Richmond, the Association of Private Enterprise Education, Linfield College, Bowling Green State University, the University of North Carolina at Chapel Hill, and Christopher Newport University for their valuable feedback on many of the arguments presented in this book.

For countless valuable discussions of this topic over the years, I especially thank Geoffrey Brennan, Bryan Caplan, David Estlund, Loren Lomasky, and Ilya Somin. Also, I greatly thank John Beverley, Jon Houston, Sean McNamara, Jake Monaghan, Paul Poenicke, and Yonatan Schreiber of the Lawless Buffalo group at the University of Buffalo for hosting a workshop on an early draft. I'm also grateful to Scott Althaus, Richard Arneson, Neera Badhwar, Christian Barry, Peter Boettke, Trevor Burrus, Elizabeth Busch, Sam Clark, Andrew I. Cohen, Andrew J. Cohen, Daniel Cohen, Ross Corbett, Ann Cudd, Richard Dagger, Vladimiros Dagkas-Tsoukalas, Ryan Davis, Christopher Freiman, Jeffrey Friedman, Michael Fuerstein, Gerald Gaus, Robert Goodin, Paul Gowder, Robert Gressis, Lisa Hill, John Holstead, Peter Jaworski, Hélène Landemore, Daniel Layman, Seth Lazar, Andrew Lister, Loren Lomasky, Aaron Maltais, Steven Maloney, Simon Cabulea May, Pierre Moraro, Tom Mulligan, Michael Munger, Guido Pincione, Aaron Powell, Dennis Quinn, Henry Richardson, Christian Rostbøll, Ben Saunders, Geoffrey Sayre-McCord, David Schmidtz, Kyle Swan, Fernando Tesón, John Tomasi, Kevin Vallier, Bas van der Vossen, Steven Wall, and Matt Zwolinski.

Thanks finally to two anonymous referees, who helped turn this into a better work.

AGAINST DEMOCRACY

CHAPTER 1

HOBBITS AND HOOLIGANS

American revolutionary and president John Adams said, "I must study politics and war that my sons may have liberty to study mathematics and philosophy. My sons ought to study mathematics and philosophy, geography, natural history, naval architecture, navigation, commerce, and agriculture, in order to give their children a right to study painting, poetry, music, architecture, statuary, tapestry, and porcelain."[1] Adams was a political animal if ever there was one, but he hoped future generations would evolve into a higher form of life.

This book explains why we should try to realize that hope.

DOES POLITICAL PARTICIPATION ENNOBLE OR CORRUPT? MILL VERSUS SCHUMPETER

The great nineteenth-century economist and moral philosopher John Stuart Mill argued that we should institute whatever form of government produces the best results. Mill advised us to examine *all* the consequences. That is, when asking whether it's best to have monarchy, oligarchy, aristocracy, representative legislatures, or other forms of government, we should focus not just on the obvious things, like how well different forms of government respect liberal rights or promote economic growth. We should also examine how different forms of government affect citizens' intellectual and moral virtue. Some forms of government might leave us dumb and passive, while others might make us sharp and active.

Mill hoped that getting people involved in politics would make them smarter, more concerned about the common good, better educated, and nobler. He hoped getting a factory worker to think about politics would be like getting a fish to discover there's a world outside the ocean. Mill hoped political involvement would harden our minds yet soften our hearts. He hoped that political engagement would cause us to look beyond our immediate interests and instead to adopt a long-term, broad perspective.

Mill was a scientific thinker. When he wrote, few countries had representative government. These few countries restricted suffrage, permitting only a nonrepresentative and elite minority to vote. In Mill's time, political participation was mostly an educated gentleman's pursuit. Mill did not quite have the evidence needed to back up his claims. At most, he had a reasonable but untested hypothesis.

That was just over 150 years ago. The test results are now in. They are, I will hold, largely negative. I think Mill would agree. Most common forms of political engagement not only fail to educate or ennoble us but also tend to stultify and corrupt us. The truth is closer to the economist Joseph Schumpeter's complaint: "The typical citizen drops down to a lower level of mental performance as soon as he enters the political field. He argues and analyzes in a way which he would readily recognize as infantile within the sphere of his real interests. He becomes a primitive again."[2]

If Mill's hypothesis is wrong and Schumpeter is right, we must ask some hard questions: How much do we really want people to participate in politics? How much should people even be *allowed* to participate?

THE UPSIDE OF DEMOCRATIC DECLINE

Many books about democracy and civic engagement complain that participation rates are falling. They note that in the late 1800s, 70 to 80 percent of eligible Americans voted in major elections. They then complain that we now muster at most 60 percent for a presidential election, or 40 percent for midterm, state, and local elections. After citing these numbers, they gnash their teeth. US democracy is more inclusive than ever, with more and more people invited to take a seat at the political bargaining table. And yet fewer people RSVP. Citizens are not taking the responsibility of self-government seriously, they say.

My response is different: this decline in political engagement is a *good start*, but we still have a long way to go. We should hope for even less participation, not more. Ideally, politics would occupy only a small portion of the average person's attention. Ideally, most people would fill their days with painting, poetry, music, architecture, statuary, tapestry, and porcelain, or perhaps football, NASCAR, tractor pulls, celebrity gossip, and trips to Applebee's. Most people, ideally, would not worry about politics at all.[3]

In contrast, some political theorists want politics to pervade more aspects of life. They want more political deliberation. They think politics ennobles us, and see democracy as a way of empowering the little person to take control of their circumstances. Some "civic humanists" regard democracy itself as the good life, or at least a higher calling.

Which side is closer to the truth depends in part on what human beings are like, what democratic participation does to us, and what problems mass political participation is likely to solve—or *create*.

THREE SPECIES OF DEMOCRATIC CITIZENS

We no longer have to speculate, as Mill did, about what politics does to us. Psychologists, sociologists, economists, and political scientists have spent more than sixty years studying how people think about, react to, and make decisions in politics. They've investigated what people know, what they don't know, what they believe, how strongly they believe it, and what makes them change their minds. They've looked into how opinionated people are, how and why they form coalitions, and what gets them to act or participate. I'll review much of this research in greater detail in the coming chapters. Here, I summarize the results.

People differ in how strongly they hold political opinions. Some people cling to their opinions with religious fervor, while others have only weakly held views. Some people maintain the same ideology for years at a time, whereas others change their minds in a heartbeat.

People differ in how consistent their views are. Some people have a unified, coherent set of opinions. Others have inconsistent, contradictory beliefs.

People differ in *how many* opinions they have. Some people have an opinion on everything, and some people have hardly any at all.

Then too, people differ in how much information or evidence they have to support their beliefs. Some people have a strong background in the relevant social sciences. Some just watch the news. Others know hardly anything about politics. They have opinions, but little or no evidence backing them up.

People differ in how they regard and respond to those with whom they disagree. Some see their political opponents as satanic, while others think they are merely mistaken. Some believe that at least some of their opponents are reasonable, while others think all of them are fools.

People also differ in how much and in what ways they participate. Some people obsess over politics the way others obsess over celebrity love affairs. Some people vote, volunteer, campaign, and donate. Others never have and never will participate. The state could revoke their political rights, and they wouldn't notice or care.

On each of these issues, citizens fall on a spectrum. But we can simplify matters for the purpose of this book. There are three broad types of democratic citizens that will be interest to us here, which I will label hobbits, hooligans, and vulcans.

- *Hobbits* are mostly apathetic and ignorant about politics. They lack strong, fixed opinions about most political issues. Often they have no opinions at all. They have little, if any, social scientific knowledge; they are ignorant not just of current events but also of the social scientific theories and data needed to evaluate as well as understand these events. Hobbits have only a cursory knowledge of relevant world or national history. They prefer to go on with their daily lives without giving politics much thought. In the United States, the typical nonvoter is a hobbit.

- *Hooligans* are the rabid sports fans of politics. They have strong and largely fixed worldviews. They can present arguments for their beliefs, but they cannot explain alternative points of view in a way that people with other views would find satisfactory. Hooligans consume political information, although in a biased way. They tend to seek out information that confirms their preexisting political opinions, but ignore, evade, and reject out of hand evidence that contradicts or disconfirms their preexisting opinions. They may have some trust in the social sciences, but cherry-pick data and tend only to learn about research that supports their own views. They are overconfident in themselves and what they know. Their political opinions form part of their identity, and they are proud to be a member of their political team. For them, belonging to the Democrats or Republicans, Labor or Tories, or Social Democrats or Christian Democrats matters to their self-image in the same way being a Christian or Muslim matters to religious people's self-image. They tend to despise people who disagree with them, holding that people with alternative worldviews are stupid, evil, selfish, or at best, deeply misguided. Most regular voters, active political participants, activists, registered party members, and politicians are hooligans.
- *Vulcans* think scientifically and rationally about politics. Their opinions are strongly grounded in social science and philosophy. They are self-aware, and only as confident as the evidence allows. Vulcans can explain contrary points of view in a way that people holding those views would find satisfactory. They are interested in politics, but at the same time, dispassionate, in part because they actively try to avoid being biased and irrational. They do not think everyone who disagrees with them is stupid, evil, or selfish.

These are ideal types or conceptual archetypes. Some people fit these descriptions better than others. No one manages to be a true vulcan; everyone is at least a little biased. Alas, many people fit the hobbit and hooligan molds quite well. Most Americans are either hobbits or hooligans, or fall somewhere in the spectrum in between.

Notice that I do not define these types in terms of how *extreme* or *moderate* their opinions are. Hooligans are not by definition extremists, and vulcans are not by definition moderate. Perhaps some Marxist radicals or libertarian anarchists are vulcans, while most moderates are either hobbits or hooligans.

More generally, I didn't define these types in terms of what ideology they espouse. Consider, for instance, all the people with libertarian sympathies. Some of them are hobbits. These hobbits lean libertarian—they are predisposed to libertarian conclusions—but they don't think or care much about politics, and most don't self-identify as libertarian. Many, perhaps most, libertarians are hooligans. For them, *being libertarian* is a major part of their self-image. Their Facebook avatars are black-and-gold anarchist flags, they only date other libertarians, and they only read heterodox cult economist Murray Rothbard or novelist Ayn Rand. Finally, a few libertarians are vulcans.

Mill hypothesized that getting citizens involved in politics would enlighten them. One way of stating his supposition is that he hoped political deliberation and participation in representative government would transform hobbits into vulcans. Schumpeter, in contrast, thought that participation stultifies people—that is, it tends to turn hobbits into hooligans.

In the chapters that follow, I examine and attack a wide range of arguments that purport to show that political liberty and participation are good for us. I contend that for most us, political liberty and participation are, on the whole, harmful. Most of us are either hobbits or hooligans, and most hobbits are potential hooligans. We would be better off—and others would be too—if we stayed out of politics.

AGAINST DEMOCRATIC TRIUMPHALISM

There is a widely shared set of views about the value and justification of democracy and widespread democratic participation. These beliefs are popular among my colleagues—that is, other analytic political philosophers and political theorists as well as a wide range of lay-people living in liberal democracies. They are less popular among empirically minded economists and political scientists, or among the more empirically minded philosophers and theorists.

Consider all the possible ways democracy and widespread political participation might be valuable:

> *Epistemic/instrumental*: Perhaps democracy and widespread political participation are good because they tend to lead to just, efficient, or stable outcomes (at least compared to the alternatives).
>
> *Aretaic*: Perhaps democracy and widespread political participation are good because they tend to educate, enlighten, and ennoble citizens.
>
> *Intrinsic*: Perhaps democracy and widespread political participation are good as ends in themselves.

What I will call *democratic triumphalism* is the view that democracy and widespread political participation are valuable, justified, and required by justice, for all three kinds of reasons. Triumphalism's slogan might be, "Three cheers for democracy!" According to triumphalism, democracy is a uniquely just form of social organization. People have a basic right to an equal fundamental share of political power. Participation is good for us; it empowers us, it's a useful way for us to get what we want, and it tends to make us better people. Political activity tends to produce fraternity and fellow feeling.

This book attacks triumphalism. Democracy doesn't deserve at least two of the three cheers it gets, and it might not deserve the last one either. I argue:

- Political participation is not valuable for most people. On the contrary, it does most of us little good, and instead tends to stultify and corrupt us. It turns us into civic enemies who have grounds to hate one another.
- Citizens don't have any basic right to vote or run for office. Political power, even the small amount of power contained in the right to vote, has to be justified. The right to vote is *not* like other civil liberties, such as freedom of speech, religion, or association.
- While there might be some intrinsically unjust forms of government, democracy is not a uniquely or intrinsically just form of government. Unrestricted, equal, universal suffrage—in which each citizen automatically is entitled to one vote—is in many ways

on its face morally objectionable. The problem is (as I will argue at length) that universal suffrage incentivizes most voters to make political decisions in an ignorant and irrational way, and then imposes these ignorant and irrational decisions on innocent people. The *only* thing that could justify unrestricted, universal suffrage would be that we cannot produce a better-performing system.

In general, the best places to live right now are liberal democracies, not dictatorships, one-party governments, oligarchies, or real monarchies. Yet this does not show democracy is the ideal or even best feasible system. And even if democracy turns out to be the best feasible system, we might be able to improve it with *less* participation. Overall, democratic governments tend to perform better than the alternatives *we have tried*. But perhaps some of the systems we haven't tried are even better. In this book, I won't try to convince you there is for sure a better alternative. I will argue for a conditional claim, however: *if* there turns out to be better a better-functioning alternative, *then* we ought to take it. To some readers, that may sound like a weak claim. Nevertheless, in the current landscape of democratic theory, this makes me radical. Most lay readers and contemporary political philosophers deny this claim; they believe we ought to stick with democracy even if some nondemocratic alternatives turn out to work better.

POLITICAL LIBERTIES ARE NOT LIKE OTHER ONES

Most North Americans and western Europeans, regardless of what party they tend to vote for, embrace a kind of philosophical liberalism. Philosophical liberalism is the view that each individual has a dignity, founded on justice, that imbues them with an extensive range of rights and freedoms—rights and freedoms that cannot easily be outweighed or overridden for the greater social good. These rights are like trump cards: they forbid others from using, interfering with, or harming us, even when doing so would produce good consequences for others. In contemporary US discourse, we sometimes use the word *liberal* to mean anyone left of center, but in political philosophy, it refers to those who think freedom is the fundamental political value.

Liberals—following in Mill's footsteps—usually hold that people should be allowed to make bad choices so long as they are only hurting themselves. To illustrate this, suppose Izzy—a single, childless man in his twenties—is imprudent. Izzy eats too much, exercises too little, and spends too much. However poor Izzy's decisions may be, he's not hurting anyone but himself. Let him live as he sees fit. His choices are bad, but we have no right to stop him from making bad choices.

Many people think that just as Izzy has the right to eat himself into a heart attack, so a democracy has the right to govern itself into an economic crisis. When a democracy makes bad, imprudent, or irrational decisions, that's just like when Izzy makes bad, imprudent, or irrational decisions.

This analogy fails. An electorate is not like an individual. It is a collection of individuals with separate goals, behaviors, and intellectual credentials. It is not a unified body in which every person advocates the same policies. Instead, some people impose their decisions on others. If most voters act foolishly, they don't just hurt themselves. They hurt better-informed and more rational voters, minority voters, citizens who abstained from voting, future generations, children, immigrants, and foreigners who are unable to vote but still are subject to or harmed by that democracy's decisions. Political decision making is not choosing for oneself; it is choosing for everyone. If the majority makes a capricious decision, others have to suffer the risks.

Thus, political decision making, whether democratic or otherwise, has a higher justificatory burden than the decisions we make for ourselves. To justify basic liberal rights, we have to explain why individuals must be allowed to harm themselves. That's a hard task, and even today some philosophers believe we should be free to stop individuals from making bad choices, even when those choices hurt no one else.[4] To justify democracy takes more work: we have to explain why some people should have the right to impose bad decisions on others. In particular, as I will show in later chapters, to justify democracy, we'll need to explain why it's legitimate to impose incompetently made decisions on innocent people.

I confine my use of the term *political liberties* in this book to include only the right to vote, and the right to run for and hold offices and positions of political power. Some people prefer to use the word in a broader way, to include the rights of political speech, assembly, and forming political parties. Here, I classify these as civil liberties, as instances of free speech and free association. For example, I classify my right to write this book about political participation as a civil rather than a political liberty.

I intend this to be a stipulation, not a point of conceptual analysis. Nothing substantive turns here on what labels we use. The reason I am interested in the rights to vote and hold office is that these rights—unlike what I am calling the civil or economic liberties—are primarily rights to exercise or attempt to acquire *power over others*. Our rights of free speech generally give us power only over ourselves, while rights to vote typically give us—as collectives, if not as individuals—significant power over others.[5]

HOW TO VALUE DEMOCRACY: INSTRUMENTALISM VERSUS PROCEDURALISM

When we ask what makes a hammer valuable, we usually ask whether it is functional for us, as we are. Hammers have a purpose—to pound in nails—and good hammers serve that purpose. Hammers primarily have *instrumental* value.

When we ask what makes a painting valuable, we generally look to its *symbolic* value. We ask whether the painting is sublime, whether it evokes various feelings or ideas. We also value some paintings more highly because of how they were made and who made them.

When we ask what makes human beings valuable, we will often say that they are ends in themselves. Sure, people can also have instrumental value—the person who makes you coffee serves a purpose—but they also have *intrinsic* value. People have a dignity, not a price.

What about democracy? Most political philosophers agree that democracy has instrumental value. It functions pretty well and tends to produce relatively just outcomes. So, they think, democracy is valuable at least in the way a hammer is valuable.

Most philosophers, however, also think we should value democracy the way we value a painting or person. They claim that democracy uniquely expresses the idea that all people have equal worth and value. They claim that democratic outcomes are justified because of who made them and how they were made, and see democracy as an end in itself. Some philosophers think that democracy is an inherently just decision-making procedure. A few go so far as to hold that anything a democracy decides to do is justified simply because a democracy decided to do it. They deny there are any procedure-independent standards by which to judge what democracies do.

On the contrary, I will argue that democracy's value is *purely* instrumental; the only reason to favor democracy over any other political system is that it is more effective at producing just results, according to procedure-independent standards of justice. Democracy is nothing more than a hammer. If we can find a better hammer, we should use it. Later in the book, I will provide some evidence that we might be able to build a better hammer than democracy. (Until we build it, though, we won't know for sure.)

One basic question about politics is *who* should hold power. What distinguishes monarchy, aristocracy, democracy, and other regimes from each other is, in the first instance, how they distribute power. Monarchy places fundamental political power in one person's hands, while democracy gives every citizen an equal basic share of political power.

But just as there are competing answers to the question of who should hold power, there are competing views about what criteria we should use to answer the question of who should hold power. The two basic views are proceduralism and instrumentalism. Proceduralism holds that some ways of distributing power are intrinsically just or unjust, or are good or bad in themselves. Instrumentalism maintains that we should distribute power in whatever way tends to promote the procedure-independent right ends of government, whatever those right ends may be.

Proceduralism is the thesis that some way (or ways) of distributing power or making decisions is intrinsically good, just, or legitimate. Or alternatively, a proceduralist might contend that some decision-making institutions are intrinsically unjust. So, for instance, the philosophers Thomas Christiano and David Estlund are both proceduralists. Christiano thinks democracy is intrinsically just.[6] Estlund doesn't argue that democracy is intrinsically just, but he thinks that certain regimes, such as monarchy and theocracy, are intrinsically unjust.[7]

Pure proceduralism, the most radical version, holds that there are no independent moral standards for evaluating the outcome of the decision-making institutions. So, for example, the political theorist Jürgen Habermas asserts that so long as we make and continue to make decisions through a particular highly idealized deliberative process, any decision we make is just. Or as the political theorist Iñigo González-Ricoy says (in a paper criticizing me), "In a democratic society no process-independent moral criteria can be referred to in order to settle what counts as a harmful, unjust or morally unjustified exercise of the right to vote, for voting is a device that is only called for precisely when citizens disagree on what counts as harmful, unjust and morally unjustified."[8]

Notice how strong of a claim González-Ricoy appears to make: people disagree about what counts as harmful or unjust. Therefore, he concludes, we may not refer to any independent standards of justice by which to judge what democracies do. Pure proceduralists believe that there are some objective, opinion-independent moral truths, but these truths concern only *how* we make political decisions, not *what* we decide.

Pure proceduralism has deeply implausible implications. For instance, suppose we had a dispute about whether citizens should be allowed to rape children. Suppose the majority votes, after following an idealized deliberative procedure, to allow adults to rape any children they please. They also vote to have the police ensure that no one stops adults from raping children. A pure proceduralist about democracy would have to say that in this case, child rape would indeed be permissible. For that reason, pure proceduralism appears to be absurd, and so I'm not going to consider it at any length in this book. Other political philosophers have already subjected the best arguments for pure proceduralism to sustained critiques, and I think these critiques are devastating and decisive.[9]

But while pure proceduralism is implausible, perhaps *partial* proceduralism is not. Later in the book, I'll examine some defenses of democracy that mix proceduralism and instrumentalism.

In contrast to proceduralism, instrumentalism about the distribution of power is the thesis that there are procedure-independent right answers to at least some political questions, and what justifies a distribution of power or a decision-making method is, at least in part, that this distribution or that method tends to select the right answer. So, for instance, in criminal law, we have an adversarial system in which one lawyer represents the state and the other represents the defendant. There is an independent truth of the matter about whether the defendant is guilty. This truth is not decided by the jury's fiat. Rather, the jury is supposed to discover what the truth is. Defenders of jury trials and the adversarial system believe that as a whole, this system tends to track the truth better than other ones.

The most radical form of instrumentalism is pure instrumentalism. It holds that no way of distributing political power is intrinsically just or unjust. Instead, according to the pure instrumentalist, there is a procedure-independent truth about what the right ends of government are, about what sorts of policies governments ought to implement or what outcomes governments ought to cause. We should use whatever form of government—or no government at all—that most reliably tracks this independent truth.

So a pure instrumentalist would say that if democracy best tracks the truth—that is, if democratic decision making is more likely to lead to good decisions than the alternatives—then we should use democracy. Otherwise, if there's a better alternative, use that. A pure instrumentalist would say that if making Aunt Betty queen leads to the most justice, make her queen. If allowing only black women between the ages of twenty-four and thirty-seven to hold office leads to the most justice, then let's do that. If allowing strange women in lakes to choose kings by dispensing swords produces the most justice, then so be it. If throwing darts at policies written on the wall works best, then do that. And so on.

One could advocate a mixed view, partly proceduralist and partly instrumentalist. For example, Estlund thinks that some alternatives to democracy—such as monarchy—are ruled out entirely on procedural grounds because they are intrinsically unjust. But he believes that procedural considerations alone are not enough to select a regime. They leave us with a few permissible choices, such as anarchy, decision by lottery, and democracy. He thinks we should use democracy instead of the other two because it is more likely to arrive at the truth about what justice requires.[10] For Estlund, proceduralist considerations rule out a few losers, yet instrumentalist considerations pick the final winner from the remaining contestants.

When I say democracy is a hammer, I mean it is a means to an end, but not an end in itself. I will argue that democracy is not intrinsically just. It is not justified on proceduralist grounds. Any value democracy has is purely instrumental.[11] (I remain agnostic about whether any forms of government are intrinsically unjust; it won't matter for my arguments here, so I take no stand.)

WHICH IS THE BETTER HAMMER, DEMOCRACY OR EPISTOCRACY?

Ample empirical research has shown that on almost any attempt to measure political knowledge, the mean, model, and median levels of it among citizens in contemporary democracies is low. I'll discuss just how low it is in chapter 2 (and to a lesser extent, chapters 3 and 7).

Thousands of years ago, Plato worried that a democratic electorate would be too dumb, irrational, and ignorant to govern well. He seemed to argue that the best form of government would be rule by a noble and wise philosopher king. (Scholars debate whether Plato was serious.) Contemporary political philosophers would label Plato an *epistocrat*.[12] Epistocracy means the rule of the knowledgeable. More precisely, a political regime is epistocratic to the extent that political power is formally distributed according to competence, skill, and the good faith to act on that skill.

Aristotle responded to Plato that while the rule of philosopher kings would be best, we'll never have any philosopher kings. Real people just aren't wise or good enough to fill that role, nor, contrary to Plato, can we reliably train them to become that wise or good.

Aristotle is right: trying to develop someone into a philosopher king is hopeless. In the real world, governing is too difficult for any one person to do alone. Worse, in the real world, if we imbued an office with the discretionary power of a philosopher king, that power would attract the wrong kind of people—people who would abuse that power for their own ends.

Yet the case for epistocracy doesn't hang on hopes of a philosopher king or guardian class. There are many other possible forms of epistocracy:

Restricted suffrage: Citizens may acquire the legal right to vote and run for office only if they are deemed (through some sort of process) competent and/or sufficiently well informed. This system has representative government and institutions similar to modern democracies, but does not imbue everyone with voting power. Nevertheless, voting rights are widespread, if not as widespread as in a democracy.

Plural voting: As in a democracy, every citizen has a vote. But some citizens, those who are deemed (through some legal process) to be more competent or better informed, have additional votes. So, for instance, Mill advocated a plural voting regime. As discussed above, he thought getting everyone involved in politics would tend to ennoble them. He remained worried, however, that too many citizens would be incompetent and insufficiently educated to make smart choices at the polls. Thus, he advocated giving better-educated people more votes.

Enfranchisement lottery: Electoral cycles proceed as normal, except that by default no citizen has any right to vote. Immediately before the election, thousands of citizens are selected via a random lottery to become prevoters. These prevoters may then earn the right to vote, but only if they participate in certain competence-building exercises, such as deliberative forums with their fellow citizens.[13]

Epistocratic veto: All laws must be passed through democratic procedures via a democratic body. An epistocratic body with restricted membership, though, retains the right to veto rules passed by the democratic body.

Weighted voting / government by simulated oracle: Every citizen may vote, but must take a quiz concerning basic political knowledge at the same time. Their votes are weighted based on their objective political knowledge, perhaps while statistically controlling for the influence of race, income, sex, and/or other demographic factors.

In recent years, Plato has made a comeback. In political philosophy, epistocracy has reemerged as the main challenger to democracy's throne. Few political philosophers embrace epistocracy; most remain democrats. But they recognize that a proper defense of democracy must show that democracy is, all things considered, superior to epistocracy. They also recognize that this is not easy to show.

In this book, I contend that the choice between democracy and epistocracy is instrumental. It ultimately comes down to which system would perform better in the real world. I will provide some reasons to believe that epistocracy would outperform democracy, although we do not yet have sufficient evidence to definitely favor epistocracy over democracy. We are forced to speculate, because the most promising forms of epistocracy have not been tried. My goal here is not to argue for the strong claim that epistocracy is superior to democracy. I am instead advocating for weaker claims. For one, if any form of epistocracy, with whatever realistic flaws it has, turns out to perform better than democracy, we ought to implement epistocracy instead of democracy. There are also good grounds to presume that some feasible form of epistocracy would in fact outperform democracy. Finally, if democracy and epistocracy perform equally well, then we may justly instantiate either system.

Epistocrats strike many people as authoritarian. They seem to hold that smart people should have the right to rule over others just because they know better. On this point, Estlund claims that defenses of epistocracy typically rest on three tenets: truth, knowledge, and authority.

> *Truth tenet*: There are correct answers to (at least some) political questions.
> *Knowledge tenet*: Some citizens know more of these truths or are more reliable at determining these truths than others.
> *Authority tenet*: When some citizens have greater knowledge or reliability, this justifies granting them political authority over those with lesser knowledge.[14]

Estlund accepts the truth and knowledge tenets, but argues that we should reject the authority tenet. The authority tenet commits what he calls the "expert/boss fallacy." One commits the expert/boss fallacy when one thinks that being an expert is sufficient reason for a person to hold power over others. But, Estlund notes, possessing superior knowledge is not sufficient to justify having *any* power, let alone greater power, than others. We can always say to the experts, "You may know better, but who made you boss?" My dietitian sister-in-law, for example, knows better than I do what I should eat, yet that doesn't mean she should be able to force me to follow a diet she prescribes. Exercise celebrity Shaun T knows better than I do how to get cut abs, but that doesn't mean he may force me to do burpees.

I agree with Estlund that the authority tenet is false. But, as I'll argue in chapter 6, the case for epistocracy does not rest on the authority tenet; it's based on something closer to an *anti*authority tenet.

> *Antiauthority tenet*: When some citizens are morally unreasonable, ignorant, or incompetent about politics, this justifies *not permitting* them to exercise political authority over others. It justifies either forbidding them from holding power or reducing the power they have in order to protect innocent people from their incompetence.

By saddling epistocrats with the authority tenet, Estlund unintentionally makes the case for epistocracy seem more difficult than it is. Epistocrats need not assert that experts should be bosses. Epistocrats need only suggest that incompetent or unreasonable people should not be imposed on others as bosses. They need only contend that democratic decision making, in certain cases, lacks authority or legitimacy because it tends to be incompetent. This leaves open what, if anything, justifies political power.

ARBITRARY VERSUS NONARBITRARY GROUNDS FOR POLITICAL INEQUALITY

Many take it as an unquestionable, nonnegotiable axiom that everyone ought to have an equal share of political power. Unequal political power is a marker of injustice.

They have a point. For most of civilized history, political power was distributed unequally, on the basis of morally arbitrary, repugnant, or evil reasons. We've made progress, and we've realized what our past mistakes were. We shouldn't imbue someone with power just because they are white, Protestant, or male. We shouldn't forbid someone from holding political power just because that person is black, Catholic, Irish, Jewish, or female, because they don't own a house, or because their parents were street sweepers. A person doesn't have the right to rule just because they are the great-grandchild of a conquering warlord. In the past, inequality in political power was almost always unjust. Past movements toward democracy were usually a step in the right direction.

That said, even if past political inequality was unjust, it does not follow that political inequality is inherently unjust. Even if, in the past, people were excluded from holding political power for bad reasons, there might be good reasons to exclude some people from holding power or grant them a smaller share of political power.

In comparison, we should not exclude citizens from driving because they are atheists, gay, or Dalits. Yet that does not mean that all restrictions on the legal right to drive are unjust. There might be *just* reasons to forbid some people from driving, such as that they are incompetent drivers who impose too much risk on others when they drive.

So it might be with political rights as well. Countries used to exclude citizens from holding power for bad reasons, such as that they were black, female, or didn't own land. But though this was unjust, it remains open that there could be good grounds for restricting or reducing some citizens' political power.[15] Perhaps some citizens are incompetent participants who impose too much risk on others when they participate. Perhaps some of us have a right to be protected from their incompetence.

"AGAINST POLITICS" NEEDN'T MEAN LESS GOVERNMENT

At one point, I considered titling this book *Against Politics*. That title could have been misleading, especially in light of some of my other work. I will argue, first, that political participation tends to corrupt rather than improve our intellectual and moral character; second, that political participation and the political liberties are not of much instrumental or intrinsic value; and third, that we would probably produce more substantively just political outcomes if we replaced democracy with some form of epistocracy.

I am not thereby arguing that we ought to reduce the scope of government, however—that is, the number or range of issues subject to political oversight and regulation. Some recent authors, such as legal theorist Ilya Somin, claim that the best way to limit the harms caused by political ignorance is to implement more limited government.[16] He might be right or wrong, but I remain agnostic about this question here.

I think most people are bad at politics and politics is bad for most of us, yet I am not arguing that therefore we should have government do less (or more). Instead, I am arguing that—if the facts turn out the right way—fewer of us should be allowed to participate. If you're a social democrat, I'm suggesting you should consider becoming a social epistocrat. If you're a democratic socialist, I'm proposing you should consider becoming an epistocrat socialist. If you're a conservative republican, I'm saying you should consider becoming a conservative epistocrat. If you're a libertarian anarcho-capitalist or left-syndicalist anarchist, I'm suggesting you should consider epistocracy a possible improvement over current democracy, even if anarchism would be even better.

Philosophers like to distinguish between "ideal" and "nonideal" political theory. Roughly, ideal theory asks what institutions would be best if everyone were morally perfect, with perfect moral virtue and a perfect sense of justice. Nonideal theory asks what institutions would be best given how people actually are—in particular, given that people's degree of virtue is to some extent a function of the institutions they live under. This is a book of nonideal theory. I am not trying to determine what a perfectly just society would look like. Rather, I am asking how we ought to think about political participation and power given that real people have pervasive moral flaws and vices, with only weak commitment to justice.

OUTLINE

In chapter 2, "Ignorant, Irrational, Misinformed Nationalists," I review the literature on voter behavior. Most democratic citizens and voters are, well, ignorant, irrational, and misinformed nationalists. I explain how the median, mean, and modal levels of political knowledge are low, how voters make systematic mistakes on many important issues in basic economics or political science, and how voters tend to be biased and irrational. I provide evidence that most citizens are hobbits, and the rest are mostly hooligans.

In chapter 3, "Political Participation Corrupts," I argue that political participation tends to make us worse, not better. Many democrats think *deliberative democracy*—a political system in which citizens frequently deliberate about politics in an organized way—would cure most of our ills. I maintain, on the contrary, that the evidence shows that deliberation tends to stultify and corrupt us; it makes us worse, not better. A fortiori, I contend that the empirical evidence is much more damning than people have realized. In response to such evidence, many deliberative democrats complain all this demonstrates is that citizens fail to deliberate the right way. But, I'll suggest, this response doesn't protect democracy from the complaint that it stultifies and corrupts.

In chapter 4, "Politics Doesn't Empower You or Me," I attack a range of arguments that purport to show that political participation and the right to vote are good for us (or are required as a matter of justice) because they empower us in some way. On the contrary, in my view none of these arguments are sound. Democracy empowers *collectives*, not individuals. One argument—popular among political philosophers who follow in John Rawls's footsteps—holds that we are owed equal rights to vote and run for office because these are necessary for us to realize our capacities to develop a conception of the good life along with a sense of justice. I show this reasoning fails to do the work Rawlsians need it to do.

In chapter 5, "Politics Is Not a Poem," I critique a range of arguments that purport to demonstrate that democracy, equal voting rights, and participation are good and just because of what they express or symbolize. These claims hold that participation has expressive value, that giving people equal voting rights is necessary to express proper respect for them, or that democracy is necessary for people to have proper self-respect. I contend that these kinds of symbolic and esteem-based arguments fail. They generally fail to show that democratic rights have any real value to us. These arguments provide no good reasons to choose democracy over epistocracy.

By the end of chapter 5, I take it that I've established that there are no good proceduralist grounds for preferring democracy over epistocracy. Of course, there are thousands of books and articles defending democracy on proceduralist grounds, and I don't respond to each of them. Instead, I'm trying to defeat some of the most significant proceduralist arguments.

In chapter 6, "The Right to Competent Government," I defend what I call the *competence principle*, which holds that high-stakes political decisions are presumed to be unjust, illegitimate, and lacking in authority if they are made incompetently or in bad faith, or by a generally incompetent decision-making body. In light of the empirical evidence examined in chapters 2 and 3, it appears that democracies systematically violate the competence principle during elections, although they might not violate it as frequently *after* the election. (The electorate acts incompetently, even if not everyone in democratic government does.) If so, I argue, then we have presumptive grounds to favor epistocracy over democracy.

In chapter 7, "Is Democracy Competent?" I examine some possible responses from democrats. On the basis of various mathematical theorems, some democratic theorists hold that the democratic electorate as a collective body tends to make competence decisions, even though many or most voters are ignorant. I argue none of these mathematical theorems succeed as defenses of democracy, in part because the theorems don't apply to real-life democracies.

Other empirically minded democratic theorists nevertheless contend—and I agree—that what democracies do is not simply a function of what the electorate wants or votes for. Based on a wide range of reasons, democratic governments tend to make fairly competent decisions over a wide range of issues, even though the electorate is systematically incompetent. There are a large number of "mediating factors" that prevent the electorate from getting its way.

In response, I explain that the competence principle is meant to apply to every individual high-stakes governmental decision. It could be that the electorate acts incompetently in most elections, even if government agents often act competently after the elections. If so, to my mind this leaves us with a dilemma: either elections still qualify as high stakes, in which case the competence principle tells us we should presumptively prefer epistocracy to democracy, or elections don't quality as high stakes. In that latter case, the competence principle by itself would leave us *indifferent* between epistocracy and democracy. But given that there are no good proceduralist arguments for democracy, we should still just prefer whatever system works better.

In chapter 8, "The Rule of the Knowers," I outline various ways we might instantiate epistocracy. I discuss some of the potential benefits and risks of different forms of epistocracy, and respond to some remaining objections to it.

Chapter 9, "Civic Enemies," is a short postscript. I conclude by saying that what's regrettable about politics is that it makes us enemies with one another. The problem isn't merely that we're biased and tribalistic, that we tend to hate people who disagree with us just because they disagree. Rather, the problem is, first, that politics puts us in genuinely adversarial relationships, and second, that because most of our fellow citizens make political decisions in incompetent ways, we have reason to resent the way they treat us. I argue that for this reason, all things considered, we should want to expand the scope of civil society and reduce the sphere of politics. The reason we should try to realize Adams's hope is not merely because, ideally, we would have no further need of politics. Instead, a major reason we should try to realize it is that politics gives us genuine grounds to hate one another.

CHAPTER 2

IGNORANT, IRRATIONAL, MISINFORMED NATIONALISTS

The typical person crosses the street only when they believe it's clear. They have every incentive to look both ways. They also have every incentive to form beliefs in a rational way about whether the street is clear. When they see what looks like a Mack truck crashing toward them, they don't dare indulge the idea that it's an optical illusion. After all, if they're wrong, they die.

Now suppose this same person is about to vote. What happens if they indulge, say, a conspiracy theory, or make an honest mistake? Alas, not much. The chances that an individual's vote will make any sort of difference are vanishingly small. An individual vote for the worst-possible candidate produces the same results as a vote for the best-possible candidate. Abstaining from voting produces the same results as voting. A well-informed vote produces the same results as a badly informed, misinformed, or irrational vote. An individual vote after careful deliberation produces the same results as voting after flipping a coin or dropping acid.

The problem is that this goes for *each* of us. People are generally well informed and rational about street traffic—and as a former insurance liability adjustor, I can assure you they're not perfect at that—because irrationality is punished.[1] But as we'll soon see, they tend to be ignorant and irrational about politics. Perhaps this is because when it comes to voting, knowledge and rationality do not pay, while ignorance and irrationality go unpunished.

If *we*, the electorate, are bad at politics, if we indulge fantasies and delusions, or ignore evidence, then people die. We fight unnecessary wars. We implement bad policies that perpetuate poverty. We overregulate drugs or underregulate carbon pollution. But the problem is that we, the electorate as a whole, don't make choices about whether to be informed or rational about politics. Individuals decide for themselves in light of their individual incentives.

This chapter begins by discussing the phenomenon of political ignorance. We'll see how little most Americans, including most voters, tend to know, and then I'll explore why they don't know much. Next, I'll provide a quick overview of the field of political psychology. Political psychology studies how people process political information. It turns out most people process political information in deeply biased and irrational ways.

In chapter 1, I claimed that many Americans are hobbits, while the others are mostly hooligans. Ignorance and apathy are the marks of the hobbit; bias and zealotry are the marks of the hooligan. At the end of this chapter, I'll explain why it's fair to estimate that Americans are about divided, roughly in half, between hobbits and hooligans.

WHAT CITIZENS DON'T KNOW

When it comes to politics, some people know a lot, most people know nothing, and many people know *less* than nothing.

You might already believe—based on anecdotes and personal experiences—that voters don't know much. But if you're not familiar with the statistics, there's a good chance you give them too much credit and that your personal experiences are misleading. When asked to think about uninformed voters, you probably picture your most ignorant acquaintances and relatives. Yet since you're reading this book, I can assume that you have or soon will have at least a bachelor's degree. Even if you attended a lower-tier university, your classmates were still the intellectual *elite* of your country. You, your friends, your relatives, and your acquaintances are probably at least among the top 10 percent most informed people in your country.

In the 1940s and 1950s, researchers at Columbia University and the University of Michigan began cataloging what typical citizens know and don't know about politics. The results were depressing.

As political scientist Philip Converse summarizes, "The two simplest truths I know about the distribution of political information in modern electorates are that the mean is low and the variance is high."[2] Somin, author of *Democracy and Political Ignorance*, says, "The sheer depth of most individual voters' ignorance is shocking to many observers not familiar with the research."[3] In his extensive review of the empirical literature on voter knowledge, Somin concludes that at least 35 percent of *voters* are "know-nothings."[4] (I stress voters because not everyone votes, and people who choose not to vote tend to know less than people who choose to vote.) Political scientist Larry Bartels observes that "the political ignorance of the American voter is one the best-documented features of contemporary politics."[5] Political theorist Jeffrey Friedman adds, "The public is far more ignorant than academic and journalistic observers of the public realize."[6] Political scientist John Ferejohn agrees: "Nothing strikes the student of public opinion and democracy more forcefully than the paucity of information most people possess about politics."[7]

I could write an entire book just documenting how little voters know. But since many others have already done that, I'll only offer a few examples:

- During election years, most citizens cannot identify any congressional candidates in their district.[8]
- Citizens generally don't know which party controls Congress.[9]
- Immediately before the 2004 presidential election, almost 70 percent of US citizens were unaware that Congress had added a prescription drug benefit to Medicare, though this was a giant increase to the federal budget and the largest new entitlement program since President Lyndon Johnson began the War on Poverty.[10]
- In the 2010 midterm presidential election, only 34 percent of voters knew that the Troubled Asset Relief Program was enacted under George W. Bush rather than Barack Obama. Only 39 percent knew

that defense was the largest category of discretionary spending in the federal budget.[11]

- Americans vastly overestimate how much money is spent on foreign aid, and so many of them mistakenly believe we can significantly reduce the budget deficit by cutting foreign aid.[12]
- In 1964, only a minority of citizens knew that the Soviet Union was *not* a member of the North Atlantic Treaty Organization. (Yes, that's right: NATO, the alliance created to oppose the Soviet Union.)[13] Keep in mind this is just a short time after the Cuban Missile Crisis, in which the United States almost went to (nuclear) war with the USSR.
- Seventy-three percent of Americans do not understand what the Cold War was about.[14]
- Most Americans do not know even roughly how much is spent on social security or how much of the federal budget it takes up.[15]
- Forty percent of Americans do not know whom the United States fought in World War II.[16]
- During the 2000 US presidential election, while slightly more than half of all Americans knew Al Gore was more liberal than Bush, they did not seem to understand what the word *liberal* means. Fifty-seven percent of them knew Gore favored a higher level of spending than Bush did, but significantly less than half knew that Gore was more supportive of abortion rights, more supportive of welfare state programs, favored a higher degree of aid to blacks, or was more supportive of environmental regulation.[17] Only 37 percent knew that federal spending on the poor had increased or that crime had decreased in the 1990s.[18] On these questions, Americans did worse than a coin flip. Similar results hold for other election years.[19]

This is sampling. I could go on for hundreds of pages documenting such ignorance, yet others have already done so at great length, as I mentioned above. In short, though, voters generally know who the current president is, but they don't know much more beyond that.

However ignorant voters tend to be, nonvoters—adult citizens who are eligible to vote but choose to abstain—tend to be worse. As the Pew Research Center summarizes, "On average, people who are not registered to vote answer 4.9 out of 12 questions correctly compared with 7.2 among voters. Just 22% of non-voters know that Republicans control the House of Representatives."[20] Less than a third of nonvoters knew in 2008 that Mitt Romney is pro-life. Only 41 percent knew that Romney opposed gay marriage. On each of the Pew Research Center's political "News IQ" quiz questions, voters scored between 10 and 25 percentage points higher than nonvoters.

Things are worse than these numbers indicate. Simple surveys of voter knowledge—such as Pew Research Center polls or the American National Election Studies (ANES)—tend to *overstate* how much Americans know.

One reason these surveys overstate voter knowledge is that they usually take the form of a multiple-choice test. When many citizens do not know the answer to a question, they guess. Some of them get lucky, and the surveys mark them as knowledgeable. Imagine I administer a twelve-question test to ten thousand voters, and each question has three choices for an answer. Now suppose the average American gets four out of twelve questions correct. It might be that the average American knows the answer to four questions, but this is indistinguishable from them guessing at random.

Yet another reason most surveys and studies overstate knowledge is that they usually don't ask citizens to identify particulars or degrees. They count a citizen as knowledgeable if they know that we spend more on social security than defense, but they typically don't check if they know *how much* more we spend. They count a citizen as knowledgeable if they know that the economy grew in 2013, but they don't check if they know roughly how much it grew.

So, for instance, even though in AD 2000, most Americans knew that the federal deficit had decreased under Bill Clinton (in fact, there was a surplus), most were not aware how much it had decreased.[21] Or while most Americans knew in 2000 that Gore was more liberal than Bush, they did not know how much more liberal he was. (Indeed, as we saw above, they appear not to know what the political label *liberal* even means.) Or even though many Americans in 1992 knew that unemployment had risen under George H. W. Bush, the majority of Americans were unable to estimate the unemployment rate within 5 percentage points of the actual figure. When asked to guess what the unemployment rate was, the majority of voters guessed it was twice as high as the actual rate.[22] When voters don't know degrees, they're likely to misallocate resources and have the wrong priorities.

Finally, the most profound reason that these studies and surveys overstate voter knowledge is that they ask *easy questions*. They investigate whether citizens know easily verifiable facts. They ask citizens to pick the current president off a list, identify which party controls the House of Representatives, or identify whether the unemployment rate has been rising or falling. These are the kinds of questions one might find on a fifth-grade civics exam. You could Google the answer to all these questions in a few minutes. While most voting Americans cannot answer such questions, these questions do not require specialized social scientific knowledge.

Knowing the answers to the easy questions is not enough to be well informed about politics. To be well informed, citizens also need to know the candidates' policy platforms, how candidates are likely to vote in Congress, what policies the candidates are likely to support, whether these votes are likely to matter or not, and how much influence the candidates are likely to have if they win.

Yet even this is not enough. To know whom to vote for, one needs to know more than what candidates stand for, what the candidates have done in the past, or what they intend to do in the future. A well-informed voter needs to be able to assess whether the candidates' preferred policies would tend to promote or impede the voter's favored outcomes. So, for example, suppose I know candidates Smith and Colbert both want to improve the economy, but Smith favors free trade, and Colbert favors protectionism. I can't make a reasonable choice between them unless I know whether free trade or protectionism is more likely to improve the economy; to know that, I need to know economics.

Or suppose candidates Friedman and Wilson both want to reduce inner-city crime, but Friedman argues we should end the war on drugs, while Wilson says we need to double down. Again, to know whom to vote for, I'd need to know about criminology, the economics and sociology of black markets, and the history of Prohibition.

Few voters have any significant social scientific knowledge. For this reason, economist Bryan Caplan begins his book *The Myth of the*

Rational Voter with, "What voters don't know would fill a university library."[23] Caplan intends his remark to be taken literally. Go to the nearest university library. Point to the history books. Voters basically don't know anything in those books. In fact, over a quarter of Americans don't even know which country the United States fought in the Revolutionary War.[24] Now turn to the economics books. Americans don't know much of anything in them. In 1776, Adam Smith published *The Wealth of Nations*, which among other things, refuted a widespread economic ideology Smith called "mercantilism." But now, 240 years later, the typical American voter more or less accepts mercantilism.[25]

Now point to the political science books. Americans don't know what's in them either. For instance, most Americans don't know what the three branches of government are, or what these branches have the power to do.[26] As Somin says,

> Compared to a sample of political scientists specializing in American politics, the public substantially underestimates the ability of the president and Congress to control the composition of the federal budget, the influence of the Federal Reserve on the state of the economy, and the impact of state and local governments on public schools.[27]

Citizens don't know who controls what, and so they're often voting on irrelevant policy differences.

Next, pull out a copy of the US Constitution. Americans revere the Constitution, but they don't know what it says. Less than 30 percent of Americans can name two or more of the rights listed in the First Amendment of the Bill of Rights. Less than a third know that Karl Marx's communist slogan "From each according to his abilities, to each according to his needs" is *not* in the Constitution.[28]

You might object, "Voters don't need to be experts in politics. They just need to know enough to throw the incumbent bastards out when the bastards are doing a bad job." But knowing whether the bastards are doing a bad job requires a tremendous amount of social scientific knowledge. Voters need to know who the incumbent bastards are, what they did, what they could have done, what happened when the bastards did what they did, and whether the challengers are likely to be any better than the incumbent bastards.

In fact, voters usually lack all this knowledge. They generally have little to no sense of who was in power, or what those people had the power to do.[29] They do not know what influence incumbents had, or how to attribute responsibility to different incumbents.[30] They frequently do not even know whether things got better or worse. For example, as mentioned above, crime—one of the biggest problems in the United States throughout the 1970s and 1980s—fell dramatically under Clinton, but most Americans did not know this. During the 2012 election, most Americans did not know that the economy grew rather than shrank the year before.[31]

What's most surprising about all this is how *stable* political ignorance is. Today, political information is cheap and easily available. But as the joke goes, "I have a device in my pocket capable of accessing all information known to man. I use it to look at pictures of cats and argue with strangers." In 1940, less than 30 percent of white people over age twenty-five had a high school diploma; now, more than 80 percent do. Although Americans are, at least on paper, better educated than ever before, and even though political information has never been cheaper or easier to acquire, people nonetheless remain roughly as ignorant about politics as they were forty years ago.[32]

MOST VOTERS AREN'T STUPID; THEY JUST DON'T CARE

Economists think it's no great mystery why voters are so ignorant. It's explained by basic microeconomics.

Acquiring information has a cost. It takes time and effort—time and effort that could be spent promoting people's other goals. When the expected costs of acquiring information of a particular sort exceed the expected benefits of possessing that sort of information, people will usually not bother to acquire the information. Economists call this phenomenon *rational ignorance*.

To illustrate this point, consider the following. Suppose there's $1 million buried somewhere in your city, there for the taking. Now suppose you know that the instructions for finding the money are inserted into the text of Leo Tolstoy's twelve-hundred-page *War and*

Peace. You'd probably be willing to read *War and Peace* to find that $1 million.

But suppose instead I just tell you the instructions are hidden, randomly, in the text of one of the books in Harvard University's seventeen-million-books library system.[33] Though it's worth $1 million to find the text, it's no longer worth your time to search for it. You might get lucky and find the instructions right away, but you're more likely to spend a lifetime reading and never find them.

Becoming an informed voter is a bit like trying to read the entire contents of Harvard's library in order to find the $1 million. You'll learn a lot along the way, but acquiring that information is not likely to pay off.

Or to put it another way, suppose a billionaire offers you $1 billion if you can ace introductory microeconomics. You'd probably be willing to do it. But suppose instead the billionaire says, "If you ace introductory microeconomics *and* introductory American government *and* US history *and* first-year constitutional law *and* can score twenty-eight or higher on the ANES civics exam, I'll then give you a one-in-sixty-million chance of winning $1 billion." If you are the typical American, you probably wouldn't bother. You'd remain rationally ignorant of those subjects.

A vote makes a difference only if there is a tie; otherwise, it usually does not matter how someone votes or whether they vote at all.[34] Yet the probability a person will break a tie is vanishingly small.[35] Some economists and political scientists estimate that you are more likely to win Powerball a few times in a row than to cast a tie-breaking vote.[36] The most optimistic estimates suggest a voter can have as high as a one-in-a-million chance of breaking a tie in a presidential election, but only if that voter lives in a swing state, and only if that voter votes for a major political party.[37] Otherwise, even on the most optimistic estimates, individual votes count for nothing. Few citizens know how to calculate the exact probability that their votes will be decisive, but they do know intuitively that their votes are unlikely to make a difference.

Individual citizens have almost no power over government, and individual votes have almost zero expected value. Citizens don't invest in acquiring political knowledge because the knowledge doesn't pay.

Regardless of whether citizens have altruistic or selfish political preferences, it is not worth their time to be well informed about politics.

SOME CITIZENS KNOW MUCH MORE THAN OTHERS

Ignorance is not uniform. As Converse says, while the mean level of knowledge is low, variance is high. Most voters are ignorant, but some are highly informed, and some are *worse* than ignorant.

The ANES surveys eligible voters on basic political information, such as who the candidates are or what these candidates stand for. There is tremendous variance in what eligible voters know. Political scientist Scott Althaus summarizes some of the results:

> Just how high [the variance is] is made clear when we add up the number of correct answers to these questions and divide respondents into knowledge quartiles. While people in the highest knowledge quartile averaged 15.6 correct answers out of 18 possible, people in the lowest averaged only 2.5 correct answers.[38]

On this test of political knowledge, the top 25 percent of voters are well informed, the next 25 percent are badly informed, the next 25 percent are know-nothings, and the bottom 25 percent are systematically misinformed.

The ANES in effect gives citizens a multiple-choice exam on basic political knowledge. As we saw above, the voting public as a whole does worse than chance on many of these questions. In the 2000 US presidential election, significantly less than half of all Americans knew that Gore was more supportive of abortion rights, more supportive of welfare state programs, favored a higher degree of aid to blacks, or was more supportive of environmental regulation than Bush. Think of what that means. Imagine you are on *Who Wants to Be a Millionaire*. The host asks you the million-dollar question, "Who was more supportive of abortion rights in 2000, Al Gore or George Bush?" Suppose you don't know, but the host gives you the option of either flipping a coin or phoning a random US voter from the year 2000. You should flip the coin; it's more reliable.

But while the public as a whole is systematically misinformed about some things, the lowest knowledge quartile is extremely misinformed.

For example, in the 1992 ANES, voters were asked to identify which party, the Democratic or Republican, was more conservative on average. Only 12 percent of people in the lowest knowledge quartile could do so. They were also asked to identify the relative ideological position of the two major party candidates, (sitting president) Bush or Clinton. Only 17.9 percent of the people in the lowest knowledge quartile could do so. Only 17.1 percent of them could identify which candidate, Bush or Clinton, was more pro-choice. Only 9.7 percent of them could identify which candidate, Bush or Clinton, wanted to expand government services or the welfare state more.[39] These answers are significantly worse than chance. In contrast, over 90 percent of voters in the top knowledge quartile get these questions right.[40]

Political knowledge and economic literacy are not evenly spread among all demographic groups. Political knowledge is strongly positively correlated with having a college degree, but negatively correlated with having a high school diploma or less. It is positively correlated with being in the top half of income earners, but negatively correlated with being in the bottom half. It is strongly positively correlated with being in the top quarter of income earners, and strongly negatively correlated with being in the bottom quarter. It is positively correlated with living in the western United States, and negatively correlated with living in the South. Political knowledge is positively correlated with being or leaning Republican, but negatively correlated with being a Democrat or leaning independent. It is positively correlated with being between the ages of thirty-five and fifty-four, but negatively correlated with other ages. It is negatively correlated with being black, and strongly negatively correlated with being female.[41] As I'll explore in chapter 8, the basis of one of the major objections to epistocracy is the fact that political knowledge is spread unevenly among demographic groups.

INFORMATION CHANGES POLICY PREFERENCES

If political ignorance had no effect on our policy preferences, if well- and badly informed people had the same political opinions, then ignorance and misinformation wouldn't matter. Yet it turns out that information does matter. What policies people advocate depends on what they know.

Political scientist Martin Gilens notes that high-information Democrats have systematically different policy preferences than low-information Democrats. High-income Democrats tend to have high degrees of political knowledge, while poor Democrats tend to be ignorant or misinformed. Poor Democrats more strongly approved of invading Iraq in 2003. They more strongly favored the Patriot Act, invasions of civil liberty, torture, protectionism, and restricting abortion rights and access to birth control. They are less tolerant of homosexuals and more opposed to gay rights.[42] High-information Democrats have the opposite preferences. They tend to have opposed the Iraq invasion and torture, and support free trade, civil liberties, gay rights, abortion rights, and access to birth control.

Using the ANES data, Althaus also finds that well- and badly informed citizens have systematically different policy preferences.[43] Althaus shows that poorly informed people have systematically different preferences from well-informed ones, even after correcting for the influence of demographic factors such as race, income, and gender. As people (regardless of their race, income, gender, or other demographic factors) become more informed, they favor overall less government intervention and control of the economy. (That's not to say they become libertarians.) They are more in favor of free trade and less in favor of protectionism. They are more pro-choice. They favor using tax increases to offset the deficit and debt. They favor less punitive and harsh measures on crime, and are less hawkish on military policy, although they favor other forms of intervention. They are more accepting of affirmative action. They are less supportive of prayer in public schools. They are more supportive of market solutions to health care problems. They are less moralistic in law; they don't want government to impose morality on the population. And so on. In contrast, as people become less informed, they become more hawkish about intervention as well as in favor of protectionism, abortion restrictions, harsh penalties for crime, doing nothing to fix the debt, and so forth.

WHY ISN'T EVERYONE IGNORANT?

Once we understand the theory of rational ignorance, political ignorance no longer seems strange. Of course people are ignorant. The democratic system incentivizes them to be ignorant (or more precisely, fails to incentivize them to be informed). What now cries out for explanation is why some people are so well informed.

The rational ignorance theory says that most people remain ignorant about politics because the expected cost of learning political information exceeds the expected benefits of possessing that information. The flip side of this is that a person will learn about politics if the benefits exceed the costs. Yet an individual informed vote is just as useless as an uninformed one. So, to explain why some people acquire political information, we have to look to different sets of incentives. The theory of rational ignorance does not imply that people will never acquire political information; rather, it suggests that most of them will not acquire it for the purpose of voting.

Hearing more and forgetting less: Educated people know more than uneducated people. Though most people forget most of what they learn in school, the more schooling one has, the more knowledge one retains. If people remember only 25 percent of what they learn in school, someone with a bachelor's degree will still know more than someone with only a high school diploma.

A belief in a moral duty to be informed: Most people believe that they have a moral duty to vote, or at least they claim to have this belief when surveyed.[44] Some of them believe that they not only must vote but also should cast an *informed* vote. Some people actually become informed for this reason, though it's difficult to say just how many.

Belonging and social class: Few people want to be the odd person out. Most want to belong to and be respected by some group. People sometimes acquire knowledge to fit in. To fit in with a various group, one might need to know a lot about football, cars, celebrities, or fashion. This also applies to political knowledge. It just depends on who the relevant peer group is.

Educated people tend to live around, associate with, befriend, and marry other educated people, while they tend to avoid uneducated people.[45] Educated people expect certain things of each other. In light of peer pressure, a typical university-educated person would be ashamed to admit they had never read William Shakespeare's work, had never attended a symphony, or preferred NASCAR to soccer. One persistent trend is that educated people expect other educated people to keep up with politics.

People sometimes start to acquire knowledge in order to fit in, but then learn to *enjoy* that knowledge. Just as a college student might start drinking beer to fit in, but over time acquire a taste for it, or another might start learning about fashion to fit in, and over time acquire a real taste for fashion, so might some people acquire a taste for political knowledge.

Political geeks: On that point, some people acquire knowledge just because they find it *interesting*. They enjoy having knowledge, understanding how the world works, and acquiring new knowledge. They take pleasure in coming to understand things they did not know.

I sometimes read encyclopedia articles about obscure topics in mathematics, physics, or physical geography—information that is unlikely to serve any greater purpose—just because I find them fascinating. I am a nerd, a geek, an infovore.

Many people are political nerds. Indeed, finding politics interesting is one the strongest predictors that a person is highly informed about politics; they just enjoy consuming political information.[46] In the test of political knowledge in the 2000 ANES, people who have a high level of interest in politics get about eleven more questions right than people who have a low level of interest in politics. In contrast, people with graduate degrees tend to get about eight more questions right than people who dropped out in middle school. Being interested in politics has a stronger effect on basic political knowledge than having a master's degree.

The problem with these three kinds of motivations, though, is that they only weakly discipline us to get our facts right. Some people have an incentive to be informed in order to fit in with their peers. But they also have an incentive to believe whatever their peers and friends believe about politics. Some people acquire political information because they find it interesting. Yet the problem here is that they might find a mistaken theory more interesting or fascinating than a true one.

POLITICAL IRRATIONALITY

Imagine how a vulcan would form beliefs about politics. Vulcans are perfectly rational. An ignorant vulcan would know they are ignorant, and thus would be almost entirely agnostic about political issues. If they decided to learn more, they would seek out information from credible sources. They would conform their beliefs to the best-available evidence. A vulcan would look not merely at evidence in favor of different views but also evidence against these views. They would change their minds whenever the evidence called for it. They would consult peers and take disagreement seriously, and would gladly accept criticism, since they want to avoid error. "Thanks for correcting me and pointing out my mistakes!" They would hold beliefs only as strongly as the evidence allows.

True vulcans are free of *cognitive bias*. A cognitive bias is a systematic pattern of deviation from rational thought. Biases are like software bugs in our brains. They prevent us from believing, thinking, or doing what we ought to believe, think, or do, given the information and evidence we have.

The overwhelming consensus in political psychology, based on a huge and diverse range of studies, is that most citizens process political information in deeply biased, partisan, motivated ways rather than in dispassionate, rational ways. Most people are much more like hooligans than like vulcans. Even the hobbits—who lack strong ideologies—are more like potential hooligans or hooligans in waiting than they are potential vulcans. (They don't care enough about politics to form opinions, but if they started to care, they'd form opinions in biased ways.)

Political psychologists Milton Lodge and Charles Taber summarize the body of extant work: "The evidence is reliable [and] strong . . . in showing that people find it very difficult to escape the pull of their prior attitudes and beliefs, which guide the processing of new information in predictable and sometimes insidious ways."[47] Political psychologists Leonie Huddy, David Sears, and Jack Levy summarize: "Political decision-making is often beset with biases that privilege habitual thought and consistency over careful consideration of new information."[48]

People tend to have bad epistemic behavior when participating in politics. They display high levels of bias when discussing or participating in politics. This may be because the human brain was designed more for winning arguments and forming coalitions than seeking truth. As psychologist Jonathan Haidt observes,

Reasoning was not designed to pursue the truth. Reasoning was designed by evolution to help us win arguments. That's why [psychologists Hugo Mercier and Dan Sperber] call [their theory of why reasoning developed] The Argumentative Theory of Reasoning. So, as they put it . . . "The evidence reviewed here shows not only that reasoning falls quite short of reliably delivering rational beliefs and rational decisions. It may even be, in a variety of cases, detrimental to rationality. Reasoning can lead to poor outcomes, not because humans are bad at it, but because they systematically strive for arguments that justify their beliefs or their actions."[49]

For a vulcan, reasoning about evidence makes them more likely to acquire true beliefs and reject false ones. But for real people, reasoning can be epistemically dangerous. We engage in *motivated reasoning*—we try to arrive at beliefs that maximize good feelings and minimize bad feelings. We prefer to believe some things as opposed to others, and our brains tend to converge on the beliefs we prefer to have.

Psychologist Drew Westen conducted one of the most famous recent experiments on motivated reasoning.[50] Westen's subjects were loyal Republicans and Democrats. The subjects were shown a celebrity's statement, followed by information potentially making the celebrity seem hypocritical. Then, the subjects were presented with an "exculpatory statement." (A test run had a quote by Walter Cronkite saying he would never do television work again after retiring, followed by footage showing he did work again after retiring, followed by an explanation saying it was a special favor.) In the experiment, the celebrities were identifiable as Republicans or Democrats. Republican subjects strongly agreed that the famous Democrats contradicted themselves, but only weakly agreed that the Republicans did so. Democratic subjects likewise readily accepted exculpatory statements from their favored party, but not the other one. Functional magnetic resonance imaging showed that subject's pleasure centers were activated when condemning members of the other party, and activated again when subjects denied evidence against members of their own party.

POLITICAL TRIBALISM

In politics (and elsewhere), we suffer from "in-group/out-group" or "intergroup bias." In-group/out-group bias means we are *tribalistic*, in the most negative connotation of that term. We are biased to form groups, and then identify ourselves strongly with that group. We tend to develop animosity toward other groups, even when there is no basis for this animosity. We are biased to assume our group is good and just, and that members of other groups are bad, stupid, and unjust. We are biased to forgive most transgressions from our own group and damn minor errors from other ones. Our commitment to our team can override our commitment to truth or morality.[51]

As an illustration, psychologist Henry Tajfel conducted experiments in which he randomly assigned subjects to groups. He would then lie to subjects by telling them that group members shared some frivolous trait. Next, he conducted experiments to see how people treated members of their own group and other groups. He repeatedly found that subjects would then show strong favoritism toward members of their own group and distrust toward members of other ones.[52]

You might have seen videos on YouTube or late-night television showing how intergroup bias and motivated reasoning work. For instance, an interviewer will ask someone if they are a Democrat or Republican. If the person answers that they are a Democrat, the interviewer will then ask them questions like, "What do you think about policy X that Obama implemented? What do you think of policy Y that Bush implemented?" The typical Democrat will then talk at great length about how great X is and how bad Y was. But then the interviewer will reveal it was a trick; in fact, Obama implemented Y, and Bush implemented X. The interviewed subject will get angry, deny everything, and stomp away.

Political psychologist Geoffrey Cohen did a number of scientific studies using this trick in order to determine how partisanship affects people's judgments about policies. As fellow political psychologist Dennis Chong sums up Cohen's work,

> The experiment presented participants with two contrasting versions—generous or stringent—of a social welfare policy. Judging

each policy on its merits, respondents preferred the version that was consistent with their ideological values. But when the policies were attributed to either the Democratic or Republican Party, liberal respondents favored the Democratic-labeled policy regardless of whether it was generous or stringent, and conservatives favored the Republican-labeled policy regardless of details.[53]

Taken in isolation, this kind of study doesn't necessarily demonstrate that people are irrational. After all, if I think that, say, the Harvard economics department is smart, and I then learn that it supports a particular policy, I might rationally defer to its opinion. If I hear that, for example, economist Andrei Schleifer disagrees with me about something in behavioral finance, I take that as strong presumptive evidence that I am wrong. Nevertheless, in the context of all the various studies on partisan biases in how we process information, it appears more likely that people are trying to be faithful to the team versus processing information in the most rational way.[54]

As I discussed above, many people acquire political information because they have a taste for politics. Somin has a good analogy: some people are political *fans*.[55] Sports fans enjoy rooting for a team. They learn player histories, stats, odds, and sports facts, not because this information will help their team win, but because doing so increases their enjoyment of the game. Sports fans, however, also tend to evaluate information in a biased way. They tend to "play up evidence that makes their team look good and their rivals look bad, while downplaying evidence that cuts the other way."[56]

This is what tends to happen in politics. People tend to see themselves as being on team Democrat or team Republican, team Labor or team Conservative, and so on. They acquire information because it helps them root for their team and against their hated rivals. If the rivalry between Democratic and Republican voters sometimes seems like the rivalry between Red Sox and Yankees fans, that's because from a psychological point of view, it very much is.

One might object that many voters claim to be independent. But in fact, study after study shows that almost all self-described independent voters are closet partisans; they belong to a team and always vote for the same party.[57]

Political scientist Diana Mutz finds striking evidence that political "fandom" is what motivates people to get to the polls. The people who are most active in politics tend to have strong hooligan characteristics. Politically active citizens are usually people who have strong opinions, but who rarely talk to people who have different opinions, and who are unable to explain the rationale behind contrary viewpoints.[58] Being exposed to contrary perspectives tends to lessen one's enthusiasm for one's own political views. Deliberation with others who hold contrary views tends to make one ambivalent and apathetic about politics, and less likely to participate.[59] What Mutz calls "cross-cutting political exposure"—exposure to contrary points of view, or talking to people who disagree—strongly decreases the likelihood that a person will vote, reduces the number of political activities a person engages in, and makes people take longer to decide how to vote.[60] In contrast, actively participating citizens tend not to engage in much deliberation and tend not to have much cross-cutting political discussion.[61] The people who participate the most are those who spend the most time in echo chambers.

If you want to see one effect of tribalism, consider how beliefs about certain political issues tend to be clustered together, even though these issues have nothing to do with each other. Consider the following topics: gun control, global warming, how to handle the Islamic State of Iraq and Syria, mandatory paid maternity leave for women, the minimum wage, gay marriage, the Common Core curriculum, and flag burning. If I know your stance on any one of these issues, I can predict with a high degree of reliability what your stance is on all the others.

If you think about that, it's rather strange. The issues are logically unrelated. The arguments for and against abortion rights have almost nothing to do with gun control. Yet if you're pro-choice, you're almost certainly pro-gun control, and if you're pro-life, you're almost certainly anti-gun control. If you want to raise the minimum wage, you probably believe global warming is a major threat, and that government needs to intervene to stop it. If you oppose raising the minimum wage, you probably believe global warming isn't real, isn't produced by humans, or isn't a big deal, and that government should do little or nothing about it. One political party and its adherents have picked one set of beliefs about these issues, while the other political party and its adherents have picked the opposite beliefs. There's rationally no reason why this should be so, since these beliefs are independent. So a good part of the explanation seems to be tribalism: the tribes have settled on answers, and people express fidelity to their tribe by adopting its beliefs.

One could imagine, say, a Democrat objecting that there is a reason why their beliefs tend to cluster together. Democrats' beliefs are all *true*, even if logically unrelated. Democrats are just people who are unusually good at getting at the truth, and so that's why Democrats tend to share a particular set of beliefs.

But even if that were so, why then would Republicans hold the opposite set of beliefs? If Democrats were just unusually good at discovering the truth, that would explain why Democrats converge on one set of logically unrelated beliefs, but it wouldn't explain why Republicans (or non-Democrats in general) converge on the opposite beliefs. We'd instead expect that Republicans would tend to have randomly distributed and disparate beliefs about most of these topics. We'd expect Democrats' beliefs to be positively correlated with one another, but Republicans' beliefs would have few or no positive correlations. We'd expect Democrats' beliefs to form a cluster, but not Republicans' beliefs. I suppose the Democrat objector might respond it's not just that Democrats are unusually good at discovering the truth, but that Republicans are unusually inclined to form false beliefs. (Some of my academic colleagues, who are unrepentant hooligans, will laugh here and say, yes, that's precisely it.)

It's *possible* that this is true. But the evidence speaks against it. If we knew that one party had high-information voters while the other had low-information ones, that fact would tend to support the hypothetical Democrat's argument. Yet while the average Republican is slightly better informed than the average Democrat, the differences in knowledge are not staggering.

On this point, consider the studies I mentioned above about how information affects our policy preferences. Althaus and others have shown that, even once we correct for whatever influence demographic factors have on our political preferences, low- and high-information voters have systematically different political preferences. We can use these studies to test the hypothesis that the reason Democrats accept one cluster of (logically unrelated) beliefs while Republican accept the opposite cluster is that one party is unusually good at tracking the truth even as the other is amazingly good at avoiding it. But Althaus doesn't find that information tends to make one converge on Democrats' or Republicans' beliefs. Rather, the enlightened US public agrees with Democrats on some issues, Republicans on some others, and rejects both Democratic and Republican stances on yet other concerns.[62]

OTHER EXAMPLES OF COGNITIVE BIAS IN POLITICS

We suffer from an impressive range of other cognitive biases, each of which impedes our ability to reason clearly about politics.

Confirmation bias and disconfirmation bias: We tend to accept evidence that supports our preexisting views. We tend to reject or ignore evidence that disconfirms our preexisting views.[63] We tend to search for and uncritically accept evidence that favors our current opinions, and ignore, reject, or are bored by or suspicious of evidence that undermines our current opinions. We give every benefit of the doubt to arguments and people supporting our views, yet we dismiss arguments and people critical of our views. We care not about the truth but instead about defending our turf. In fact, many political partisans are so biased that when they are presented with evidence that they are mistaken, they double down—they come to believe even more strongly that they were right.[64]

Confirmation bias explains how we consume news and information. Most people only read news that supports their preexisting opinions. Left-liberals read the *New York Times*. Conservatives flock to Fox News.

Law professor Dan Kahan recently did an ingenious experiment that shows just how corrupting politics can be.[65] He wanted to answer the question, When laypeople come to mistaken conclusions about social scientific matters, is it because they aren't smart enough to understand the evidence, or because they are too biased to process the evidence properly?

To test this, Kahan recruited a thousand subjects, gave them a basic mathematics aptitude test, and then surveyed their political views. He then asked them to reason through some scientific problems. The first problem was politically neutral. In it, he described a hypothetical study testing the effect of a skin cream on rashes. The subjects understood it was a hypothetical study and that they were being asked what conclusion the data would tend to support if true. Kahan purposefully made the mathematics tricky. Not surprisingly, only subjects with high mathematical aptitude scores figured out the right answer. Liberals and conservatives did equally well.

This gave Kahan a baseline by which to judge how people's political loyalties affect their ability to reason about evidence. Kahan reworded the math problem; he made it about gun control as opposed to skin cream. In one version, the hypothetical data would support the conclusion that bans on concealed handguns failed to decrease crime. In another, the data would support the conclusion that bans succeeded in decreasing crime. The math was exactly the same as with skin cream. So presumably people who got the answer right in the first case should get it right in the second.

On the contrary, people overwhelmingly concluded that the hypothetical data supported their preexisting beliefs about handguns and crime. Conservatives tended to believe that the math showed that allowing people to carry concealed handguns decreases crime. Liberals tended to believe the math proved that allowing people to carry concealed handguns fails to decrease crime. Kahan gave half the liberals the version that supported their belief, and half the version that undermined it. In both cases, the liberals concluded the hypothetical data supported their preexisting belief. Even when the data implied that concealed handguns decreased crime, liberals concluded overwhelmingly that the data said that concealed handguns failed to decrease crime. Kahan similarly gave half the conservatives the version that supported their preexisting belief, and half the version that undermined it. Again, in both cases the conservatives concluded that the data just supported their preexisting belief. Even when the data implied that concealed handguns failed to decrease crime, conservatives overwhelmingly concluded that the data said that concealed handguns succeeded in decreasing crime. Worse, the better people were at math—the higher they scored on the aptitude test—the more *biased* they were.

Availability bias: A few years ago, the news media realized Americans love stories about kidnapping. Soon, the national media started covering every child kidnapping in the United States. Because there was near-constant television coverage of kidnappings, most Americans believed that there was a kidnapping epidemic. The soft rock band Train sang that it was "calling all angels" because "children need to play inside so they don't disappear."[66] But in fact, kidnappings had been going down, not up; only about a hundred children a year are kidnapped by strangers in the United States. Kids are actually safer now than they were in the 1960s, and not just because their parents have recently become too paranoid to let them play outside.

The problem here is that we are terrible at estimating probabilities. When we are asked, "How frequently does X occur?" we use a cognitive shortcut: if we find it easy to think of examples of X, then we assume X must be common. If we find it difficult to think of examples, we assume X must be uncommon.

Psychologists Amos Tversky and Daniel Kahneman call this phenomenon "availability bias" or the "availability heuristic."[67] Vivid things—plane crashes, shark attacks, terrorist attacks, and Ebola—come to mind easily, so we assume these things are much more common than they are. Things that aren't vivid—deaths from the flu or pneumonia—do not come to mind easily, and so we wrongly conclude these things are uncommon.

Availability bias is dangerous in politics. It causes us to focus our attention and money on the wrong things.

Consider that in the past fifty years, there have been only about thirty-five hundred deaths from terrorism in the United States. The 9/11 attacks cost $30 billion in cleanup, property damage, and lost income to businesses. We might compare these lost lives and financial losses to the War on Terror itself. So far, fighting this war has killed over six thousand US soldiers, over two thousand US contractors, and over a hundred thousand (or maybe over two hundred thousand) innocent civilians in Afghanistan, Pakistan, and Iraq. The Watson Institute at Brown University estimates the total real monetary costs of the wars on terror at $3 to $4 trillion.[68] Political scientist John Mueller and civil engineer Mark Stewart say that to justify the expense of the Homeland Security Administration, the agency would need to prevent nearly seventeen hundred major terrorists events per year, which of course it doesn't.[69] The US War on Terror doesn't survive cost-benefit analysis. But Americans are bad at estimating probabilities, and so few wish to abolish Homeland Security.

Affective contagion and prior attitude effect: I characterize vulcans as dispassionate. Some political theorists might rebel against this; they might think that passion is a good thing in politics, and might complain that Western political philosophy has long had a bias against emotion.[70] But the psychological evidence indeed shows that passion corrupts our thinking. When people feel strongly about an issue, they are more likely to evaluate arguments about it in a polarized, biased way. Moreover, when people are feeling emotional (sad, angry, joyful, etc.), this corrupts their ability to think about politics.[71] How you evaluate political information, what conclusions you draw, depends on your mood. Experiments show that emotion causes us to ignore and evade evidence, or rationalize political beliefs. It leads to biased and motivated thinking.

Framing effects: How people evaluate information depends heavily on how the information is presented. Psychologists call this a framing effect.

Consider the following two questions.[72]

1. There is a disease that is expected to kill six hundred people. There are two possible programs that authorities can use to fight it. Program A will save exactly two hundred people. Program B has a one-third chance of saving all six hundred people, but a two-thirds chance that no one will be saved. Which program is better, A or B?

2. There is a disease that is expected to kill six hundred people. There are two possible programs that authorities can use to fight it. If program alpha is adopted, exactly four hundred people will die. If program beta is adopted, there is a one-third chance that nobody will die, but a two-thirds chance that everyone will die. Which program is better, alpha or beta?

If you look closely, you'll realize that questions 1 and 2 are the same. They describe exactly the same scenario and probabilities, but use different wording. Question 1 asks about saving people, and question 2 asks about letting them die. A perfectly rational person, a vulcan, would recognize this and give the same answer to both questions. But Americans aren't vulcans. When we ask them question 1, they prefer option A. When we ask them question 2, they prefer option beta. But option beta in question 2 is simply option B in question 1, worded differently.

In fact, such framing effects are persistent and expansive.[73] *How* questions are posed has a major effect on what opinions people form. A psychologically savvy person—a pollster, newscaster, pundit, politician, moderator in a deliberative forum, or person writing up a referendum question on a ballot—can use framing effects to get voters to pick one choice over another.

Peer pressure and authority: Other people's testimony matters. I believed Australia existed long before I ever set foot on Australian soil. I was justified in believing Australia existed because I had good, reliable testimony from others that it existed. So it often makes sense for us to listen to each other. Vulcans listen to others.

That said, we are biased to conform our opinion to that of the majority (or that of whatever group we want to be part of), even when it is irrational to do so. Perhaps the most famous example of this is the Asch experiment. In Solomon Asch's experiment, eight to ten students were shown sets of lines in which two lines were obviously the same length, and the others were obviously of different length. They were then asked to identify which lines matched. In the experiment, only one member of the group is an actual subject; the rest are collaborators. As the experiment proceeds, the collaborators begin unanimously to select the wrong line.

Asch wanted to know how the experimental subjects would react. If nine other students are all saying that lines A and B, which are obviously different, are the same length, would subjects stick to their guns or instead agree with the group? Asch found that about 25 percent of the subjects stuck to their own judgment and never conformed, about 37 percent of them caved in, coming to agree completely with the group, and the rest would sometimes conform and sometimes not.[74] Control groups responding privately in writing were only one-fifth as likely to be in error. These results have been well replicated.

For a long time, researchers wondered whether the conformists were lying or not. Were they just pretending to agree with the group, or did they actually believe that the nonidentical lines were identical because the group said so. Researchers recently repeated a version of the experiment using functional magnetic resonance imaging.[75] By monitoring the brain, they might be able to tell whether subjects were making an "executive decision" to conform to the group, or whether their perceptions actually changed.[76] The results suggest that many subjects actually come to see the world differently in order to conform to the group. Peer pressure might distort their eyesight, not just their will.[77]

These findings are frightening. People can be made to deny simple evidence right in front of their faces (or perhaps even come to actually see the world differently) just because of peer pressure. The effect should be even stronger when it comes to forming political beliefs.

WHY POLITICAL IRRATIONALITY IS RATIONAL

Political psychology shows that we are not disposed to be vulcans. But we can overcome our cognitive biases with effort. The problem, though, is that we have weak incentives to surmount our cognitive biases when thinking about politics. Just as it is instrumentally rational for most people to remain ignorant about politics, it is instrumentally rational for most of them to indulge their biases. They are, in Caplan's terms, *rationally irrational*.[78]

A person is rationally irrational when it is *instrumentally rational* for that person to be *epistemically irrational*. Instrumental rationality is about taking courses of action that serve one's ends. Epistemic rationality is about forming beliefs with the goal of seeking truth and avoiding error, using a scientific evaluation of the best-available evidence. It can sometimes be useful—instrumentally rational—for us to form our beliefs in an epistemically irrational way. So, for instance, suppose one lived in a fundamentalist theocratic monarchy or something close to it, such as most of Europe in the Middle Ages or Saudi Arabia right now. In those cases, it would be in your best interest to conform your beliefs to whatever the theocracy wanted, even if the evidence didn't support these beliefs.

In our day-to-day lives, we tend to get punished for being epistemically irrational. If you think looks are all that matters in a mate, you'll have a string of bad relationships. A person who indulges the belief that buying penny stocks is key to financial success will lose money. The Christian Scientist who indulges the belief that pneumonia can be cured by prayer might watch their children die. And so on. So reality tends to discipline us into thinking more rationally about these things.

Unfortunately, in politics, our individual political influence is so low that we can afford to indulge biases and irrational political beliefs. It takes time and effort to overcome our biases. Yet most citizens don't invest the effort to be rational about politics because rationality doesn't pay.

Suppose, for the sake of argument, that Marxist economic theory is false. Imagine that electing a Marxist candidate would be an absolute disaster—it would destroy the economy, and lead to widespread death and suffering. But now suppose Mark believes Marxism on epistemically irrational grounds—he has no evidence for it, but it caters to his preexisting biases and dispositions. Suppose Mark slightly *enjoys* being Marxist; he values being Marxist at, say, five dollars. Mark would be willing to overcome his biases and change his mind, but only if being Marxist started to cost him more than five dollars. Now suppose that Mark gets an opportunity to vote for the disastrous Marxist candidate or a decent run-of-the-mill Democrat. While it's a disaster for Mark if the Marxist wins, it's not a disaster for him to vote Marxist. Since Mark's vote counts for so little, the expected negative results of voting for the Marxist are infinitesimal, just as the expected value of voting Democrat is infinitesimal. Mark might as well continue to be and vote Marxist.

The problem, again, is that what goes for Mark goes for us all. Few of us have any incentive to process political information in a rational way.

AT LEAST VOTERS MEAN WELL, SORT OF

Political scientists have conducted numerous empirical studies of voter behavior, using a wide variety of methods. They overwhelmingly conclude that voters do *not* vote selfishly.[79] Instead, voters tend to be nationalist and sociotropic. That is, they tend to vote for what they *perceive* to be in the national interest rather than in their self-interest.

This may seem surprising. After all, most people are predominantly selfish in their daily lives. So if they are altruistic as voters, this cries out for explanation. Fortunately, we have the explanation in front of us. As I just discussed, individual votes don't matter. Rational, selfish people would not vote selfishly. They wouldn't vote at all, because the costs of casting a selfish vote exceed the expected benefits of voting. To illustrate this, suppose one presidential candidate promises to give me $10 million if elected. While it's worth $10 million to me for them to win, it's not even worth a penny for me to vote for them. I better promote my interests by staying home to drink Laphroaig than by voting.

So it goes with other citizens. If citizens do bother to vote, it will be out of a sense of duty or belonging, to express their ideologies, or to demonstrate their commitment to their political tribe. Since none of our votes matter, it doesn't cost us anything *extra* to cast an altruistic vote as opposed to a selfish one.

Voters generally want to promote the common good instead of their own narrow self-interest, but that doesn't mean they in fact succeed in doing so. When voters vote, they have both what we might call policy preferences and outcome preferences:

Policy preferences: The set of policies and laws they want candidates to support, such as increasing the estate tax, cutting spending, increasing tariffs, or escalating the war in Afghanistan.

Outcome preferences: The consequences they want candidates to produce, such as improving the economy for everyone, reducing the amount of criminal violence, increasing economic equality, or reducing the danger of terrorism.

To say that voters are nationalist and sociotropic is to make a claim about their outcome preferences. It tells us they want their elected officials to serve the common good of their country rather than their narrow self-interest or the common good of the entire world. But that doesn't mean that voters know enough to have good policy preferences. We sometimes mistakenly believe a policy will promote our favored outcomes, when that policy will in fact undermine those outcomes. So, for example, in 2008, Republicans sincerely believed cutting taxes and government spending would stimulate economic growth. Democrats sincerely believed increasing taxes and spending would stimulate economic growth. They can't both be right.

HOBBITS AND HOOLIGANS

In chapter 1, I argued that the public is split between hobbits and hooligans. To review, hobbits generally have low information and typically don't care much about politics. Hooligans generally have higher information and have strong opinions about politics, but they are biased in how they evaluate and process political information.

In this chapter, I've reviewed a number of findings from political science and political psychology. I showed:

- The overwhelming majority of people lack even an elementary knowledge of politics, and many of them are misinformed.
- Some people tend to have more knowledge than others. Knowledge is strongly tied to interest. That is, people acquire political knowledge primarily because they find it interesting.
- Most people process political information in a biased way—a way that reinforces their current ideology.
- The most active people in politics tend to be true believers who rarely talk to people who have contrary points of view and cannot articulate why someone might disagree with them.

These facts alone come close to dividing American almost in half along hobbit and hooligan lines. Pretty much everyone is disposed to be biased and irrational. Somewhat more than half of Americans, however, know nothing or less than nothing about politics, while the rest know a moderate amount about politics. All we need now to complete the picture is information about the *strength* of people's ideological preferences.

In one of the most famous studies of political opinion, Converse found that on any particular issue of broad political importance, the public could be partitioned into one of two groups: the first made up of citizens who possess genuine opinions and hold onto them tenaciously; the second and much larger group composed of citizens who are quite indifferent to the issue in question and who, when pressed, either confess their ignorance outright or, out of embarrassment or misplaced civic obligation, invent an attitude on the spot—not a real attitude, but a "nonattitude." Converse concluded that sizable fractions of the public "do not have meaningful beliefs, even on issues that have formed the basis for intense political controversy among elites for substantial periods of time."[80]

That's not to say that literally only a minority of people have any opinions. Rather, it's that there is a continuum. High-information citizens tend to have many strong opinions. Low-information citizens tend to have fewer and weaker opinions. The average citizen is somewhere in between. Subsequent studies have tended to confirm this.[81]

Today, fewer and fewer Americans regard themselves as political partisans. In a recent Gallup Poll, a record 42 percent of Americans identify as politically independent rather than Republican or Democrat.[82] Over the past forty years, the trend is that an increasing percentage of citizens identify themselves as independent. Yet further research shows that almost all these people who now classify themselves as independent are weak partisans versus true independents.[83] Weak partisans think of themselves as independent, but they almost always vote for the same political party. Weak partisans are halfway between hobbit and hooligan. Weak partisans, people who lean independent, and genuine independents participate less in politics, and are less likely to vote than strong partisans, but they also know less.[84]

CONCLUSION

Democracy empowers each person with an equal basic share of political power. But this is a small share indeed. Because the share is so small, citizens have little incentive to use their power responsibly.

Voting and air pollution have a lot in common. Consider that right now, Washington, DC, where I work, is one of the smoggiest cities in the United States. There is little heavy industry in the area, so almost all the smog comes from tailpipe emissions. DC's rush hour traffic is infamous. While drivers collectively cause the pollution, no single driver makes any significant difference. If I were the only driver, I could drive my turbocharged sports sedan to my heart's content and never cause any noticeable pollution. And the same goes for every other driver. How much *we* pollute makes a huge difference, but for each person, how much *they* pollute make no real difference. So each individual person has little incentive to stop polluting.

Democracy is much like that. Voters remain ignorant and irrational because democracy incentivizes them to remain ignorant and irrational. So we have to ask, What should we do about it?

Some political theorists and political scientists think we need to get people to talk. If people talk, they could overcome their ignorance and irrationality. In chapter 3, I'll argue that such talk tends to make things worse, not better. Others say we needn't worry, because democracy as a whole behaves as if people were vulcans, even though most voters are hobbits and hooligans. In chapter 7, I'll contend they're largely wrong about that.

If they are mistaken, then we need to ask, Just as we regulate emissions in order to control air pollution, should we regulate voting in order to control voting pollution?

CHAPTER 3

POLITICAL PARTICIPATION CORRUPTS

Mill worried—correctly, as we just saw in chapter 2—that most people tend to be poorly informed about history, the social sciences, and politics. He thought the typical British subject of his time was a hobbit. I think there's nothing wrong with being a hobbit, but Mill was an elitist and perfectionist.[1] He wanted to transform Britain's hobbits into vulcans. Mill hoped that getting citizens involved in politics would induce them to take on broader perspectives, empathize with one another more, and develop a stronger concern for the common good. He hoped political engagement would develop their critical thinking skills and increase their knowledge.

For these reasons, Mill advanced what I will call the education argument.[2] In its broadest and most generic form, it goes as follows:

1. Civic and political activity requires citizens to take a broad view of others' interests, and search for ways to promote the common good. This requires long-term thinking as well as engagement with moral, philosophical, and social scientific issues.
2. If so, then civic and political activity will tend to improve citizens' virtue and make them better informed.

3. Therefore, civic and political activity will tend to improve citizens' virtue and make them better informed.

The education argument is popular. Nineteenth-century historian and author of *Democracy in America* Alexis de Tocqueville also advanced it, though with many reservations.[3] Many contemporary political theorists also accept some version of it.[4] Most contemporary theorists try to make the premises more exact and rigorous, perhaps by specifying particular forms of participation that they think will enlighten or educate us.

The education argument sounds plausible. But whether the argument is sound or not depends on what people are like. It's possible that engaging with politics tends to improve people. It's possible it tends to have no effect. It's also possible that getting them to participate makes them worse.

In this chapter, I maintain that most common forms of political engagement are more likely to corrupt and stultify than to ennoble and educate people. Political engagement is more likely to turn a hobbit into a hooligan than into a vulcan. It is more likely to make hooligans even worse hooligans than to transform them into vulcans. Many advocates of the education argument will agree on this point, but then object that this just shows we need to find the right way to structure political activity and discussion. In response, I'll argue that while it is of course possible in principle to structure civic and political activity in ways that tend to educate and enlighten people, we don't seem to know how to do so, and most of the activities that my colleagues advocate tend to fail.

THE EDUCATION ARGUMENT DEPENDS ON THE FACTS

The education argument is popular among philosophers and theorists, but is not really a philosophical argument. We cannot determine whether it is sound by analyzing concepts, consulting intuitions, exploring the implications of our moral values, or reading the history of political theory and seeing how the discussion has unfolded over time.

Instead, the education argument is a social scientific one. The argument says that engagement is valuable *because* it produces certain desirable consequences. Whether it in fact produces those results is something we can, in principle, test using social scientific methods. So anyone advancing the education argument needs to supply us with the relevant evidence. In the absence of that, we should remain agnostic about whether the argument is sound or not.

The most charitable way to read the education argument is that it makes a controversial yet possibly correct empirical claim. It asserts that participation causes people to learn more and become more rational. Since the education argument rests on a controversial, positive claim, anyone advancing it thus bears the burden of proof. One must offer evidence, sufficient to withstand normal social scientific scrutiny, that participation does indeed have these positive effects. One must provide strong empirical evidence that when citizens participate more, they will tend to take a broad view of others' interests, search for ways to promote the common good, engage in long-term thinking, and grapple with moral, philosophical, and scientific issues.

Ideally, someone who advances the education argument would supply us with specific proposals about just what forms of participation are supposed to ennoble and educate. That person would explain just how and in what ways those forms of participation are supposed to ennoble and educate us. Finally, they would provide sufficient empirical evidence that those forms of participation do ennoble and educate us in just those ways. Otherwise, in the absence of compelling evidence, we must not accept the education argument.

Now suppose we don't know how to measure what participation does to us, and so we just don't know whether Mill is right or wrong. In that case, we should still not accept the education argument. Just as we should not accept, without proper evidence, that the paleo diet makes us healthier, so we should not accept, without proper evidence, that political participation cures ignorance and vice.

MERE PARTICIPATION DOES NOT IMPROVE KNOWLEDGE

Does merely getting people to vote cause them to become better educated?

As we saw in chapter 2, citizens who choose to vote tend to be better informed than those who choose not to vote.[5] But that does not suffice to show that participation *causes* people to be better informed. Chapter 2 demonstrated that people who are more interested in politics are both more likely to be well informed and more likely to participate. That evidence implied that voters know more not because they vote; rather, they vote more and they know more because they like politics. To support the education argument, we need evidence that political participation causes us to learn more.

Compare this issue to another, similar one. Many philosophy departments try to convince people that they should major in philosophy because it will make them smarter. As a matter of fact, philosophy majors get the best overall scores on the GRE, and some of the best scores on the LSAT, MCAT, and GMAT.[6] Philosophy majors tend to be smart. Yet test results, by themselves, provide no evidence that philosophy makes anyone smarter. The problem is that students choose their majors; the majors aren't chosen for them. Students tend to major in things they find interesting and are good at. So it's both possible and plausible that philosophy students excel at these standardized tests simply because the students who choose to major in philosophy are already good at logic, mathematics, and critical reasoning—precisely the things these standardized tests test. To use the language of psychology, if we see philosopher majors get high scores, this leaves open whether philosophy majors' high scores result from a *treatment effect*—that is, philosophy makes you smart—or *selection effect*—that is, smart people tend to major in philosophy.

In fact, we already have strong evidence of a selection effect. High school students who say they intend to major in philosophy have higher average SAT scores than those who are drawn to any other intended major, except physics.[7] Still, it's possible that there is a treatment effect on top of the selection effect—that is, that philosophy majors start off smart, but studying philosophy makes them even smarter.

In principle, we could test whether studying philosophy actually makes anyone smarter. We could run an experiment over a huge number of undergraduates, in which we collect their baseline scores, force them to major in different subjects, and then see how this affects their final scores. This experiment, however, would never pass a university's institutional review board.

Fortunately for the current discussion, governments are not bound by university institutional review boards' ethical standards. Some governments force citizens to vote, and this allows us to test whether getting citizens to vote causes them to acquire greater levels of knowledge.

The test results are negative. Political scientist Sarah Birch, in her comprehensive book *Full Participation*, reviews nearly every published paper examining whether compulsory voting improves voters' knowledge. She concludes that it does not. Birch also concludes that it has no significant effect on the individual propensity to contact politicians, the propensity to work with others to address concerns, or participation in campaign activities.[8] In a related work, political scientist Annabelle Lever recently reviewed the empirical studies on compulsory voting, and concluded that it had "no noticeable effect on political knowledge or interest [or] electoral outcomes."[9]

In short, if citizens start voting, this does not by itself cause them to take a greater interest in politics or learn more. This kind of participation does not have an educative benefit. We have no evidence that it has an aretaic benefit either.

DELIBERATIVE DEMOCRACY

Many advocates of the education argument will be nonplussed by these results. They would say that for participation to educate and enlighten us, it's not enough to vote. We need to talk. What we need is deliberative democracy.

Deliberative democracy refers to various forms of democracy in which people come together to advance ideas, argue about those ideas, weigh pros and cons, listen to one another, and criticize each other's ideas with an open mind. Most deliberative democrats advocate an ideal under which citizens argue with one another in a dispassionate, scientific way, and then, as a result, reach a consensus about what ought to be done. Deliberative democrats believe democracy should be inclusive—it should include a range of people of all races, gender identities, religions, socioeconomic status, and so on.

Hélène Landemore says, "Deliberation is supposed to . . . [e]nlarge the pools of ideas and information, . . . [w]eed out the good arguments from the bad, . . . [and lead] to a consensus on the 'better' or more 'reasonable' solution."[10] Bernard Manin, Elly Stein, and Jane Mansbridge contend that democratic deliberation is a process of training and education.[11] Joshua Cohen claims "the need to advance reasons that persuade others will help to shape the motivations that people bring to the deliberative procedure." Cohen also holds that *ideal* deliberative procedures can be expected to "shape the identity and interests of citizens in ways that contribute to the common good."[12] Jon Elster asserts that in democratic deliberation, people will need to advance their proposals by appeal to the common good, and will find it difficult to defend their proposals in such terms unless they really are concerned with the common good (rather than just paying lip service to it).[13] Amy Gutmann and Dennis Thompson maintain that even when deliberation fails to produce consensus, it will generally cause citizens to respect one another more.[14]

Deliberative democrats don't just want people to talk about politics; they want them to deliberate. Deliberation connotes an orderly, reason-guided process. Deliberative democrats tend endorse a demanding ideal of how political deliberation ought to go. So, for example, Habermas says deliberators should observe the following rules:

- Speakers must be consistent; they must not contradict themselves.
- Speakers must treat like cases alike.
- Speakers should use terms and language in a consistent way so as to make sure they are all referring to the same things. (There should be no equivocating or switching definitions in ways that would interfere with communication.)
- Speakers must be sincere; they must assert only what they believe.
- Speakers must provide reasons for introducing a subject or topic into the discussion.
- Everyone who is competent to speak should be allowed into the discussion.
- Speakers should be allowed to discuss any topic, assert whatever they like, and express any needs—so long as they are sincere.
- No one may coerce or manipulate another speaker.[15]

Cohen advocates similar rules. Participants should have equal voice. Everyone must offer reasons for their views, and only the reasons expressed during the deliberation should determine the outcome of the deliberation. Everyone should reach consensus, or if that's not possible, they should take a vote.[16]

WHAT DELIBERATION DOES TO US DEPENDS ON OUR PSYCHOLOGY

The claim that deliberation will educate and enlighten us has intuitive appeal. Imagine how vulcans would deliberate. Vulcans are perfectly scientific thinkers. They apportion belief according to the evidence. They seek out new evidence for and against their beliefs. Vulcans have no loyalty to their beliefs; they readily abandon those beliefs once the evidence stops supporting them.

Now think about how hobbits would deliberate, if hobbits were perfectly rational. Hobbits are poorly informed. If hobbits were rational but merely ignorant, however, then deliberation would tend to turn them into vulcans. They probably each have a little bit of information. If they would just share it with one another, they could learn a huge amount.

Now imagine what would happen if we put perfectly rational hobbits and vulcans together. The vulcans know they know more than the hobbits, and the hobbits know they know less than the vulcans. But the vulcans would also acknowledge that hobbits might have some information that they, the vulcans, lack. They would recognize that even hobbits have good ideas, opinions, and criticisms. The hobbits recognize this about themselves, too. When ideally rational hobbits and vulcans deliberate together, everyone will be better off.

This is the model of discourse that many deliberative democrats have in mind. If people are sincere, rational, offer reasons for their views, give every voice proper respect, and so forth, then of course deliberation will educate people. If people were to follow Habermas's or Cohen's rules, then they would deliberate the way vulcans would deliberate. *Of course* deliberation would educate and enlighten them.

But as philosopher Michael Huemer comments, deliberative democracy so described looks like fantasy: "If there is one thing that stands out when one reads philosophical descriptions of deliberative democracy, it is how far these descriptions fall from reality. Of the four features of deliberative democracy that Cohen identifies, how many are satisfied by any actual society?"[17] Huemer thinks the answer is none.

Habermas and Cohen say that citizens must advance reasons for their proposals. They believe citizens should decide what to do solely on the basis of the reasons advanced during deliberation. They claim the best argument should win. But in actual democracies and deliberation, no one is literally required to state reasons for their policy proposals. People in fact do advance policy proposals without offering good reasons, or any reasons at all. Indeed, people often are swayed by rhetoric, charisma, and good looks rather than by the "force of the better argument."[18]

Consider instead how hooligans would deliberate, if we even want to honor their discussions with that label. Hooligans would try to dominate the discussion. They would ignore, jeer at, and dismiss one another during disagreements. They would insult one another, or at least mutter insults under their breath. Hooligans would fail to both offer reasons for their views and accept others' reasons, even when they *should*. They would happily manipulate one another, use language in a deceitful way to confuse people, and lie, if doing so helps their side. In the face of contrary evidence, hooligans will just dig in their heels and get angry. When hooligans deliberate, the "force of the better argument" is impotent. What matters are rhetoric, sex appeal, and promoting the team. When hooligans deliberate, they get *worse*.

As I discussed in chapter 2, political psychology shows that most of us are much more like hooligans than like vulcans. We suffer from a number of biases, including:

Confirmation bias: We tend to accept evidence that supports our preexisting views.

Disconfirmation bias: We tend to reject or ignore evidence that disconfirms our preexisting views.

Motivated reasoning: We have preferences over what we believe, and tend to arrive at and maintain beliefs we find comforting or pleasing, or whatever beliefs we prefer to have.

Intergroup bias: We tend to form coalitions and groups. We tend to demonize members of other groups, but are highly forgiving and charitable toward members of our own groups. We go along with whatever our group thinks and oppose what other groups think.

Availability bias: The easier it is for us to think of something, the more common we think that thing is. The easier it is for us to think of an event occurring, the more significant we assume the consequences will be. We are thus terrible at statistical reasoning.

Prior attitude effect: When we care strongly about an issue, we evaluate arguments about the issue in a more polarized way.

Peer pressure and authority: People tend to be influenced irrationally by perceived authority, social pressure, and consensus.

Given these prevalent biases in political psychology, real-life political deliberation could easily corrupt and stultify rather than ennoble and enlighten us. Deliberation presents citizens the opportunity to confront new ideas and information in a rational way. But similarly, frat parties present college students with the opportunity to practice and cultivate the virtue of temperance.

EMPIRICAL WORK ON DELIBERATIVE DEMOCRACY

There is large amount of empirical work on how democratic deliberation actually proceeds, and what it actually does to people. The results are largely discouraging for deliberative democracy and the education argument.

In a comprehensive survey of all the extant (as of 2003) empirical research on democratic deliberation, political scientist Tali Mendelberg remarks that the "empirical evidence for the benefits that deliberative theorists expect" is "thin or non-existent."[19] In her survey, Mendelberg finds:

- Deliberation sometimes facilitates cooperation among individuals in social dilemmas, but it undermines cooperation among groups. When people self-identify as members of a group, including as members of political groups, deliberation tends to make things worse, not better.[20] (Remember that in the real world, people tend to self-identify as members of a political group.)

- When groups are of different sizes, deliberation tends to exacerbate conflict rather then mediate it.[21] (Note that in realistic circumstances, political groups tend to be different sizes.)
- Deliberation does tend to make people more aware of others' interests. Nevertheless, other empirical work shows that if groups simply state their preferences *without* any discussion, this is just as effective as stating their preferences *with* discussion.[22] So deliberation per se isn't itself helpful in this case.
- Status seeking drives much of the discussion. Instead of debating the facts, people try to win positions of influence and power over others.[23]
- Ideological minorities have disproportionate influence, and much of this influence can be attributed to groups' "social appeal."[24]
- High-status individuals talk more, are perceived as more accurate and credible, and have more influence, regardless of whether the high-status individuals actually know more.[25]
- During deliberation, people use language in biased and manipulative ways. They switch, for example, between concrete and abstract language in order to create the appearance that their side is essentially good (and any badness is accidental) while the other side is essentially bad (and any goodness is accidental). If I describe my friend as kind, this abstract language suggests that they will regularly engage in kind behavior. If I say that my enemy donated some money to Oxfam, this concrete language leaves open the question of whether this kind of behavior matches my enemy's character and could be expected again.[26]
- Even when prodded by moderators to discuss controversial matters, groups tend to avoid conflict, focusing instead on mutually accepted beliefs and attitudes.[27]
- When a discussant mentions commonly held information or beliefs, this tends to make them seem smarter and more authoritative to others, and thus tends to increase their influence. As such, Mendelberg concludes, "in most deliberations about public matters," group discussion tends to "amplify" intellectual biases rather than "neutralize" them.[28]
- Deliberation works best on "matters of objective truth"—when citizens are debating easily verifiable facts and statistics, such

as information one could find on the US Census Bureau's website. During "other times"—when citizens debate morals, justice, or social scientific theories meant to evaluate those facts—"deliberation is likely to fail."[29]

Mendelberg describes significant evidence of motivated reasoning by deliberators. Deliberators who expect to have an unpopular position tend to do more research before deliberation begins and tend to come actively prepared to listen. They nonetheless seek out evidence that will support their view while overlooking evidence against it. They come prepared to listen only because they want to find ways to convince the majority of their side. In contrast, deliberators who expect to be in majority positions do not come prepared to listen and do not do any homework ahead of time.[30] Other studies have shown that when presented with new research on the deterrent effects of capital punishment, both those for and against capital punishment interpret the studies in favor of their preexisting viewpoints.[31]

After surveying many other examples of motivated reasoning in politics, Mendelberg concludes that

> the use of reasoned argument to reinforce prior sentiment is a widespread phenomenon that poses a significant challenge to deliberative expectations. Motivated reasoning has considerable power to interfere with the motivation that deliberative theory cherishes—the motivation to be open-minded, evenhanded, and fair. Deliberators can hardly pursue truth and justice if they view everything in favor of their priors through rose-tinted glass and everything against it through dark ones.[32]

In short, people tend to deliberate like hooligans, not like vulcans. Mendelberg therefore ends her review by observing,

> When groups engage in discussion, we cannot count on them to generate empathy and diminish narrow self-interest, to afford equal opportunities for participation and influence even to the powerless, to approach the discussion with a mind open to change, and to be influenced not by social pressures, unthinking

commitments to social identities, or power, but by the exchange of relevant and sound reasons.[33]

Mendelberg's take on the empirical literature is not unusual. Other reviews of the extant political literature—including by people who *favor* deliberative democracy—find similar results.[34] For instance:

- Deliberation tends to move people toward more extreme versions of their ideologies rather than toward more moderate versions. Legal theorist Cass Sunstein calls this the "Law of Group Polarization."[35]
- Deliberation over sensitive matters—such as pornography laws—frequently leads to "hysteria" and "emotionalism," with parties to the debate feigning moral emergencies as well as booing and hissing at one another.[36]
- In actual deliberation, some groups get a greater voice than others, and leaders are often chosen in sexist or racially biased ways.[37]
- Deliberation often causes deliberators to choose positions inconsistent with their own views—positions that the deliberators "later regret."[38]
- Deliberation frequently causes deliberators to doubt there is a correct position at all. This leads to moral or political skepticism or nihilism.[39]
- Deliberation often makes citizens apathetic and agnostic about politics, and thus prevents them from participating or acting. Exposure to contrary points of view tends to induce citizens to disengage with politics, thereby reducing their degree of civic participation.[40]
- During deliberation, citizens frequently change their preferences and reach consensus only because they are manipulated by powerful special interests.[41]
- Consensus often occurs only because citizens purposefully avoid controversial topics, even during organized deliberative forums designed to make them confront those topics.[42]
- Rather than causing consensus, public deliberation might cause disagreement along with the formation of in-groups and out-groups.[43] It can even lead to violence.[44]

- Citizens prefer *not* to engage in deliberative modes of reasoning and prefer that deliberation not last long.[45] They dislike deliberating.

Overall, the empirical literature on deliberation looks bad for deliberative democrats. Most studies find that actual deliberation fails to deliver the results deliberative democrats would like to see. In fact, it frequently delivers the *opposite* ones. These results therefore tend to undermine the education argument. On its face, the empirical evidence seems to show us both that people are too hooliganish to deliberate properly and that deliberation makes them *more* hooliganish.

Some deliberative democrats advocate replacing or at least supplementing mass voting with "deliberative polling." In a deliberative poll, one brings together, say, a thousand citizens to deliberate about a given topic. The citizens are selected at random, although the poll's organizers try to ensure that the demographics of the deliberative body are similar to those of the community or nation as a whole. The organizers give the deliberators relevant informational sources, such as news articles, social scientific papers, and philosophical arguments for various sides. A moderator helps spur participants to deliberate and do so properly. The moderator tries to ensure that people stick to the topics at hand and that no one dominates the conversation. There is some evidence that this kind of moderated deliberation can work, at least in the laboratory and even in some real-world scenarios.

Yet if we try to export these experiments to real-world decision making, deliberative polls are ripe for abuse. It's one thing to have moderated, controlled deliberate polls when nothing is at stake. It's another when such polls might actually choose policy. In the real world, politicians and others will seek to control the agenda, frame the debate in a way that is favorable to their position, distribute informational materials that favor their side and make the other side look dumb, and so on. As I explored in chapter 2, *how* a question or debate is phrased can easily lead people to switch their positions.

Consider how professors teaching classes on politics will tend to select materials from many points of view, but still tend to select stronger materials for their own perspective and tend to teach in a way that favors their own opinions. They tend to do this even when they want to be fair, because it's hard to be fair to the other side. This happens when *nothing* is at stake. What happens when deliberation actually matters, such as when it can decide law?

That said, the research on deliberative polling shows promise. It may be able to overcome many of the problems of mass participation and mass democracy. But advocates of deliberative polling don't yet have sufficient evidence to proclaim it a solution to our troubles or counterexample to my general thesis that political participation tends to corrupt.

In the end, I am an instrumentalist about the choice between democracy and epistocracy. If democracy with deliberative polling (with whatever abuses and flaws it suffers) turns out to produce better results than the best form of epistocracy (with whatever abuses and flaws it suffers), then I'll advocate democracy with deliberative polling. If the results come out the other way, I'll advocate epistocracy. As I said in the introduction, and as I'll argue more in later chapters, we don't have the evidence to know for sure which works better. But the extant work on deliberative democracy is not promising.

WHY A NEUTRAL RESULT IS A NEGATIVE ONE

As we saw, there is ample empirical evidence that deliberation often stultifies or corrupts us, that it frequently exacerbates our biases and leads to greater conflict. For the sake of argument, however, suppose none of this evidence existed. Suppose instead that all we had were neutral results. That is, suppose empirical political scientists had continually tried to test the thesis that deliberation educates and enlightens, but continually failed to find evidence that it does. It would be tempting in that case to conclude that deliberation is pointless and ineffective, but at least not *harmful*.

Researchers often present their findings this way. Sometimes, researchers say that while they didn't find positive results, they at least didn't measure negative ones. The results were neutral.

On the contrary, I'll contend here, a neutral result is usually a negative one. If people deliberate together, but this fails to educate or enlighten them, then this means they are actually *worse off* as a result of deliberation. If I am right, then the existing empirical work on deliberative democracy is much more damning than other philosophers, political theorists, and political scientists have realized.

What is rational for you to believe or not depends on the evidence available to you. Imagine a child has led a sheltered life, with no exposure to history, geology, biology, physics, or cosmology. They believe, on the basis of their young Earth creationist parents' testimony, that the universe is six thousand years old and that all animals were created six thousand years ago. But suppose this child then takes sixteen years of classes in history, geology, biology, physics, and cosmology. Along the way, they get to sequence DNA, re-create Gregor Mendel's pea experiment, handle fossils, and the like. After sixteen years of intense study, though, suppose they continue to believe the world is six thousand years old and that all animals were created as they currently are.

In this case, from an epistemological standpoint, they got *worse*. After all, they encountered an overwhelming amount of evidence confirming evolution and disconfirming young Earth creationism. They *should* have changed their mind, but didn't. After sixteen years of study, the gap between what they believe and what they ought to believe increased. Their beliefs are less justified now than they were sixteen years ago, before taking the classes and doing the experiments. They have thus violated their epistemic duties. They added further wrongdoing to their epistemic tally sheet. They are more epistemically delinquent after getting new evidence than they were before. In that case, it would be a mistake to report that taking classes had a *neutral* effect on their epistemic situation. This person is actually worse off.

Now consider what happens during deliberation. When someone learns that other smart, well-informed people disagree with them about some issue, they might question whether they should reduce their confidence in their own beliefs.[46] If they encounter new information and evidence, they should revise their beliefs accordingly. Even in badly run, badly functioning deliberations, most citizens encounter new arguments and new information—arguments and information that *should* cause them to revise their beliefs or weaken their degree of confidence. Citizens should weigh other citizens' testimony on the basis of how expert, reasonable, and reliable those citizens are likely to be, and revise their own beliefs accordingly. If the citizens do not revise their beliefs accordingly, then their epistemic situation has worsened. Deliberation made them more delinquent.

As such, when deliberation has *no* effect on citizens' beliefs or their degree of credence in their beliefs, we should generally interpret this as showing that deliberation made them worse, from an epistemic viewpoint. Just as a university-educated young Earth creationist is epistemically inferior to an uneducated young Earth creationist, so a person who does not revise their beliefs or degrees of belief after deliberation is (usually) epistemologically inferior to their situation before deliberation.

Deliberative democrats must conclude that similar remarks apply to citizens' *moral* status postdeliberation. Deliberative democrats usually hold that the rules of proper deliberation are moral. They believe citizens have moral *duties* to abide by the rules of deliberative democracy. In their view, citizens are obligated to deliberate properly. Given this, if we find that most citizens are not deliberating properly, the deliberative democrat should conclude that the gap between what the citizen ought to have done and did in fact do has widened. The citizen has added further moral wrongdoings to their lifetime moral tally sheet. After deliberation, they are more defective from a moral point of view than they were before.

"PEOPLE JUST AREN'T DELIBERATING THE RIGHT WAY"

Mutz remarks, "It is one thing to claim that political conversation has the *potential* to produce beneficial outcomes if it meets a whole variety of unrealized criteria, and yet another to argue that political conversations, as they actually occur, produce meaningful benefits for citizens."[47] Real people (whether in town hall meetings or laboratory experiments) do not usually follow Habermas's or Cohen's rules for proper deliberation. Deliberation doesn't typically generate the intended results either.

Since the empirical work on deliberation generally returns negative results, one might guess that most deliberative democrats would become disillusioned and give up being deliberative democrats. One might expect that most deliberative democrats would advocate deliberation cautiously or with reservations, only in those cases where we had solid evidence it works.[48]

On the contrary, deliberative democrats tend to be nonplussed by the empirical results described above. (For what it's worth, the empirically minded deliberative democrats behave much better here than the philosophers and theorists.) They tend to assume the benefits of deliberation will be revealed in due time. They presume we are just about to discover a method to ensure that real people deliberate in a vulcan-like as opposed to hooligan-like fashion. Mendelberg notes that despite the "thinness of evidence showing that deliberation . . . works as expected," and despite the dangers that deliberation might make matters worse, many theorists want to create more rather than fewer opportunities for real-life deliberation.[49]

Many political theorists say we just need *proper* deliberation. The empirical studies do not falsify or disconfirm the purported benefits of deliberative democracy, because as the research itself shows, *people aren't deliberating the right way*—the way that the deliberative democrats say they should.[50] For instance, Landemore maintains that these studies merely show we need to find ways to "set up the optimal conditions" to produce "genuine deliberation with others."[51] Even Mendelberg speculates that by doing proper empirical research on deliberation, we "can hope to create conditions that allow deliberation to succeed."[52]

Deliberative democrats can rightly assert that the research hasn't falsified their views, because people aren't deliberating properly. After all, as anyone who has taken introductory logic should know, these two sets of claims are compatible:

A. If people deliberate properly, this will tend to educate and ennoble them.
B. People do not deliberate properly, and improper deliberation fails to educate and ennoble them. In fact, it stultifies them and exacerbates their biases.

The evidence I discussed above tends to verify B, but verifying B doesn't disprove A. The statement "If P then Q" is *not* falsified by evidence of "not-P and not-Q." So the empirical research doesn't show that proper deliberation fails to educate or ennoble. Deliberative democrats can continue to claim that *if* people would follow, say, Habermas's rules of proper discourse, *then* deliberation would deliver certain educative and aretaic benefits. The evidence itself just shows that people do not follow those rules.

This response is correct. Still, deliberative democrats should not rest secure. To see why, let's parody the debate here.

Sigma Alpha Epsilon "strives to give young men the leadership, scholarship, service and social experiences they need to excel." Chapters of this fraternity "strive to mold [their] members into gentlemen so they can set an example in today's society."[53] Sigma Nu stylizes its members as "knights" who "believe in the life of love, walk in the way of honor, and serve in the light of truth."[54] Beta Theta Pi intends to "develop men of principle for a principled life."[55] Phi Delta Theta "was built on three pillars that haven't budged an inch since" the fraternity was founded, including the pillar of "the attainment . . . of a high standard of morality."[56]

Fraternities are usually founded on high-minded ideals. They strive to transform ordinary men into extraordinary men, to bring out the best in each of them. Most fraternities have extensive educational programs meant to cultivate virtue, scholarship, and a commitment to service among their brothers. College social fraternities are supposed to make men into better men. These fraternities are supposed to serve both educative and aretaic functions.

Frats tend to fall far short of these ideals. Many college frats are full of drunken men who take advantage of drunken women. Fraternity men are disproportionately represented among men who commit rape or sexual assault on a college campus.[57] Men who join fraternities drink more, and drink more frequently, than other college males.[58] Fraternity men are more likely to engage in academic dishonesty than men who do not join fraternities.[59] Though most fraternities' mission statements say they are dedicated to high standards of scholarship, first-year fraternity men tend to have worse GPAs and do worse on various tests of cognitive ability than nonfraternity men, although this gap tends to shrink over time.[60] It's possible these are all just selection effects, but when doing a literature search, I could find no evidence that joining a fraternity tends to *improve* men's GPAs.

Not all fraternities are the same, of course. Some individual fraternity chapters on some campuses are better than others. Yet the evidence seems to show that fraternities tend to undermine rather than support their aretaic and educative goals. Fraternities seem to be more of a disease than a cure, however noble their founders' intentions were.

Imagine a conversation in which a critic of college fraternities advanced all these concerns. The critic complains about the drunkenness, abuse of pledges, sexual exploitation of women, homophobia, and poor academic performance. Now imagine that the executive director of Sigma Alpha Epsilon responds,

> Sure, most *actual* fraternities tend to corrupt men instead of ennobling them. But fraternities *would* educate and ennoble college men, if only fraternity men acted properly and went through the fraternity experience the right way. The college fraternity experience provides an excellent opportunity for men to develop into true gentlemen, who live with honor, who hold themselves to the highest moral standards. It's just too bad that men do not properly take advantage of this opportunity. Still, I think it's important that we keep providing them with the opportunity, as much as possible. It's also important that we keep researching ways to induce men to use the fraternity experience the correct way. In fact, we're doing that now, as we're trying to put more restrictions on our members' behavior. We're actively researching how to generate better behavior from our members.

There's a sense in which the executive director's response is absolutely correct and yet misses the point. The director is probably correct that fraternities would ennoble and educate, if only the men who joined them behaved appropriately. The director is also correct that there should in principle be a way to create fraternities that generate consistently good outcomes. The director, too, is right to assert that if such a method of running fraternities were discovered, then we might reasonably hope that all men join them.

At the same time, the director fails to take the criticisms of fraternities seriously. Critics of fraternities do not deny that in principle, or that under highly idealized circumstances, fraternities *could* educate and ennoble. Instead, they are complaining that as a matter of fact, fraternities *don't* educate and ennoble; they stultify and corrupt. They tend to do more harm than good. In theory, we could discover how to make fraternities function well, but we don't seem to know how to do so right now, and the current research is not altogether promising.

Deliberative democrats want to avoid this mistake. If they say, "Sure, actual deliberation messes people up, but proper deliberation would improve their character and knowledge," that's not much different from stating, "Sure, actual fraternities mess men up, but proper fraternities would improve their character and scholarship."

Politics *can* serve an educative or aretaic function. Lots of things—joining the Bloods, shooting heroin, or dropping out of high school—*can*. But overall, the education argument for political participation seems on par or worse than the education argument for fraternity participation. The most common forms of political participation are more likely to corrupt than ennoble us. Now perhaps in the future a political scientist will discover a form of participation that in fact tends to ennoble most people, and could be implemented without abuse on a large scale. Similarly, a reformer could one day discover how to make fraternities work better, not just in principle, but with reforms we could feasibly implement on a large scale. That day hasn't yet come.

CONCLUSION: AGAINST POLITICS

Sometimes it is better for a person's epistemic character if they remain ignorant and apathetic. Sometimes even as people gather information, they do so in a biased and corrupted way. Perhaps the disposition to be corrupted lies there all along, but it's better that it remains dormant.

For these reasons, we have strong presumptive grounds against encouraging more and more citizens to participate in politics, spend time thinking about politics, watch political news, or engage in political deliberation. If political engagement tends to be corrupting versus edifying, that's a count against it. It may be that this presumption can be overcome, however, if widespread participation produces some other, more important good, or if participation turns out to be some sort of end in itself. Let's turn to arguments to that effect.

CHAPTER 4

POLITICS DOESN'T EMPOWER YOU OR ME

A man is no less a slave because he is allowed to choose a new master once in a term of years.

—*Herbert Spencer, "The Right to Ignore the State"*

Political participation tends to have a corrupting effect on our moral and epistemic character, but perhaps it provides some other benefit that outweighs this cost. It's the devil's bargain, yet maybe we should take it.

I had a housemate in college who sincerely believed she was a witch and possessed the power to alter the weather in subtle ways. She no doubt felt empowered when casting one of her fake spells. The feeling was real, but the belief was an illusion.

I'm worried something similar happens to voters in democracies. Many laypeople and theorists believe that political liberty and engagement are good for us, as *individuals*, because they empower us (again, as individuals) in some way. Suffragist and feminist leader Elizabeth Cady Stanton claimed, "The right of suffrage is simply the right to govern one's self. Every human being is born into the world with this right."[1] More recently, philosopher Michael Cholbi claimed that the right to vote is essential to the right of self-determination, by which he means "the right to shape the conditions of one's own existence."[2]

In this chapter, I'll look at five ways that, according to various philosophers and lay thinkers, possessing the political liberties and participating in politics could empower individuals:

Consent: Your political liberty and participation allow you to consent to government.

Interests: Your political liberty and participation make government responsive to your interests.

Autonomy: Your political liberty and participation give you increased autonomy.

Nondomination: Your political liberty and participation prevent others from dominating you.

Moral development: Your political liberty and participation are essential for you to develop a sense of the good life and capacity for a sense of justice.

I contend instead that your political liberties and participation do not enable to you consent to government, do not usually advance your interests, do not increase your autonomy in any meaningful sense, do not protect you from domination, and do not contribute to your moral development as a free and equal person. Save for in exceptional circumstances, you are more empowered by finding a five-dollar bill on the sidewalk than you are by possessing the rights to vote or run for office, or participating in politics. Stanton and Cholbi are wrong. When suffragists succeeded in getting women the right to vote, they empowered women as a group, but for the most part, they didn't empower any individual women, except for the tiny minority that won political office.

These five arguments are used for two different purposes. First, many democratic theorists think these arguments show that democratic participation is valuable for most citizens. Second, many democratic theorists think these arguments might explain why, as a matter of justice, citizens should be empowered with the right to vote and run for office, even if the majority of them are incompetent. That is, perhaps citizens have such a strong interest in voting rights that it is worth letting them impose incompetently made decisions on their fellow citizens. If political rights were in some way essential to personal autonomy, for instance, this might be a reason to prefer democracy with universal suffrage to an epistocratic system that tries to prevent incompetent decision making.

Thus, some of the "democracy empowers us" claims are meant to demonstrate that democratic participation is good, while others are meant to show that failing to imbue everyone with equal political rights is unjust. Yet if I'm right that political rights do not empower us in any meaningful sense, then this accomplishes two goals for me. First, it removes a set of objections to my thesis that most of us should just minimize the extent to which we engage in politics. Second, it removes a set of objections to epistocracy.

Note that my focus here is in explaining how democracy does not empower you as an individual. If I'm right, then if you lost the right to vote in an epistocracy, epistocracy would not thereby disempower you as an individual in any interesting way. But notice the difference between these two questions:

- Do your political liberties empower you?
- When large groups of people possess the political liberties, do these liberties empower the group as a whole?

These are distinct questions. The answer to the first one might be "no" even if the answer to the second might be "yes." Of course democracy empowers groups in certain ways—after all, the majority possesses significant power—even if it doesn't thereby empower the individuals who form part of that majority. Suffragist Susan B. Anthony said, "Women, we might as well be dogs baying to the moon as petitioners without the right to vote!"[3] Anthony might be right that women as a group become more than mere petitioners when many members of that group possess the right to vote. I'll argue, though, it's still the case that even with the right to vote, each individual woman—and also each other individual—remains a mere petitioner.

LIBERALISM AND POLITICAL RIGHTS

In this chapter, I'm asking whether democratic rights and political participation tend to empower individual citizens in any meaningful way. It's important to be clear on just what the question is.

There does appear to be a tight connection between democracy and liberal freedom. That is, as a matter of fact, existing democratic countries tend to do a better job protecting citizens' civil and economic liberty than nondemocratic ones, and liberal countries in turn tend to be more democratic. There is a tight positive correlation between the extent to which a country has free and open elections, and extent to which it protects civil rights. There is a weaker though still robust positive correlation between the degree to which countries have free and open elections, and degree to which they protect economic liberty. I don't dispute these connections; on the contrary, in other work, I've shown that such correlations exist.[4]

Liberal freedom and democracy are not connected on a conceptual level. A political regime could be liberal but nondemocratic, or democratic but illiberal. In the real world, we have some instances of nondemocratic but liberal countries, and many cases of illiberal democracies. Existing democracies nonetheless tend to be more liberal than less democratic ones. Just why this is so is disputed. Some think it is just a positive correlation. Perhaps the background conditions that tend to produce liberal politics also tend to produce democratic political structures. Some think there is causation. Perhaps liberalism causes democracy, democracy causes liberalism, or they are mutually reinforcing.

In this chapter, though, I'm asking whether the connection between democracy and freedom is even deeper than that. Many people—including most American laypeople—insist that democracy is more than a useful instrument for promoting liberty. They believe that democratic politics itself is an important kind of freedom, that democracy is essential to freedom, or that the rights to vote, run for office, and participate are themselves constitutive of what it means to be free.

An epistocracy could in principle fully realize liberal freedoms. (Indeed, in later chapters, one reason I will advocate experimenting with epistocracy is that I think epistocracy would protect and promote liberal freedoms better than democracy does.) But if this deeper connection between democracy and epistocracy exists, then epistocracy would always mean a loss of an important kind of freedom for some citizens. As I'll argue in this chapter, however, there's little reason to think that the equal rights to vote or run for office are important for personal freedom or autonomy.

THE CONSENT ARGUMENT

I'll start by attacking the weakest argument in favor of thinking that democracy empowers us. In fifth grade, my social studies teacher told me that democracy rests on the consent of the governed. Every year thereafter, my social studies and history teachers told me the same thing. Then, in college, I took a political philosophy class and learned they were wrong. Philosophers—both those who favor and those who disfavor democracy—have thoroughly debunked the claim that democracy rests on the consent of the governed; indeed, they debunked this claim before the modern democracies were even founded. Still, lay readers may not know why the consent argument fails. So it's time to once again kill this zombie before moving on to more challenging arguments.

The consent argument holds that it is valuable for me to possess the political liberties and participate in politics so that I can express consent to government, or so I can have a consensual relationship with my government. The argument goes as follows:

1. Democracy rests on the consent of the people.
2. A citizen cannot consent to government unless they have the right to vote or run for office.
3. A citizen who does have the right to vote or run for office, and who exercises that right, can consent to government.
4. It is valuable to each citizen to live under a political system to which one consents.
5. Therefore, political participation along with the rights to vote and run for office are valuable to each citizen.

The problem with this reasoning, though, is that for the overwhelming majority of us, our relationship to our government and its law is not, and cannot be, consensual.

To see why, let's consider what it would take to have a genuinely consensual relationship or transaction. Recently, I consented to buy a Fender American Deluxe Telecaster. All the following were true:

A. I performed an act that signified my consent. In this case, I ordered the guitar from a dealer. The outcome—I lost money yet gained a Telecaster—would not have occurred but for my performing the act that signified consent.
B. I was not forced to perform that act; I had a reasonable way to avoid doing it.
C. Had I explicitly said, "I refuse to buy a Fender Telecaster at that price!" the exchange never would have taken place.
D. The dealer was not entitled to take my money unless it sent me the guitar; it had to hold up its end of the bargain.

Had any of these conditions failed to obtain, it would not have been a consensual transaction. Substitute any one of the corresponding conditions a–d below for A–D above:

a. The dealer just sends me the guitar and takes my money, even though I never placed an order.
b. The dealer puts a gun to my head, telling me I must buy the guitar or die.
c. I tell the dealer I don't want a Telecaster, but it sends it to me anyway.
d. The dealer takes my money, but keeps the guitar.

If we replace any of conditions A–D with conditions a–d, the transaction was *not* consensual. Under conditions a or b, it's theft. In c, the dealer has just given me a gift without my consent. If the dealer sends me a bill, I don't have to pay it, since I have not consented to pay it for the guitar. In d, the dealer commits fraud, or at least does not live up to its end of the bargain. I did not consent to give the dealer my money; I consented to give it my money *only if* I also get a guitar.

When you, as an individual voter, vote for a candidate, policy, or political outcome, is it more like conditions A–D or a–d? When you participate in politics by campaigning, donating money, writing letters to the editor, and so forth, is it more like A–D or a–d?

Remember, if you replace any item from A–D with the corresponding item from a–d, the relationship is no longer consensual.

Now consider that as in a, if you don't vote or participate, your government will just impose rules, regulations, restrictions, benefits, and taxes on you. Except in special circumstances, the same outcome will occur regardless of *how* you vote or what policies you support. So, for instance, I voted for a particular candidate in 2008. But had I abstained or voted for a different candidate, the same candidate would have won anyway. This is not like a consensual transaction, in which I order a Telecaster and the dealer sends me the guitar. Rather, this is more like a nonconsensual transaction in which the dealer decides to make me buy a guitar whether I placed an order or not, and no matter what I ordered.

As in b, the government forces you to abide by its rules, no matter what you do, and will fine, imprison, beat, or even kill you if you resist. You have no reasonable way of opting out of government control. Governments control all the habitable land, so we have no reasonable way to escape government rule. You can't even move to Antarctica—the governments of the world forbid you to live there. At most, a small minority of us—those who have the financial means and legal permission to emigrate—can choose *which* government will rule us.

Even that—choosing which government will rule you—does not signify real consent. Imagine a group of men said to a woman, "You must marry one of us, or die, but we will let you chose whom you marry." When she picks a husband, she does not consent to being married. She has no real choice.[5]

As in c, if you actively dissent, the government will just impose the rules on you anyway. Suppose you smoke marijuana. You dissent from marijuana criminalization laws and believe it is deeply immoral to throw people in jail for possessing marijuana. The government will still throw you in jail for possession. This is unlike a consensual transaction, where saying "no" means no. For the government, your "no" means yes.

The government will sometimes yield if *many* people dissent through voting, but it will not usually respond to *your* dissent. This is different from what happens in situations involving real consent. Imagine my guitar dealer says, "I'm making you buy a Telecaster against your will, unless, of course, the majority of Americans tell me not to." We wouldn't consider that a consensual transaction on my part, regardless of what happens. Or if a person says to me, "I will force you to marry me unless a majority of Americans tell me not to," we wouldn't consider my subsequent forced marriage to be consensual.

Finally, as in d, governments require you to abide by their rules and will force you to pay taxes, even if they do not do their part and keep up their end of the transaction. So, for example, if the government fails to provide adequate education or protect you, it will still force you to pay taxes and comply with its rules. As Huemer notes, the US Supreme Court has repeatedly ruled that the government has no duty to protect individual citizens. Suppose you call the police to alert them that an intruder is in your house, but the police never bother to dispatch someone to help you, and as a result the intruder repeatedly rapes you. The government still requires you to pay taxes for the protection services it chose not to deploy on your behalf.[6]

Laypeople and politicians tend to say that voting expresses consent. Political philosophers regard this as, well, silly. Christopher Wellman mocks the idea:

> To say a citizen is bound to a law since she voted . . . is like saying that a person has consented to being shot since she expressed a preference that her abductor shoot her rather than stab her! . . . Just as the abductee will be killed no matter how she responds (and even if she does not answer the abductor's questions), the citizen will be subjected to coercive laws no matter how she votes (and even if she does not vote).[7]

For each of us, our relationship to government lacks *all* the normal features of a genuine consensual relationship. It's not just that our relationship to government lacks *some* of the features of consent.

Note that in some countries, such as Australia and Bolivia, citizens are *forced* to vote or punished for not voting. Australians who fail to vote pay a twenty-dollar fine. If citizens take their case to court and lose, they pay fifty dollars.[8] Repeat offenders pay increasing penalties. In Bolivia, citizens who fail to vote are barred from holding public employment, conducting many bank transactions, or getting a passport for ninety days.[9] Thus, Bolivia deprives its citizens of their civil liberties—including the right of exit—unless they vote. In Brazil, nonvoters are barred from receiving state-funded education. Hence, in countries with compulsory voting, voting is even *less consensual*.

For voting and political participation to make one's relationship to government or the law consensual, our relationship would need to be radically different. It would have to be more like the relationship we have with our favorite restaurants or friends.

The good news, though, is that the right to run for office does involve genuine consent. No democracy forces citizens to hold political office (unless you count soldiers or jurors as political positions). You hold office only if you want to. Of course, for most people it is extraordinarily difficult to win a political office. But this does not make it nonconsensual.

Note that I do not assert the strong claim that because our relationship to government is nonconsensual, governments are therefore unjust, illegitimate, or lack authority. I am not suggesting that we should be anarchists because we cannot consent to government. Democracy doesn't rest on the consent of the governed, and neither would epistocracy. Rather, I am just attacking the view that political participation is in some way valuable or just because it allows us to consent.

CONSENT VERSUS INFORMED CONSENT

The preceding worries listed all the standard objections to the consent argument. Even if, heroically, all these objections could be overcome, there is nevertheless an additional worry about consent.

As I discussed in chapter 2, there is overwhelming evidence that the majority of citizens are ignorant and misinformed about politics. Most citizens know hardly any of the basic political facts, such as who holds power, what those people have done, and what the challengers

want to do. Even fewer citizens have the background in social scientific knowledge needed to evaluate politicians' proposed policies,
though most of them subscribe to a wide range of social scientific
beliefs anyway. If so, then there's another worry about voting and
participation: it does not signal *informed* consent.

Suppose you go to your physician for a routine checkup. Your doctor pokes a doodad in your ear and then pronounces, "Ah, you've got
a case of gooberiasis. Unless we remove your polydactylpendix, you'll
die." You immediately agree to the procedure. Did you consent?

The consensus view in medical ethics is no, you did not consent.
You said "yes," but you have no idea what you're getting into. As
Matt Zwolinski observes, "[It] is a truism among medical ethicists
that patients . . . must do more than merely *say* 'I consent' in order
to morally authorize treatment. . . . People need to know what their
options are, and at least something about what these various options
entail."[10] In short, genuine consent is informed consent.

Ruth Faden and Tom Beauchamp, two leading bioethicists, say
that informed consent requires:

Disclosure: The physician must provide the patient sufficient information for the patient to make an autonomous choice about
whether or not to undertake the procedure.

Understanding: The patient must not just have access to sufficient
information but also must *understand* that information.

Capacity: Accordingly, the patient must have the capacity to understand that information.

Voluntariness: The patient must not be coerced, manipulated, or
bribed into making the decision.[11]

Informed consent is required whenever a high-stakes decision is
being made—that is, whenever the physician is recommending an
invasive procedure that carries with it the risk of harm. The physician
is not allowed to perform the procedure unless they can demonstrate
that their patient has informed consent.

Government decisions often look like the kinds of decisions that
would require informed consent in the medical fields. After all,
most government decisions are high stakes, invasive, and carry the

risk of great harm. Governments do not simply decide things like what the national anthem will be. Instead, government decisions determine who can work where, who gets money and who doesn't, whether one can purchase certain items or not, who can marry or not, whether we go to war or not, whether we will be forced to buy health insurance or not, and so on. Government decides matters of basic liberties, life and death, peace and war. So if we care about consent, we should thus not just want citizens to consent but to express informed consent, too.

For most voting citizens, the conditions of informed consent listed above are not met. Politicians do not disclose all relevant information. In fact, they often hide or suppress parts of their agenda, and try to prevent citizens from gaining access to relevant information. So democracies frequently violate the disclosure condition.

Second, as I discussed at great length in previous chapters, even when the information citizens would need to consent is disclosed, most citizens fail to acquire or understand it. The median voter is ignorant, and the median nonvoter is even worse than ignorant. Many citizens are wrong; they know less than nothing. Not only are citizens mistaken about or ignorant of basic, easily verifiable facts (such as the size of the federal budget or who their current congressperson is), they lack even a rudimentary understanding of the social sciences needed to evaluate those facts. As such, democracies systematically violate the understanding condition of informed consent.

Third, not only do citizens lack understanding; it's not clear that many of them could acquire that understanding. It might turn out that only people with an IQ of over, say, 110 can understand econ 101. But unless someone understands basic economics, they are usually not in a position to evaluate different presidential candidates. So democracies might systematically violate the capacity condition.

Fourth, it's clear that politicians routinely do manipulate voters. President Obama, for instance, repeatedly lied to the US public to get it to support the Affordable Care Act: "If you like your insurance, you can keep it." During the 2012 presidential campaign, Republicans lied to and manipulated voters by quoting Obama's "you didn't build that" out of context. Obama merely meant that government was partly responsible for the background institutions and infrastructure that make small businesses possible, but Republicans deliberately cultivated the impression that what Obama meant was that government built people's small businesses for them. George W. Bush lied about torturing detainees. Clinton lied about his extramarital sexual affairs. And so on. Political leaders not only routinely make promises they never keep but also frequently use outright deception and manipulation to win votes. If a physician did that—if they lied by stating, "You definitely need expensive breast enhancement surgery in order to help improve your eyesight"—that would clearly violate the voluntariness requirement.

In recent years, certain bioethicists have begun to challenge the dominant theory of informed consent. They worry it is too stringent or demanding. They think it's unlikely that most patients could meet all four of these conditions, and if so, that seems to suggest that many or even most vital medical procedures are unjust. Some bioethicists thus argue for a slightly less demanding view of informed consent. I'm not a bioethicist, and I don't intend to take a stance on that debate here. Instead, my point is more generic: if you think political rights are important because they allow citizens to express consent, then presumably you should care about informed consent, whatever the correct theory of informed consent turns out to be. Given how stubbornly ignorant most voters are, it seems implausible that their votes are a means of expressing informed consent.

As we saw in the previous section, to say that citizens consent to government seems false. Even if we ignore all the other problems with the consent argument, however, it's clear that most citizens do not express informed consent. The relationship we have to government, even in a democracy, is about as nonconsensual as a relationship can get. Given this, democracy does not empower us by creating or maintaining a consensual relationship.

THE POWER TO ADVANCE ONE'S INTERESTS

Another popular argument holds that political liberty and participation are valuable because they help us advance our interests. Consider the following:

1. The government will not be responsive to your interests unless you have the right to vote and run for office, and unless you participate in politics.
2. It is valuable to have the government be responsive to your interests.
3. Therefore, it is valuable to have the right to vote and run for office as well as participate in politics.

Among many citizens in democracies, the outcomes argument is a common justification of the claim that the political liberties and participation are valuable.

This claim fails in part because individual votes in fact have almost no instrumental value. The outcomes argument overstates the value of an individual's political liberties in terms of their ability to make government responsive to their interests.

As I discussed in chapter 2, for any individual voter, it makes no difference whether they vote or abstain. The probability that our votes will make a difference is vanishingly small. It is not as though the government will help you just in case you vote or ignore you just in case you abstain. As individuals, our single votes do not influence whether our elected leaders decide to help, ignore, or hurt us.

One might object that individuals can influence electoral outcomes even when they do not cast the deciding vote. One might contend instead that by voting, you can at least change the margin of victory (or loss) and then help determine whether a candidate "enjoys a mandate."[12] If you vote against the bad candidate, then, even if they win, you at least reduce their effectiveness in office by reducing their mandate. If you vote for the candidate, then, even though they would have won without you, you at least increase their effectiveness by increasing their mandate. Let's call the claim that candidates can enjoy mandates that increase their political effectiveness the mandate hypothesis.

Empirically minded political scientists have submitted the mandate hypothesis to numerous and varied tests, and found it wanting. The evidence soundly favors rejecting the mandate hypothesis.[13]

Similar remarks apply to the right to run for political office. The probability that a random American, if they tried, could secure a significant public office is low. In part, this is because there are few seats to go around. There are over 700,000 Americans for every seat in Congress. Even smaller, less important offices (such as town alderperson) tend at best to have ratios of a single seat for every 2,000 citizens. If offices were distributed randomly at any given time, these would be bad odds.

Of course, offices are not randomly distributed; rich, attractive, well-connected citizens have much better odds than other people. The average US senator has a net worth of almost $14 million, and the average member of the House of Representatives has a net worth of $4.6 million.[14] In contrast, the average American *household* has a net worth of under $70,000.[15] Political offices are for rich people. This tends to hold true even in more egalitarian countries such as Sweden, where, for example, one recent prime minister, Fredrik Reinfeldt, has a net worth of about $8 million, and other politicians are still significantly richer than average.[16] So normal folk like you or I might decide to run for office, but politicians aren't cowering at the thought, and it isn't keeping them in line.

While exercising the right to vote and run for office does little to empower us, one might still hope that broader forms of participation, such as campaigning, donating, deliberating, or writing, do more to help advance our interests. But again, here we face the same problem: most citizens have little chance of making any difference. Some people, such as Paul Krugman or Stephen Colbert, have significant influence over how others vote, and, in turn, how politicians behave. Some college professors at elite universities can influence politics by influencing their students, some of whom will become future leaders. Some activists, such as Martin Luther King Jr., have had enormous influence. But most don't. And most of us could not come to acquire that much influence even if we tried, just as most of us could not become professional baseball players or pop stars no matter how hard we try.

It *feels* great to discuss justice and freedom with the League of Women Voters. It feels empowering to march around Pennsylvania Avenue or Wall Street while wearing Guy Fawkes masks. No doubt the Occupy protesters felt empowered when camping out in public parks and corporate-owned plazas. Sending a letter to one's senator complaining about the National Security Agency feels like an accomplishment. I sometimes enjoy complaining about the injustices of the US police state on Facebook with my like-minded friends, and when I publish an article on resistance to state injustice, I feel like I took a stand.

But unfortunately, outside exceptional circumstances, our individual actions have no perceivable effect. For any one of us, things would go on at the macro level exactly as they do even if we abstained from participating or even if we participated by rallying for the opposite sides. The Occupiers might as well rally for capitalism rather than against it. I might as well advocate and vote *for* the drug war instead of against it. You might as well switch parties. The average political blogger might as well switch sides. Except in unusual circumstances, regardless of how you vote and how you participate, you make no difference. Your participation does not make government respond to your interests.

Large *groups* of people certainly can have power in democracies. (I'll discuss this issue in later chapters.) But individuals normally do not. Indeed, that's a feature, not a bug, of democracy. Democracy isn't meant to empower individuals; it's intended to disempower all the individuals in favor of large groups or collections of individuals. Democracy empowers *us*, but not you or me.

PARTICIPATION AND AUTONOMY

Intuitively, there seems to be some connection among political liberty, political participation, and empowerment. This link is described in the autonomy argument:

1. It is valuable for each person to be autonomous and self-directed, and live by rules of their own making.
2. In order for each person living in a shared political environment to be autonomous and self-directed, and live by rules of their own making, they need to possess the political liberties and make use of them. Participation helps them be autonomous and self-directed.
3. Therefore, each person living in a shared political environment needs to possess the political liberties and make use of them.[17]

This argument maintains that the political liberties and participation are instrumental to, or perhaps even constitutive of, maintaining one's autonomy. If autonomy is valuable, then so are the political liberties and political participation.

Some think the connection between voting and autonomy is that by voting, a person is in part the author of the laws. If a person abstains from voting, then they have no partial authorship over the laws, and thus the laws are in some way imposed on them.

Notice, however, that on this kind of reasoning—that you become partial author of the laws by voting—voting confers autonomy on you only if your side wins. After all, if your side loses, then you are not in part the author of the laws. (If you were, that would be rather horrifying. Imagine you vote against the war hawk because they're a hawk, but they win anyway. When they start a war, you'd be partly the author of that war.)

The autonomy argument nevertheless overstates the degree of autonomy that the rights to vote and run for office confer. I've made quite a few autonomous decisions in my life. I've made autonomous decisions over petty things: what to wear each day, what to eat, what color toothbrush to have, and what to watch on television. I've made autonomous decisions over important things: what to write about for my dissertation, where to go to college and graduate school, and which job offers I would accept. I've made autonomous decisions over momentous things: whom to marry, whether to have a child, and what to choose for a career.

Suppose these choices had been subject to democratic decision making. We'd regard that as taking away my choice and giving it to the democratic body. Even if I had an equal vote in this body, it would be a severe loss of autonomy. Even if the democratic body didn't just vote but instead actively deliberated over the best choices (and listened to me give my reasons), having it make the decisions would mean a severe loss of personal autonomy for me.

It's not just that I have more autonomy when I make decisions alone as opposed to when a democratic assembly (of which I am a member) makes the decisions. Obviously I have more autonomy as an individual than as a voting member of a large group. It's that when a democratic assembly (of which I am a member) makes the decisions, I don't have much autonomy at all.

There is a surefire way to determine that you do not have autonomous control over situations. No matter what you choose or what you decide, the same thing happens anyway; your decisions make no difference. To illustrate this point, while writing this paragraph, I conducted an experiment. I decided that the moon would turn purple. I repeated this experiment many times over a few weeks. Alas, the moon did not turn purple. I conclude that I have no autonomous control over the color of the moon.

So it goes with voting. Regardless of whether you choose to vote or not, and regardless of how you decide, the same result will occur. We might as well be willing the moon to turn purple.

In contrast, today I also chose to eat raisin bran for breakfast. After making the decision, I did in fact eat raisin bran. For lunch, I chose to eat curry—and did in fact eat curry. My experiments allow me to conclude that I have real autonomy over what I eat.

The concept of autonomy is rather nebulous. I've focused on one common idea of autonomous control here: *autonomy as difference making*. On this concept, an agent has autonomous control over some object or state of affairs only to the degree that their actions can change, affect, or make a difference regarding that object or state of affairs.

The *Stanford Encyclopedia of Philosophy* documents many other concepts of autonomy, most of which have to do with different theories of freewill or intentionality, and that are thus irrelevant to the discussion here. Nevertheless, there may be some other plausible view of autonomy out there that is in some way relevant to whether political liberty or the right to vote is valuable. The general challenge is this, though: first, the type of autonomy in question must plausibly be valuable or owed to people as a matter of justice; and second, it must be something that an individual without a right to vote necessarily lacks.

BEING AT HOME IN THE WORLD

Christiano offers a more nuanced and plausible version of the autonomy argument. He holds that the political liberties can serve each person's fundamental interest "in making the world a home for [themselves]."[18] One is "at home in the world" when "one is able to make sense of the world one lives in and have a sense of how one fits in with it and is connected with it."[19] People have an interest in seeing the world correspond to their view of what's right and good. And to some degree, they want the world to be a product of their own making. They don't just want to the world to *conform* to their judgments (perhaps by coincidence) but also to *be responsive* to their judgments.

Reasoning like this often leads to versions of what I call the social construction argument:

1. Each person has a fundamental interest in living in a world in which they can feel at home.
2. In order to serve this interest, each person needs their world to be adequately responsive to their judgments, and they need to take an adequate part in the process of social construction.
3. In order to make the world adequately responsive to their judgments and take an adequate part in the process of social construction, each person needs to possess the political liberties and be able to exercise them with others as equals. Each person needs to participate with others as equals.
4. Therefore, each person needs to possess the political liberties and be able to exercise them with others as equals.[20]

I do not mean to suggest that the social construction argument is equivalent to Christiano's own contention on behalf of democracy or the value of the political liberties.[21] It's a strand of his argument, but his argument has other strands as well, including strands of other arguments I consider in later chapters. Instead, I present the social construction argument here because it captures one reason both philosophers and laypeople tend to think that the political liberties are valuable.

Premise three above claims that I need the political liberties in order to take part in the process of social construction and make the world adequately responsive to my interests. The social construction argument is meant to be distinct from the outcomes argument. We should not interpret it as claiming that an individual's right to vote is instrumentally valuable because it has a significant expected utility in terms of its propensity to produce favored political outcomes. As we saw above, this claim is false.

Hence, a more plausible interpretation of the third premise of the social construction argument might say that when I have the right to vote and run for office, I thereby acquire the power to *help cause* the government to be responsive to my interests. I cannot cause the government to be responsive all by myself, yet by acting in concert with others, I can still be *part of the cause* of the government being responsive to my interests. If my favored political outcomes occur, I can say to myself, "I helped make that happen."[22] This might make me feel more at home in the world.

One problem with this claim, though, is that it relies on controversial views about causation. Suppose ten of us throw rocks at a window, and our ten rocks simultaneously hit and break the window. Did I cause the window to break? Did you? Did the ten of us collectively cause it to break, but none of us as individuals did so? Metaphysicians continue to debate these questions. The answers aren't clear. Ideally, the question of whether the political liberties or political participation are valuable won't depend on a difficult debate in the metaphysics of causation.[23]

Fortunately, there is a plausible interpretation of the third premise, and it relies on less controversial metaphysics. Premise three can be interpreted as claiming that by having the right to vote and run for office, I can thereby participate in producing preferred outcomes. This interpretation makes a weaker metaphysical claim: even if I don't cause the window to break or a candidate to be elected, at least I participate in the collective activities of breaking the window or electing the candidate.

The social construction argument might explain why some citizens could find their political liberties valuable. A person might *enjoy* taking part in democratic processes. If one enjoys these enough, then even once opportunity costs are taken into account, it can be worthwhile to vote or run for office. If so, then having the political liberties can be valuable. On this view, to vote is much like deciding to "do the wave" at a sports game. The wave will happen with or without one's own participation, but it can be enjoyable or worthwhile to participate.

Still, politics provides a weak outlet for social construction, in part because there are no niches. Democratic political decisions apply to all equally, and if one dislikes the outcomes, there is usually no escape. In trying to explain why the political liberties are valuable, Christiano (and political theorist Michael Walzer, whom Christiano recruits as an intellectual ally here) uses the metaphor of "being at home."[24]

The political liberties are supposed to help us feel at home. But this seems misleading. Our homes are niches. Most of us are at home in our homes because we may unilaterally shape our homes to reflect our preferences. Our homes are governed by principles we endorse. We don't have to deliberate in public and justify our furniture arrangements to others in society. Many of us can shape our work environments to a significant extent as well, at the very least by choosing where we work. And even if we don't feel completely at home in society, we can at least usually find niches within society where we do feel at home. In politics, however, there are no real niches. I find marijuana criminalization and farm subsidies stupid and unjust, but there's no niche to accommodate me (or it is prohibitively expensive for me to relocate to that niche).

Politics provides a weak outlet for social construction in part because individual citizens are nearly powerless. They have so little power that they are faced with a choice: conform to the majority's position, and thus "help to produce favored outcomes," or go against the majority's position, in which case the voter has at most helped to signal dissent from the majority's position. In light of this powerlessness, it is difficult to take seriously the claim that engaging in politics is a valuable way of participating in social construction.

If you vote with the majority, then you participate in producing the electoral outcome. But the empowerment offered by voting seems like a sham. Consider this metaphor. Suppose you're swimming at the beach. A large wave heads your way. You can choose to stand your ground or you can swim with it, but you can't push it back. If you decide to ride with the wave, you might be said to participate in the wave, and if you give the water a push, you might even help cause some of that water to reach the shore sooner. Yet to think of any of this as sharing control seems implausible.[25] If you feel at home in the water, it's because you accommodated yourself to the water, not because the water accommodated itself to you.

Also, even if we grant that voters for the winning candidate count as helping to cause that candidate's election, voters for losing candidates do not even get this benefit. For losers, the right to vote is at best an opportunity to help cause a favored candidate to win in the future. Persistent minorities—people whose favored candidate or position loses year after year—lack even this opportunity. To get a chance to help cause a candidate to win, you need to accommodate yourself to what other voters favor. In the United States, individual voters can choose to ride the Democrat or Republican wave. If they dislike both parties, they can't do much to change what's in the ocean.

In summary, once again, the political liberties and political participation empower us only in special circumstances. The autonomy and social construction arguments fail for many of the same reasons the outcomes argument failed. To succeed, individual citizens would need to have much more power and influence as individuals than they in fact do.

STOPPING DOMINATION

As "neo-republican" philosopher Philip Pettit asks us to consider, Why is the master-slave relationship morally wrong? (Note that the "republicanism" I discuss in this section is a political philosophy that advocates a particular conception of liberty along with a theory of how the political process might protect that liberty. I am not referring to the American Republican Party. Few philosophical republicans are American Republicans.) It is not merely that the master might be cruel to the slave or might interfere with the slave's plans. To see why, imagine you are a slave with an unusually kind and permissive master. The master never issues any orders or interferes with you in any way. Pettit says, though, that you remain in some important sense *less* free than nonslaves. While the master does not interfere with or control you, the master retains the right and ability to do so.

Pettit thinks this shows a defect in what he considers the liberal conception of freedom. Classical liberal Isaiah Berlin claims that he and other liberals tend to define freedom as the absence of interference from others.[26] Pettit points out that this conception of liberty cannot properly explain everything that is wrong with the master-slave relationship. After all, in the case of the kindly and permissive master, no one interferes with the slave, but intuitively, the slave remains unfree. Pettit thinks we therefore need a new conception of liberty: liberty as nondomination. Freedom is not the absence of interference; it is the absence of *domination*.

One person (call them the dominator) is said to have the capacity to dominate another person (call them the victim) when the following conditions obtain:

- The dominator has the capacity to interfere with the victim's choices.
- The dominator can exercise this capacity at will, with impunity.[27]

This applies to groups as well. A group can dominate an individual, a group can dominate another group, or an individual can dominate a group.

Philosophical republicans hold that democracy of the right sort is essential to realizing freedom as nondomination. Like liberals, they advocate due process of law, checks and balances, separation of powers, and constitutionally protected rights of free speech and assembly.[28] Like liberals, they worry that these devices are imperfect. Government agents—from police officers to bureaucrats to senators—continue to enjoy some degree of arbitrary power over others.

To reduce the degree to which government agents wield this arbitrary power, republicans believe that citizens must be actively engaged with politics. Philosopher Frank Lovett says,

> The standard republican remedy [to the problem of arbitrary power] is enhanced democracy. . . . Roughly speaking, the idea is that properly-designed democratic institutions should give citizens the effective opportunity to contest the decisions of their representatives. This possibility of contestation will make government agents wielding discretionary authority answerable to a public understanding of the goals or ends they are meant to serve and the means they are permitted to employ. In this way, discretionary

power can be rendered non-arbitrary in the sense required for the secure enjoyment of republican liberty.[29]

To "enhance" democracy in this way, republicans hold we need two major sets of changes. First, there must be *greater public deliberation*. Political decision makers, such as legislative bodies, courts, or bureaucracies, routinely should present the rationale behind their decisions in public forums, where the public may challenge and debate these reasons. Some republicans argue that some such forums should serve as "courts of appeals," in which citizens can object to or even overturn decisions.[30]

Whether this is a solution or not of course depends on how deliberation actually proceeds. As we saw in chapter 3, the empirical work on deliberation seems discouraging. It's one thing for republicans to say that ideal or close-to-ideal deliberation could fix other problems in realistic, nonideal governments, but it's another thing to state that realistic deliberation in realistic government could solve problems.

Second, republicans claim there should be greater *inclusion and real political equality*. All citizens must have an equal right to participate in such public contestation. Republicans hold that formal political equality is not enough. Some citizens (by virtue of wealth, family, or prestige) have more de facto influence and power than others. To ensure that all citizens can participate on an equitable basis, there should be limits on campaign financing, advertising, and lobbying. Republicans, in short, think that regular, contested, competitive elections are not enough. They think we need deliberative democracy both before and after decisions are made. We need to protect the political sphere from being unduly influenced by money, fame, or other irrelevant factors.

Given this, republicans, unlike liberals, deny that citizens under a benevolent liberal dictator would be free. Republicans advocate what they regard as a distinct and superior conception of liberty, and hold that a robustly participatory and deliberative democratic regime of the right sort is essential to realizing this form of freedom.

The main theoretical motivation for republicanism was supposed to be a defect in the traditional liberal conception of freedom as noninterference. Supposedly, liberals cannot adequately explain just what makes slaves unfree. Recall Pettit's point: even if a master never interferes with or controls the slave, the master *could* do so with impunity.

While I don't have any ideological opposition to conceiving of freedom as nondomination, and I favor some of Pettit's policy proposals for different reasons than he does, I'm nonetheless not sure Pettit has found a problem with liberalism, but rather with Berlin's way of describing how liberals conceive of freedom. After all, liberals have long argued that a person is not free simply because no one interferes with them. They should also be seen as possessing *rights against interference*. Liberals can thus respond to Pettit that a slave—even one with a kind and liberal master—is unfree because the master violates their rights. So it seems that liberals possess a prior explanation for why even slaves with kind, liberal masters are still unfree. The situations that Pettit portrays as exposing citizens to domination, the situations that are intended to convince the liberal that the liberal conception of freedom is inadequate, are those in which liberal rights are insecure or inadequately protected. A liberal might respond to Pettit that Berlin *misconstrued* the liberal conception of freedom. For liberals, a person is free when they have adequately protected rights against interference. This does not appear to be a revision of the liberal conception of freedom in response to Pettit but instead the conception liberals have had all along.

I won't dwell on this issue, because the real concern for us here is whether active political engagement among equals of the sort Pettit envisions is essential to preventing domination. The thought is that we can protect citizens from domination only by imbuing each of them with strong and equal political liberties as well as encouraging them to participate as equals. If Pettit is right, then political participation, not to mention democracy, is instrumentally valuable as a means of preventing domination, and failing to imbue citizens with equal political rights within a republican regime is unjust because it exposes them to unjust domination.

Pettit's views seem right when we talk about *large collections of individuals*. If we deprive all black people of the right to vote and run for office, then this will help facilitate people of other races in exploiting, dominating, and oppressing blacks. Yet this doesn't show that it's valuable for any individual black person to possess the political liberties or participate in politics. Instead, at most it demonstrates that it's valuable to each black person that a sufficient number of black people possess the political liberties. Because individual votes and individual participation almost never matter, a black person should be nearly indifferent between situations A and B:

A. All black people *except an individual* have the political liberties.
B. All black people (including the individual) have the political liberties.

If A isn't enough to stop the individual black person from being dominated, then, except in unusual circumstances, neither is B.[31] The political liberties and political participation may very well empower a *group of which I am a part*, but it doesn't follow that they empower *me*.

Empowering *people like me* to vote tends to protect me only if the people like me tend to vote in ways that protect me. I am a member of many different groups; there are many different overlapping groups that qualify as people like me. Some of these groups are large, while others are small. Some of these groups tend to vote in groupish ways (i.e., membership in that group turns out to affect voter behavior), while others do not. Whether the voting behavior of a group tends to protect or promote individuals' interests within that group is a complicated empirical question. We don't want to gloss over it by imagining that empowering everyone within a group to vote protects that group. After all, that depends on how they vote, including whether they are well informed enough to vote in ways that protect their interests. It also depends on how others outside the group vote, including whether they vote to harm other groups or not.

In the end, it seems false that *I* need the political liberties to prevent others from dominating and exploiting me. What prevents me from being dominated is that *other* citizens either choose to restrain themselves or are in some way restrained. If they decide to act badly, my rights to vote or run for office can't stop them. The moral majority stops the unjust minority, the courts stop them, various procedural checks and balances stop them, or they stop themselves. Yet if tomorrow everyone in my country decides they want to interfere with me or subject me to their collective will, my political rights provide me no more protection than a bucket provides against a flood.[32]

Further, it's unclear why republicans should favor democracy over epistocracy. Epistocracy appears to be compatible with republican liberty. Consider a form of epistocracy in which suffrage is restricted only to citizens who can pass a test of basic political knowledge. Suppose the top 95 percent of citizens pass the exam, but the bottom 5 percent fail. Will this top group of voters thus dominate the others? It seems unlikely. An epistocracy could retain the other "enhancements" republicans favor—deliberative forums, citizens' courts of appeal, limits on campaign spending, and so on. If these procedural checks and balances would prevent government officials or special interest groups from dominating citizens when everyone is allowed to participate, it is not clear why they would suddenly fail if the most ignorant or misinformed citizens were not allowed to vote. The republican idea is that one enjoys freedom as nondomination when there are sufficient institutional checks in place that prevent anyone from just dominating you at will. But there's no plausible reason to think your individual right to vote or participate is essential to stopping domination.

Republicans might complain that even in an epistocracy that copied their favored institutions (checks and balances, contestatory deliberative forums, etc.), citizens would lack equal status.[33] But that's a complaint about equality and status, about the expressive meaning of unequal political rights. It's not a complaint about freedom or power, and so I put it aside here. I consider these issues at great length in the next chapter.

DEVELOP TWO MORAL POWERS?

So far, each of the arguments (about how democracy might empower us as individuals) I've considered is based on widely shared beliefs and moral intuitions. This section explores a claim that is much more esoteric and theory driven: I'll respond to a view that many analytic political philosophers, but pretty much no one else, hold. Lay readers may wish to skip this section.

Rawls, the most important analytic political philosopher of the past century, developed a theory of justice (called "justice as fairness") that features two major moral principles. The first principle, the "liberty principle," requires that each citizen enjoy a "fully adequate" set of basic rights and liberties.[34] (Rawls's second principle of justice won't concern us here.)

For Rawls, once a society has reached a level of development in which everyone can lead a decent life, this liberty principle tends to trump everything else. So, for instance, Rawls thinks that even if, through some strange causal chain, restricting one person's free speech would improve GDP growth by 3 percent a year for ten years, it would be unjust to do so.[35]

What's most relevant for us here is how Rawls treats *political liberty*, specifically the rights to vote and run for office. In Rawls's theory of justice, the rights to vote and run for office have a special, privileged position, above that of even the other already-privileged basic rights and liberties. Rawls says that justice requires that citizens be guaranteed the "fair value of their political liberties."[36] As leading Rawls scholar Samuel Freeman explains, the fair value of political liberties is "a requirement of . . . justice, that the value of equal political rights of participation be fairly secured for all citizens by measures that neutralized the effects of wealth and social position and influence on the political process; including publicly financed campaigns, prohibitions on private contributions to candidates, etc."[37]

I'm not concerned here with Rawls's policy recommendations, such as his belief that we should have public funding of elections. (That said, I'm worried that many Rawlsians are insufficiently versed in the empirical political science literature on the effects of campaign contributions.)[38] Rather, what's of interest here is first that Rawls holds that the rights to vote and run for office are among our basic liberties, and second, that these political rights have a higher status than our other liberties. Why think that?

Rawls's final philosophical test for whether something is a basic liberty or not has to do with whether it has the right connection to what Rawls calls our "two moral powers." The two moral powers are, according to Rawls, a capacity to develop a sense of the good life, and a capacity for a sense of justice. The first—also called rationality—is the capacity to "have a rational conception of the good—the power to form, revise, and to rationally pursue a coherent conception of values, as based in a view of what gives life and its pursuits their meaning." The second—also called reasonableness—is the capacity to "understand, apply, and cooperate with others on terms of cooperation that are fair."[39] For Rawls, these two powers are what make humans *moral beings* worthy of special consideration. They are what separate us from, say, the "lower" animals. It's plausible these powers in some way explain why human beings might have more stringent and demanding moral rights than cats or worms.

In Freeman's view, the connection between the basic liberties (including political rights) and moral powers is supposed to be this: "What makes a liberty basic for Rawls is that it is an essential social condition for the adequate development and full exercise of the two powers of moral personality over a complete life."[40] Freeman elaborates that a liberty is basic only if it is necessary for *all* citizens to have that liberty in order to develop the two moral powers.[41] Let's call this the Rawls-Freeman test of a basic liberty: some liberty X qualifies as a basic liberty just in case X turns out to be an essential social condition for all citizens to adequately develop and fully exercise their two moral powers over a complete life. What, if anything, passes this test?

To illustrate the Rawls-Freeman test, let's take a look at a debate between political theorist John Tomasi and Freeman on what counts as a basic liberty. Tomasi thinks Rawls's list of basic liberties is too short. Rawls believes certain civil rights are among the basic liberties, but denies that any capitalist economic rights count as basic liberties, except for the right to own some personal property and a right to choose one's occupation. Tomasi argues we should expand the list of basic liberties to include certain capitalist economic rights, such as freedom of contract or the right to own productive property. He claims that such rights are essential for *many* citizens to develop their conception of the good life or exercise their sense of justice.

But, Freeman responds to Tomasi, even if owning a factory were essential to *some* people's conception of the good life, that doesn't mean there's a basic liberty to own productive property. After all, Freeman continually stresses, *not all* citizens need capitalist liberties to lead their conceptions of the good life.[42] For something to be a basic liberty, Freeman says, it must be essential to *every* single reasonable person's capacity to develop a sense of the good life or justice. Freeman says that Tomasi has at most shown us that these capitalist freedoms are essential to many or some people's capacities to develop these two moral powers, but not all. This means capitalist liberties fail the Rawls-Freeman test.

Freeman is perhaps the most important Rawls scholar and interpreter around. It's possible he's mistaken about Rawls, but I'm inclined to defer to him about what Rawls was up to. That is, I trust his judgment about what Rawls means more than I trust my own judgment. So I will assume Freeman's interpretation of Rawls to be correct.

Let's say that Freeman's response to Tomasi is decisive. Capitalist rights of freedom of contract or to own factories don't pass the Rawls-Freeman test. The problem, I'll now argue, is that it's not clear *anything* passes that test. If the Rawls-Freeman test is correct, it's unclear much of anything counts as basic liberty.

Remember, Freeman responds to Tomasi by claiming that unless literally everyone needs certain economic freedoms to develop and fully exercise their sense of justice or the good life, then these liberties don't count as basic (on the Rawls-Freeman test). Yet if Freeman can make that move against Tomasi, then I can make similar moves against him.

Freeman might remark to Tomasi that people in Denmark and Switzerland enjoy much more economic liberty than people in Russia. But this does not mean it's impossible or even particularly difficult for Russians to develop a sense of justice or conception of the good life. Most Russians do indeed develop a sense of justice and capacity for a sense of the good life. In fact, perhaps only about ten countries allow citizens to have the range of economic liberty Tomasi thinks crucial, yet despite that, most citizens in those countries can and do develop the two moral powers. This means Tomasi's argument for expanding the list of basic liberties doesn't work; it doesn't pass the Rawls-Freeman test.

That's no victory for Rawls and Freeman, though. The reasoning for rejecting capitalist freedoms as basic liberties applies equally well against left-liberal freedoms, including political liberties. After all,

Rawls and Freeman think people have a basic right to extensive freedom of speech, freedom of participation, to vote and run for office, and so on. But it is also implausible that it is necessary to have these or other Rawlsian basic liberties in order to develop a sense of justice or conception of the good life.

Again, only a small handful of countries in the world actually afford their citizens the full scope of Rawlsian basic liberties, and few, if any, guarantee the fair value of political liberty. In the overwhelming majority of the unjust countries, however, the overwhelming majority of people do develop (and the rest *could* develop) a sense of justice and conception of the good, despite lacking these basic liberties, or not having the liberties protected at the level Rawls and Freeman believe they should.

Consider that I, Jason Brennan, have an adequately developed sense of the good life and capacity for a sense of justice, as adequately developed as Rawls's or Freeman's. (Certain Rawlsians might deny this, as some have a cruel tendency to dismiss their good faith intellectual opponents as morally unreasonable.) Yet I don't care much about having the right to vote or participate in politics. I would gladly sell my right to vote for a hundred dollars. The right to vote or run for office doesn't figure in any way into my conception of the good life, even though I'm a professional political philosopher who has published two books and a bunch of articles with the word *voting* in their titles. Do I qualify as a counterexample or disproof of the Rawls-Freeman test? Does my existence suffice to show that the political liberties are not basic?

Or consider that to many nonreligious people, religious liberties don't much matter. They need freedom from religion, but not freedom to practice religion. Or to most people, the rights to engage in free scientific inquiry mean little; they will never take advantage of these rights. And so forth. The problem is that few liberties are essential to everyone. (At this point, some Rawlsians might complain that I've misinterpreted Rawls or Freeman. I'll get back to that.)

In fact, it seems very little liberty is strictly speaking necessary for the typical person (let alone all people, as Freeman would have it) to develop the two moral powers. People in deeply authoritarian or totalitarian regimes may have a harder time than I do in accessing the proper evaluative horizons for them to develop the moral powers, but even in such countries, it's not impossible or even all that hard. To develop the two moral powers, you don't need much freedom of speech, freedom of marriage rights, freedom of association, or political liberty. You don't need to have the right to vote or run for office. You don't need to have full freedom of bodily integrity, and you don't need to be free of physical harassment from state officials. You don't need to have the right to choose your own occupation. Indeed, it's easy to imagine people developing the two moral powers without having much liberty. The Stoic philosopher Epictetus probably developed his two moral powers more than almost anyone who has ever lived, and managed to do so while literally being a slave. Aleksandr Solzhenitsyn developed his two moral powers despite living in a totalitarian regime and being imprisoned in the gulag; he seems to have developed his two moral powers as much as he did precisely because he was deprived of his basic liberties. And you can find other historical examples of people who have developed their two moral powers in spite of lacking much freedom. So it seems that if Rawls and Freeman are right about what makes something a basic liberty, then basically nothing is a basic liberty. Practically no freedom is actually necessary for all people to develop the moral powers. It looks like the Rawls-Freeman test must be too strong. Nothing passes the test.

Now Rawls and Freeman could try to respond by redefining or elaborating on the moral powers such that it turns out that possessing certain freedoms isn't merely instrumentally useful, as an empirical matter, for some people to develop these moral powers but is instead constitutive, as a matter of logic, of what it means to develop these powers. But without seeing the argument to that effect, I can't imagine how they'd make this move without thereby begging the question.

Rawlsians might complain that I'm misunderstanding the Rawls-Freeman test. The Rawls-Freeman test isn't just about *developing* the moral powers but also about *exercising* them. I might be right that the rights to vote or run for office aren't necessary for all, or even most, people to develop their two moral powers. Rawls and Freeman nevertheless say that something is a basic liberty just in case it is necessary for all people to develop *and* exercise the two moral powers.

I'm forgetting the exercise part. Perhaps that's the part of the proviso that does the work in justifying the rights to vote and run for office.

This response doesn't work, at least not with the Rawls-Freeman test as stated. Rawls and Freeman say something is a basic liberty if, and only if, it's necessary for all people to develop and exercise their capacity for their sense of justice. But let's do a little formal logic here: $\Box(P \; \& \; Q) \supset (\Box P \; \& \; \Box Q)$. That is, necessarily the conjunction of P and Q implies necessarily P and necessarily Q. If something qualifies as a basic liberty only if it necessarily meets conditions P and Q, then it fails to be a basic liberty if it fails to meet *either* condition.

Rawls and Freeman say that something is a basic liberty just in case it's necessary for all people to develop their two moral powers *and* exercise their two moral powers. It follows that if something is not necessary for all people to develop their two moral powers, it is not a basic liberty, even if it is necessary for all people to exercise their two moral powers. The class of potential basic liberties necessary to both develop and exercise the two moral powers is equal to or smaller in size than the class of potential basic liberties necessary simply to develop the two moral powers.

I think this means that Rawls and Freeman made their test more demanding than they intended. On their behalf, let's change the "and" to "or." Let's replace their test of whether something is a basic liberty with a new, less demanding test:

> What makes a liberty *basic* is that it is an essential social condition for *all people* for the adequate development *or* full exercise of the two powers of moral personality over a complete life.

This new test gets around the problem I outlined above. Sure, hardly any liberty is needed to develop the two moral powers, but perhaps full and equal rights to vote are needed to exercise them. On this revised formulation of the Rawls-Freeman test, the "necessary for all people to exercise their moral powers" proviso does nearly all the work, since, as we saw, almost no liberty is necessary for all people to develop their moral powers.

But this new test won't do the work Rawls and Freeman need it to do. On this new formulation, left-liberal civil and political liberties might pass the Rawls-Freeman test, but then we have equally good grounds to think that capitalist economic freedoms (such as extensive freedom of contract and the right to own private property in the means of production) pass the test, for all the reasons Tomasi offers in *Free Market Fairness*. Tomasi's arguments almost exactly mirror Rawls's and Freeman's. Rawls and Freeman, though, want the Rawls-Freeman test to be broad enough to include left-liberal liberties yet narrow enough to exclude classical liberal economic liberties. Tomasi could merely say, paralleling Rawls or Freeman, that while people can easily develop their two moral powers without full capitalist freedoms, they can't fully exercise their two moral powers without such freedoms.

If Rawls and Freeman want to dispute this, they'll probably have to use an ideologically loaded conception of what counts as exercising the two moral powers. I doubt they'd be able to offer such a nonquestion-begging interpretation; I haven't seen any Rawlsians do it yet. On the contrary, Tomasi's view of what counts as fully exercising a capacity for a sense of justice is more intuitive and pretheoretically plausible than Rawls's or Freeman's, simply because Tomasi has a more expansive perspective. Tomasi has a big list of things that intuitively seem like they have something to do with exercising a capacity for a sense of justice or developing the good life. Rawls and Freeman cut that list in half, and simultaneously assert that this amputated list counts as full.

Now consider political rights. Let's try to ask what it means to exercise one's sense of justice and capacity to develop and act on a sense of the good life from a commonsense perspective rather than from a stance that's clearly loaded toward one side of this debate. From a commonsense perspective, it seems apparent that at least one person somewhere, and a fortiori most people, could effectively exercise their senses of justice and the good life without having the right to vote or run for office. Removing your right to vote or run for office might be (for other reasons) unjust, it might (for other reasons) be an affront to your dignity, or whatnot, but surely there is at least one person who could lose such rights yet still have and exercise their sense of justice and the good life. After all, as I've been discussing over the course of this chapter, these rights rarely enable individuals to do much. To exercise a sense of justice, rights of free speech and association matter far more; these rights actually tend to give us each power to *do* stuff that shapes our individual lives. But again, Rawls and Freeman say that for something to be a basic liberty, it must be essential to all people.

This seems to apply just as well to other basic liberties, not just the rights to vote or run for office. The typical person could effectively exercise their sense of justice and the good life even if we arbitrarily placed a bunch of restrictions on their freedom of religion or occupational choice. Suppose, for example, the United States forbade Americans from worshipping Zeus. Surely this is a violation of freedom of religion. But since pretty much no one wants to worship Zeus, this won't actually impede anyone from exercising their moral powers.

Again, Rawls and Freeman could insist that by definition, a person can't truly exercise their moral powers unless they have these rights, but I don't see how they could make this move in a nonquestion-begging way. Rawls and Freeman intended to use intuitive ideas of what it means to develop and exercise the moral powers to determine what our basic liberties are; we're not supposed to load the idea of exercising one's sense of justice with ideological baggage. At any rate, if they want to just assert that a person can't truly exercise their moral powers without such rights, then they are vulnerable to Tomasi saying that same thing about the capitalist rights they exclude from the list of basic liberties.[43]

So Rawls and Freeman must further modify their test. They need to look for a different explanatory relationship between basic liberty and the two moral powers. Fill in the blank: Some sphere of freedom counts as a basic liberty just in case it _____ the two moral powers. Some candidates:

> *Might be useful for developing or exercising* . . . . This proposal sounds
> good at first, but on reflection, it is far too broad. There are
> many things that might be useful for developing and exercising
> the moral powers that no liberal would plausibly hold is a basic
> liberty. For instance, suppose it turned out, empirically, that in
> order to develop one's moral capacities, it was useful to get ten-
> year-olds to have experience hurting other people. (They might

react in horror to seeing others suffer, and thus, from a sense of guilt, better develop empathy and a sense of fairness.) It would still be absurd to suggest that we make the right to hurt other people (even if it's only allowed as part of an education program at a suitable age) a basic liberty. But the present proposal implies exactly that. As such, this proposed modification of the Rawls-Freeman test is too broad and must be rejected.

Tends to be conducive to developing or exercising . . . . This proposal is stricter than the last, but is still too broad. The problem that I discussed with the last proposal applies here; it might turn out, empirically, that allowing people to do certain harmful things to one another will tend to help them develop their moral powers. Even if so, we wouldn't want to say that the right to hurt others is among the basic liberties. But the present proposal says they should. The present proposal is also in another way too narrow for Rawls's and Freeman's purposes. After all, Rawls and Freeman want to argue that equal rights to vote and run for office are not merely basic liberties but instead the most important basic liberties. As we saw in chapters 2 and 3, however, the available evidence in political psychology strongly suggests that exercising political rights (and rights of political speech) tends to impede rather than promote most people's capacity to develop their two moral powers. Politics tends to be bad for most of us and makes most of us worse people, as judged by Rawlsian standards.[44]

Tends to maximize the development or exercise of . . . . This proposal suffers from the same problem as the last.

The Rawls-Freeman test of whether a liberty is a basic liberty is that it must be necessary for all people to develop and fully exercise their capacity for a sense of justice and the good life.[45] Freeman tells us that Rawls means necessary for all people, though Rawls does not explicitly say this in the passage Freeman refers to.

It's unclear to me that Rawls and Freeman even try to apply their test of basic liberties to the things they call basic liberties. They both try to illustrate why certain possible rights—such as the right to free speech or vote—might be basic liberties, according to the test, by showing us that certain rights might useful in developing the powers, or that constraints on these rights might get in the way.[46] For instance, they say a person will have difficulty assessing different conceptions of the good life if the government forbids them from reading about alternative lifestyles. Yet the problem for Rawls and Freeman is that it wouldn't be *impossible* for that person to do so, and it might not even be that hard. Rawls and Freeman think justice forbids censorship, but people can easily develop their senses of justice under a regime with significant censorship, if perhaps not a North Korean level of censorship.

The Rawls-Freeman test for basic liberties doesn't seem to work. We haven't found any good connection between the political liberties and the development and exercise of the two moral powers.

In this book, I am arguing that the choice between epistocracy and democracy is largely instrumental; we should choose the system that works better. I don't accept Rawls's or Freeman's theory of what makes something a basic liberty. Still, as the exercise above has shown, I could use their theory on my behalf. According to Rawls and Freeman, something is a basic liberty just in case everyone needs it to develop and exercise their two moral powers. But people don't need the rights to vote or run for office to develop and exercise their two moral powers. Accordingly, Rawls's first principle of justice contains no objection to epistocracy. Rawls may have *other* objections to epistocracy—I'll look at some in the next chapter—but this particular one doesn't succeed.

SUMMARY: ESSENTIAL POWERLESSNESS

In a democracy, every citizen has equal fundamental political power. While democracy grants each citizen an equal share of fundamental political power, this nonetheless is a small share indeed.

Define the variable P as the full power of the government. In an absolute monarchy, the right to rule resides in one person. De jure, the monarch has P power, while everyone else has 0 power. (Of course, de facto, the monarch will have less than P and some subjects will have greater than 0.)

In a representative democracy, by law, every citizen has a P/Nth share of the total power, where N = the number of citizens. Of course, how much de facto power citizens have varies. Presidents, members of parliament, lobbyists, influential celebrities or pundits, and so on, have more power, while others have less.

Yet even if such unequal influence could be eliminated, saying that each citizen in a democracy holds P/Nth share of power is misleading. The modal or average citizen, in their capacity as a voter or potential candidate for office, is better said to have δ, an infinitesimal amount of power > 0. Most citizens have a vanishingly small chance of making any difference through their political activities.

I have approximately 1/210,000,000 of the legal voting power in the United States. I have actively opposed my country's military endeavors for the last ten years. It is not as though by voting against hawkish candidates, I reduced US bellicosity by 1/210,000,000th. I have stopped not a single bullet from being fired. I have had no effect whatsoever. Similarly, I would prefer to reduce capital gains taxes to zero and instead instantiate higher value-added taxes. My activities, however, have not changed any taxes of any sort by any amount. Finally, I am a strong advocate of open borders. Yet not a single individual has been admitted to the United States as a result of my votes, nor has a single individual been allowed to stay a single second longer in the United States before being deported. My political activities have had *no* effect whatsoever on law or policy, and most likely, they never will. And unless you are in a better position, the same goes for you.

One of the complaints about epistocracy, compared to democracy, is that it deprives some citizens of their share of power. But we're not denying citizens a slice of the pie of power. We're denying them crumbs.[47]

The idea that democracy empowers us is intuitive, but it probably rests on an unnoticed fallacy of division. Democracy certainly does empower *us* in a way dictatorships do not. But although democracy empowers us, it doesn't empower you, or me, your friends, your mom, or your adult children. Democracy does not empower *individuals*. It disempowers individuals and instead empowers the majority of the moment. In a democracy, individual citizens are nearly powerless.[48]

Recall two of the basic questions I'm asking:

- Are the political rights and political participation good for individuals?
- Are individuals owed the right to vote and hold office as a matter of justice?

The idea that democracy empowers you in some way is supposed to justify giving a "yes" answer to both these questions. But since democracy doesn't actually empower you or me, we haven't yet discovered a reason to answer either question in the affirmative.

A 2015 Monmouth University poll finds that Americans are increasingly skeptical of whether their individual political participation is valuable as a means of producing change.[49] Fifty-four percent believe "they can be more effective in the world around them by getting involved in nonpolitical activities," while a mere "28 percent say that being involved in government and elections is the way to go in order to effect change in their communities."[50] Some take this as evidence that the US public has grown cynical. Perhaps it is, but in this case, people's cynicism has made their beliefs more reasonable and realistic.

CHAPTER 5

POLITICS IS NOT A POEM

The instinct of worship is still so strong upon us that, having
nearly worn out our capacity for treating kings and such
kind of persons as sacred, we are ready to invest a majority
of our own selves with the same kind of reverence.

—*Auberon Herbert, "State Education: a Help or Hindrance?"*

Years ago, in a previous book on voting ethics, I wrote the following:

> The value of the right to vote consists in something [other than
> its instrumental value]. It is not that individual votes have much
> practical utility. It is, rather, that the right to vote is a badge of
> equal personhood. The Nazis made Jews wear the Star of David
> as a badge of inferiority. The right to vote is a metaphorical badge
> of equality.[1]

At that time, I accepted the common view that equal voting rights
have some sort of symbolic value. Just as we might express the equal
dignity of each citizen with a statue in the town square or poem, so

POLITICS IS NOT A POEM   **113**

we might express their equal dignity by giving them each a right to vote. I now believe this way of thinking is seriously inadequate.

The previous chapter examined whether democracy empowers individuals in any significant way. I turn now to a different class of arguments on behalf of democracy and political participation. These arguments focus broadly on the symbolic power of democracy, what giving them equal political rights expresses, what giving them unequal rights expresses, and what effects such expressions have on people's self-esteem and social status. These arguments are meant to show both that democracy and participation are *good* for individuals, and that individuals are owed the right to vote and run for office as a matter of justice.

Many people regard it as axiomatic that all people share a fundamental moral equality. At the very least, many are convinced that just governments ought to act as if everyone's life is of equal worth. Many want to ground their arguments for democracy or against epistocracy on this fundamental equality. As Elizabeth Anderson says, "Pressure toward universal inclusion [in the franchise] follows from the demands of equality . . . whereby each adult actively recognizes everyone else's equal authority to make claims concerning the rules under which all shall live."[2]

In this chapter, I primarily attack what I will call *semiotic* arguments for democracy and against epistocracy. Semiotic arguments for democracy rely on the idea that imbuing everyone with equal fundamental power expresses, communicates, or symbolizes respect. Relatedly, semiotic objections to epistocracy depend on the idea that failing to imbue people with power (or equal power) expresses, communicates, or symbolizes disrespect. Many philosophers and laypeople alike find it plausible that imbuing each citizen with the same basic political power rightly expresses the idea that each citizen has the same basic moral worth. Many also find it plausible that formally imbuing citizens with unequal power wrongfully expresses the idea that citizens have unequal moral worth.

Proper semiotic arguments, as I define them, are independent of *other* arguments for democracy or against epistocracy. Semiotic arguments are about what democracy signals, not about whether democracy performs better than the alternatives or is especially fair.

To test semiotic objections, to see whether they have any independent force, we have to put nonsemiotic objections to the side. Thus, when comparing democracy to epistocracy or other forms of government on semiotic grounds, we must imagine that there are no other worries about epistocracy other than what it signals or expresses.

Suppose it turned out that some sort of epistocracy—say, one in which some low-information voters were excluded from voting—consistently outperformed democracy. Many democratic theorists and laypeople would be still be tempted to conclude that there is just something plain disrespectful about labeling some citizens as more politically competent than others. Epistocracy seems to express a kind of immoral elitism. This kind of worry appears to be a genuine semiotic objection to epistocracy. Something like this could be used to ground a proper semiotic argument for democracy.

As an example of a semiotic objection, consider the following passage from political theorist Pablo Gilbert. Gilbert says that nondemocratic political structures by their very nature would *insult* the dignity of citizens:

> Being rendered a second-class citizen (which is normally the case in a nondemocratic regime) is arguably injurious to an individual's dignity, or a failure of due consideration. It is insulting to be told, or treated in a way that pragmatically implies, something like the following: "Our fundamental collective decisions are yours just as much as everyone else's, although you deserve fewer rights to participate in shaping them than some others." . . . Regardless of whether one actually takes offense, it is in fact an affront to one's dignity to be subject to a basic political structure within which one has less than equal rights of participation.[3]

Here, Gilbert is not talking about whether democracies do a better job of protecting liberty or promoting social justice than other forms of government. He instead means to point out that unequal political power signals inferiority and sends an offensive message.

Similarly, philosopher Christopher Griffin claims that a "denial of an equal share of power in the context of disagreement about the basic ground rules of social life is a public declaration of second-class citizenry."[4] Estlund complains that epistocracy involves "invidious comparisons," as it relies on the idea that some are more fit to rule than others.[5] Or consider this passage from Robert Nozick, who in the middle of his philosophical career became impressed with symbolic arguments:

> Democratic institutions and the liberties coordinate with them are not simply effective means toward controlling the power of government and directing these toward matters of joint concern; they themselves express and symbolize, in a pointed and official way, our equal human dignity, our autonomy and powers of self-direction. We vote . . . in part as an expression and symbolic affirmation of our status as autonomous and self-governing beings whose considered judgments or even opinions have to be given equal weight to those of others.[6]

Although Nozick remained a libertarian throughout his career (talk of his apostasy is incorrect), one of the things he found inadequate about his earlier expressions of that philosophy was his inattention to the expressive value of politics.

Political theorists, philosophers, and laypeople have adduced an impressive range of symbolic or semiotic reasons to prefer democracy to the alternatives:

- Democracy is necessary to express that all citizens are equal.
- Democracy is necessary for proper social recognition or recognition of one's agency.
- Democracy is necessary as a social basis for self-respect.
- Democracy is necessary as a social basis for being respected by others.
- Democracy is necessary for proper inclusion as a full member of society.
- Nondemocratic structures, regardless of how well governed they are, are an affront to citizens' dignity.

In this chapter, I maintain that these kinds of symbolic, semiotic, and esteem-based claims fail to show that democratic rights have any real value to us. They do not provide good reasons to choose democracy over epistocracy, or to think that democracy is more inherently just than epistocracy.

THE TRUTH BEHIND SEMIOTIC CLAIMS

Semiotic arguments have the most force when they are describing explicitly immoral attitudes. Thus, imagine a republic in which the written constitution explicitly gave voting rights to all whites but not to blacks. Suppose the founders did so transparently out of racism. Suppose also that there is no legal procedure for amending this constitution.

Now one clear worry is that such a government would lead to bad outcomes—that is, it would consistently neglect, harm, or exploit blacks. But this is *not* a semiotic objection to political apartheid. It concerns how well the political regime performs, not what the regime expresses. In principle, a regime that excludes blacks from voting could (aside from the exclusion itself) treat blacks better than a system that allows them to vote. So let's put this concern aside here.

Instead, imagine that after a few generations, no one in this imagined society is even slightly racist. Imagine that every member of society is now fully informed and has a perfect sense of justice. Suppose the white voting electorate now votes for political policies that fully respect blacks' equal civil and economic rights, and advances their interests equally. That is, imagine that aside from the issue of voting rights, blacks have no other complaints about any of the policies the government enacts; the government does exactly what blacks themselves support.

Even still, in this situation, blacks have a real complaint about the semiotics of the constitution. The adopters of the constitution quite literally meant the constitution to express that blacks are inferior. So of course they should feel disrespected.

Yet the kinds of epistocracies that I along with Mill, Caplan, and Claudio López-Guerra have provisionally advocated as alternatives to democracy are not like this.[7] We don't want to exclude people, or reduce their power, in order to express wrongful contempt or disrespect for any individuals, groups, or races. Instead, our goal is to produce better, more substantively just policy outcomes.

Therefore, this apartheid example is not a victory for semiotic arguments. If someone does something with the explicit intention of signaling racist attitudes, and if everyone knows the actor has this intention, then it's not surprising that the action will signal racist attitudes. That's not an exciting result. But as we will see below, those who rely on semiotic arguments want to contend that such reasoning succeeds *regardless of the authors' intentions*. They want to assert that democracy inherently signals respect while epistocracy inherently signals disrespect, notwithstanding what any person actually feels, believes, or intends to express, even if the purpose of implementing epistocratic regimes is to generate more substantively just results.

WHAT DEMOCRACY EXPRESSES

Suppose I believe that in some sense every person's life is worth as much as any other's. Or suppose I believe that a just political system ought to treat every citizen as if their life and interests were equally important; a government ought not favor some over others. There is no obvious logical entailment from these general commitments to equality to a commitment to democracy or representative government of any form. On its face, it looks like an open, empirical question as to which political system best promotes these kinds of equality. It could turn out that epistocracy ends up being smarter than democracy, and for that reason does a better job of promoting equal outcomes. So, for instance, US voters tend to be ignorant of the effects of the drug war on minorities, about how and why crime rates are falling, and how being "tough on crime" tends to cause disproportionate harm to minorities. An epistocracy might alleviate this problem, because epistocratic voters are more likely to know that US crime and drug policies are counterproductive.

In an ideal, properly functioning democracy, every citizen has equal fundamental political power. Democracy, in that way, is egalitarian. One might assert that by virtue of imbuing everyone with equal voting rights, democracy expresses the idea that every person is equal. But even if that's true, we have to ask, Why should we think there is any moral requirement to express equality *that way?*

There are lots of ways to express that everyone is equal. Societies could put equality signs on their flags. They could erect statues of equality in their major cities. They could have a national equality day in which every schoolchild talks about equality. Or they could even put their money where their mouths are and commit to choosing whatever form of government turns out, as a matter of fact, to produce properly equitable results (even if that form turns out to be epistocratic).

Almost everyone believes in equality, but just what the ideal of equality requires is heavily disputed. Some hold it necessitates equal material resources. Others believe it *forbids* equal material resources; since people are different, to ensure that everyone has equal material outcomes, we would have treat people unequally, they say. Others claim it requires equal opportunity to acquire resources. Others say it merely requires that departures from material equality be to everyone's benefit. Still others maintain it is essential that all citizens have equal rights, but then they disagree about just what rights all citizens ought equally to have. Rawls thinks equality necessitates social democracy. Gerald Cohen thinks equality requires a socialist anarchist society. Libertarians think equality requires a capitalist anarchist society, or a minarchist or night watchman state.[8] Each of them thinks that their society expresses citizens' fundamental moral equality and other forms of government fail to do so.

There's a sense in which these disputants are all correct: each of these ways of distributing political power, material resources, and property rights can indeed be grounded on one kind of equality, so each society is egalitarian in its own right. The disagreement here isn't over whether people should be regarded and treated as equals but rather over *which* ways they should be treated as equals and which ways they should not be. A basic commitment to human equality severely underdetermines what a good society will look like.

I've opened here by expressing in general why I'm skeptical that a commitment to the equal status and value of all persons has any direct connection to democracy. But over the next few pages, I'll examine and rebut specific arguments that try to explain just what this connection is.

JUDGMENTS OF SUPERIORITY

Christiano bases an argument for the duty to obey democratic laws in part on semiotic grounds. He contends that if I choose to disregard or refuse to obey a democratic law, "I am in effect saying that my judgment on these matters is better than [my fellow citizens']. . . . I am in effect treating myself like a god or the others like children."[9] By refusing to obey democratic law, I fail to treat their judgment as equal to mine.[10] By refusing to obey democratic laws, I would be "putting [my] judgment ahead of others [and] . . . in effect expressing the superiority of [my] interests over others."[11] It is morally wrong to express such attitudes and therefore wrong to disobey democratic laws.[12] Christiano isn't the only prominent philosopher with such worries. As I noted above, Estlund is similarly troubled that epistocracy would involve invidious comparisons.

In the passages I just cited, Christiano's goal is to defend a moral duty to obey democratic laws. He is not in the first case trying to make a semiotic objection to epistocracy. Nevertheless, I bring up his argument here because it suggests that epistocracy is objectionable on semiotic grounds. Christiano believes that the choice to violate a democratic law with which one disagrees expresses contempt for one's fellow citizens' political judgment and an immoral attitude of superiority. His reasoning thus suggests that to refuse the franchise to the incompetent expresses even greater contempt and an even stronger view of superiority.

Restricted suffrage and other forms of epistocracy do indeed communicate the idea that some citizens have better political judgment than others. After all, one way or another, epistocracies attempt to apportion political power on the basis of political competence. Epistocratic institutions may not express the view that some are like gods and others like children, but they do express the view that some people have better judgment than others when it comes to political matters.

Christiano thinks it is morally wrong to express such views. Presumably, in his opinion, the views defended in this book are not simply mistaken; I do something morally wrong by writing this book. But Christiano's position is puzzling for a number of reasons.

First, Christiano makes the perplexing claim that by viewing one person's judgment as superior to that of others, one thereby "in effect" regards that person's interests as more valuable. Christiano's main argument for this claim seems to be that people suffer from self-serving biases. So if we privilege the political judgment of some over others, the privileged will exercise power in ways that promote their interests at the expense of others' interests.

While people are generally biased to be overconfident in their own judgment, as I discussed in previous chapters, the empirical evidence overwhelmingly shows that voters are not biased to vote in their self-interest. On the contrary, as I reviewed in chapter 2, the empirical evidence overwhelmingly demonstrates that citizens vote in what they regard as the national interest. Remember that the evidence does not simply show that voters *believe* themselves to be voting for the national interest. Rather, political scientists overwhelmingly find that citizens' voting behavior is not predicted by what the political scientist would independently define as in the citizens' interests. So long as the voting population in an epistocracy is in the thousands or greater, we can expect epistocratic voters to vote altruistically as opposed to selfishly.[13]

Beyond that, if Christiano is worried about self-serving biases, this doesn't seem to call for a categorical rejection of epistocracy. It instead leaves open as an empirical question whether epistocracy does a better or worse job of promoting justice than democracy, given whatever biases people have. If people are biased, this calls for comparative institutional analysis and picking whichever system works better.

Second, it is unclear why it would be unjust or wrong to express the view that some citizens have inferior normative or political judgment to others.[14] I agree with Christiano that all citizens have equal basic moral rights. In addition, I agree that governments should not privilege the interests of some over others. None of this precludes me from thinking that some people have inferior judgment to others on political matters—both about specific topics and in general.

Concerning almost any topic inside or outside politics, some people have superior judgment to others. Despite disagreement, diversity, and self-serving cognitive biases, we can and do form justified true beliefs that some people have superior judgment to others. I justifiably believe my surgeon brother-in-law has superior medical judgment than I do. I justifiably believe my information systems technician brother has superior judgment about computers than I do, and my plumber has superior judgment about pipe fitting. I justifiably believe that Qantas pilots have superior judgment about piloting than I do. And while I no doubt suffer from some degree of confirmation and self-serving bias, perhaps I justifiably believe that I—a named professor of strategy, economics, ethics, and public policy at an elite research university, with a PhD from the top-ranked political philosophy program in the English-speaking world, and a strong record of peer-reviewed publications in top journals and academic presses— have superior political judgment on a great many political matters compared to many of my fellow citizens, including to many large groups of them. If I *didn't* believe that about myself, I'd feel like a fraud every time I teach a political economy course.[15]

Note that such judgments (that on some topic, one person knows more and has better judgment than the other) need not carry with them the further judgment that some people are better than others, tout court. I think my plumber is better at plumbing than I am, but I don't think he is better than I am, period. I think I'm better at economic reasoning than my plumber, but I don't think I'm better than he is, period.

Judging that one has superior normative or political judgment seems especially unproblematic once we examine empirical work on what citizens know. As we saw in chapter 2, the empirical evidence demonstrates that on even the most basic questions about politics, most citizens know nothing, and many know less than nothing. We have evidence that the public makes systematic mistakes about social scientific matters. The US public sets the bar low. My five-year-old son, Keaton, is agnostic about economics, while the average and modal American is a mercantilist. This means that on many questions of economics, Keaton is superior to the US public as a whole. He is merely ignorant, while they're *mistaken*. Keaton might not understand much about economics, yet at least he's not a mercantilist, like almost everyone in the United States.

In light of these objections, a semiotic defender of democracy might agree that it is not essentially disrespectful to judge that some have superior judgment to others, but then object that it is usually disrespectful to *express* such judgments. It is fine to believe that some have better judgment than others, though we should keep this belief to ourselves and avoid expressing it through our institutions.

As an illustration of this, my surgeon brother-in-law, David, correctly believes that he has superior medical judgment to most people. It is not morally wrong for him to have this belief. But that does not mean he should walk around Target, telling everyone he meets that he has better medical judgment than they do. This would express arrogance or contempt.

There are times when something important is at stake, however. In such cases, it can become permissible or even mandatory that one publicly judge and express who is superior to others along some dimension. Indeed, democrats seem to agree; most seem to think that when we're voting for elected officials, we're supposed to look for the better candidates—those better fit to lead.[16]

If someone, for instance, starts choking in front of David during his Target shopping trip, he should not be modest. Someone's life is at stake. He should declare that he is a doctor—thus expressing that he has superior medical judgment to others—and should be charged with helping the choking customer. Suppose bystander Bob, who has no medical training, says, "Hey, *Doctor* David, I want to help the choking person too! It's disrespectful of you to insist *you* help him. You and I are equals. We should flip a coin to determine who will help. Otherwise you're hurting my feelings." In this scenario, Bob acts badly. David should take charge, and Bob should get over himself. Even if Bob sincerely believed he and David are equals, Bob is negligent in holding this belief, and shouldn't act on it.

It can be immoral or disrespectful under *some* conditions to express the view that some have better judgment than others, but under *other* conditions, it can be permissible or even mandatory. Let us apply this to a political illustration. Suppose an evil demon said, "I will cast a spell condemning all of you to lower-quality government—and hence more unjust wars, bad economic policies that harm the poor, more bigotry, and more poverty and suffering—unless you do a moderately decent job identifying which citizens tend to have better political judgment from others." In this case, under the demon's threat, we would have good reason to try to distinguish the more from the less competent. If people feel insulted, it is just too bad, and they need to grow up. The point of distinguishing the more from the less competent is not to insult the incompetent but rather to save us from the bad government the evil demon will inflict on us.

Yet this is more or less the situation epistocrats claim we are in, except that in the real world, the evil demon is democracy. Now epistocrats may be wrong about this—perhaps it turns out that democracy functions better than epistocracy—but the issue we're currently considering is whether epistocracy has disrespectful semiotics. (Remember, the semiotic arguments for democracy are meant to show that we should use democracy instead of epistocracy, even if epistocracy performs better.) If epistocrats are right about the dangers of democracy and advantages of epistocracy, then they are just as justified in expressing the view that some have superior political judgment as David was in expressing the perspective that he has superior medical judgment. If this offends voters, they are acting like Bob in the story above and are morally obligated to get over it. We cannot let the country choke simply because people are sensitive about or have unjustified beliefs about their political competence. It seems strange to hold that we should have less just policies, greater chances of unjust war, greater poverty, and so on, in order to avoid expressing the view that some people have better judgment about politics than others, especially when that judgment is true.

In response to worries like this, Christiano says that justice must not only be done; it must also be seen as being done.[17] If fundamental political power is distributed equally, then citizens will tend to believe that everyone's interests are being promoted equally. If power is distributed unequally, then citizens will tend to believe (or be suspicious) that the government favors some over others.[18] If some citizens are granted the right to vote but others are not, people might be suspicious that the former's interests are being promoted while the latter's interests are not.

But such suspicions are not enough to ground a theory of justice in the distribution of political power. One problem for Christiano is that to see is a success verb. One cannot see a ghost in the shadows unless there actually is a ghost. One cannot see justice being done unless justice is actually being done. So suppose it turned out—as it well may—that epistocracy is superior to democracy at promoting just outcomes. If so, then instantiating democracy over epistocracy would not cause citizens to see justice done; it would at best cause them to mistakenly believe they are seeing justice done. Christiano's objection gets off the ground only if citizens' suspicions of epistocracy are well grounded—that is, only if democracy actually performs better than epistocracy in promoting all citizens' interests equitably. In that case, the semiotic concerns would no longer be decisive. We instead should have democracy simply because it works better. If epistocracy would perform better than democracy, though, then in order for citizens to see justice being done, they would need to see epistocracy.

Now suppose Christiano modified his view to say that it's important that people *believe* justice is being done, and in some situations, it might be more important that people falsely believe justice is being done than that justice actually be done. For instance, suppose it turned out that people are terribly stubborn. Even if we had overwhelming proof that epistocracy produces more substantive justice than democracy does, these people would still regard epistocracy as unjust, and as a result, epistocracy would be less stable than democracy. If the instability is bad enough, perhaps that would be outweigh whatever substantive benefits epistocracy would bring and would be reason to favor democracy over epistocracy. But notice here that we've moved away from a semiotic argument for democracy to the instrumentalist question of which system performs better, all things considered.

EQUAL POLITICAL POWER AND THE SOCIAL BASES OF SELF-RESPECT

Rawls contends that justice requires all citizens be afforded equal basic political power. I disposed of one of his arguments for this conclusion in chapter 4. Here, I focus on a second, semiotic argument.[19]

As philosopher Stephen Wall summarizes Rawls's argument, Rawls "holds that the fair value guarantee of the political liberties is essential to securing the self-respect of all citizens in a liberal society." Rawls's argument "begins with the plausible thought that political institutions established in a society bear importantly on the social component of self-respect. Some institutional arrangements do better than others in encouraging citizens to view one another as moral equals. . . . The public expression of . . . the fair value of political liberty is an affirmation of the equal status of all citizens."[20] Notice the semiotic language: encourage citizens to view one another, public expression, and affirmation.

Freeman claims that

> Rawls contends that the status required for self-respect in a well-ordered democratic society comes from having the status of equal citizenship, which in turn requires the equal basic liberties. It would not be rational for less advantaged persons to compromise this primary ground for their self-respect, by giving up the right to vote for example, for this would "have the effect of publically establishing their inferiority. . . ." This subordinate ranking would indeed be humiliating and destructive of self-esteem.[21]

This is a strongly semiotic argument. Rawls and Freeman do not merely assert that democracy is one way of expressing the public equality of citizens. They think democracy is essential to express this equality. Rawls and Freeman (who concurs with Rawls) believe that it would be *irrational* for the relatively disadvantaged to give up the right to vote, even if that would massively improve their welfare, because this would be "humiliating," "destructive of self-esteem," and would *express* the idea that they are subordinate.

There's something strange about these self-esteem-based arguments for democracy. Remember that to give citizens the right to vote is not just to give them some modicum of power over themselves but also to imbue them with a modicum of power over others. It makes them part of the collective that in turn can push people around and force them to do things against their will. Giving a person or groups of people control rights—even weak control rights—over a stranger has to be justified.

Democracy is not a poem or painting. Democracy is a political system. It is at base a method for deciding how and when an institution claiming a monopoly on legitimate violence will exercise violence.

As Rawls himself believes, government and political structures are meant to help secure the benefits of cooperation, advance justice, and ensure the peace. They are not in the first instance institutions intended to boost, maintain, or regulate our self-esteem.

Suppose a citizen was repeatedly rejected from serving on a jury on the grounds that they were mentally unfit to be a juror. Suppose they are not insane or mentally disabled. Rather, in each case, the prosecutor or defense attorney reject them because they are identifiably irrational or biased. Now suppose they complain, "This hurts my self-esteem. It makes me feel bad about myself that you think I'm not competent to serve on a jury. Also, when I tell my friends I was rejected again, they will laugh at me. It hurts my social standing." Here the citizen isn't being rejected because of their race, sexual orientation, gender, sex, or any indelible characteristics. They're being rejected because everyone rightly and justifiably concludes that they would do a bad job. They could choose to do a good job—they could overcome their flaws—but they aren't willing to put in the effort. If that hurts their self-esteem and social standing, most of us will conclude that it's just too bad.

Suppose similarly that a shoe salesperson has been repeatedly rejected from serving as a justice in their state supreme court on the grounds that they don't have any background in law. Now suppose this makes them feel bad about themselves. They also complain that this hurts their social standing, since justices of the court have a higher standing than shoe salespeople. If they feel bad that they can't be a supreme court justice, that's just too bad. The best response isn't to lower the standards to allow anyone to serve on the supreme court but instead for them to *get over it*. Alternatively, they could study law and become qualified.

Or consider that for men in the United States today, having sex with a large number of conventionally attractive women confers significant social standing. In contrast, being a forty-year-old heterosexual virgin makes you the subject of jokes. People will call you a loser. Now suppose a forty-year-old virgin, Andy, feels deeply ashamed of his involuntary celibacy. Suppose his friends learn he is a virgin, and respond by mocking him. Even then, we shouldn't, in order to protect Andy's social standing or self-esteem, imbue Andy with some degree of control over women's bodies. This may seem like an irrelevant example, but it's not. Political power is control over other people's bodies. Modern polities make a greater number of decisions about what people are allowed to eat, what drugs they can take, where they are allowed or required to go, and even whether they can have consensual sex with other adults.

Even if we accept that imbuing some people with less political power than others, or failing to give everyone equal political power, might harm people's self-esteem or lower their relative social status, it's not yet clear why this matters from the standpoint of justice. We do not in these other cases think that in order to protect people's social status or self-esteem, it is appropriate to give them *any* power or control rights over others. So we need some further argument that shows the rights to vote or run for office are different.

One further problem with Rawls's semiotic argument is that it seems to rely on highly contingent views of what democracy expresses. While it is not arbitrary that we should signal respect for one another and avoid signaling disrespect, the practices, gestures, and words by which we signal such things are arbitrary—unless, of course, those actions are harmful, exploitative, rights violating, corrupting, or conducive to the misallocation of goods. Otherwise, if there are no *other* problems, then what our actions communicate seems merely to be a socially constructed fact. So, for instance, shooting you signals disrespect *because* it harms you and violates your rights. But my giving you the middle finger signals disrespect simply because we happen to have imbued the gesture with that meaning. There is no additional reason to regard it as disrespectful. We could have imbued the middle finger with patriotic, religious, or romantic meaning instead. We could have made the middle finger a form of salute.

This is not to deny that there is a fact about what we communicate but rather to affirm that in the absence of nonsemiotic concerns, these facts appear to be contingent and in principle open to revision. Societies construct codes that imbue certain behaviors with meaning. In light of those codes, some behaviors will signify morally bad meanings.

As a matter of fact, most human beings tend to associate political power with a kind of majesty. They tend to think that a person's fundamental moral standing is expressed through their political standing, and vice versa. Nation-states are like clubs, and people tend to treat the rights to vote and run for office as signifying full membership in the national club. Most people believe that citizens who lack these rights are like junior members of the national club. When people lack the political liberties, most people look down on them. Those who lack the right to vote might then feel humiliated by their lesser status. And so it seems plausible that the social bases of self-respect really do depend on equal political power. But perhaps that is just a contingent feature of how we Western liberal democrats happen to think.

To illustrate why, imagine that in our culture, or in the human race in general, we tended to associate being given a red scarf by one's government as a mark of membership and status. You aren't fully in your national club until you get your government-issued red scarf at age eighteen.

Now suppose the government gives red scarves to everyone, except homosexuals. Homosexuals would be upset; they would claim that the government's refusal to grant them red scarves shows that homosexuals are considered second-class, inferior people. The government's behavior would tend to induce people (including homosexuals themselves) to regard homosexuals as having low status and being less valuable. Homosexuals and their sympathetic allies would have reason to take to the streets and demand that homosexuals be granted scarves. Given how everyone thinks about red scarves, it in some sense becomes crucial to have one.

At the same time, we can say, "There's no deep reason to attach status and standing to red scarf ownership. Human dignity doesn't actually depend on scarves. It's just a silly, contingent psychological or cultural fact that people think this way. They needn't think this way." The red scarves are valuable only as a result of a social construction, and an *odd* one at that.[22] In the absence of that social convention, they would lack the value they have.

Perhaps we can say the same thing about the political liberties and associating moral standing with political power. (The political liberties are, after all, rights to political power.) Maybe there is no intrinsic or essential connection between one's fundamental status and political power. Perhaps it's merely a contingent psychological or cultural fact that people tend to associate human dignity with the right to vote.

This association is only contingent; there is, as far as I can see, no intrinsic or essential connection between status and political power. It is a contingent, psychological or cultural fact that people tend to associate human dignity with political power, or more specifically with the right to vote. We can easily imagine a world otherwise like ours, in which people lacked these kinds of attitudes. Instead of viewing the president as majestic or the office of the presidency as deserving reverence, people merely think of the president as the chief public goods administrator. Instead of holding that the rights to vote and run for office express a lesser kind of majesty, or that such rights signify membership in the national club, people could regard these rights as licenses, no different from driving, hairdressing, or plumbing licenses. We can imagine people who do not associate national status with international political power and do associate personal status with power. In fact, not only can we envision such people, such people actually exist! I am one of them. It's not difficult to imagine an epistocratic society in which everyone regards one another as having equal status. Perhaps they endorse epistocracy because they think it tends to produce more equitable results, and for that reason think their commitment to epistocracy expresses a commitment to equality.

So it appears that equal voting rights expresses respect for equal human dignity only as a result of contingent attitudes or a contingent social construct. If so, this leaves open the question of whether these are good attitudes or a good social construct. Perhaps, on the contrary, they're *bad* attitudes or a bad social construct, which we ought to change.

A world in which political power conferred no status might be a better one than ours. We tie esteem to political power. But doing so has a terrible track record.[23] Just think of the abuses and injustices entire nations, kings, emperors, presidents, senators, district attorneys, police officers, and average voters have gotten away with throughout history, all because we attach standing, reverence, and status to political power, and defer before such majestic standing. Moreover, one reason why kings, presidents, and district attorneys commit such abuses in the first place is that they associate status with power. Henry

VIII's wars, for example, had no chance of increasing his (or most of his subjects') personal wealth or comfort. He committed these atrocities in large part because he wanted the prestige and status that attach to increased political power. Most people revere power, more than they would admit to themselves. The romance of power and authority partly explains why people have so often willingly collaborated with government-sponsored injustices.

Most people attach symbolic meaning to the rights to vote and run for office. Yet there is no moral requirement to accept, uncritically, the meaning people attach to these rights. Instead, we may be morally required to revise the semiotics we assign to voting rights.

To see why, note that most Rawlsians believe people should be prohibited from practicing medicine without a government license. But we can imagine a culture or society that attaches the same semiotics to the right to practice medicine as Americans happen to attach to the right to vote. We can thus envision a society in which being denied a medical license on grounds of incompetence would be humiliating or destructive of self-esteem. Perhaps some people actually think this way. For instance, some libertarians think that all such licensing requirements express contempt for people's dignity.

Still, Rawlsians would be unmoved. They would not agree that in order to avoid signaling disrespect, we should simply let everyone be a medical doctor. They would instead say that the point of licensing medical doctors is to protect people's health. They would assert that there are compelling consequentialist grounds for this practice. The culture in question should just modify its views about what counts as signaling respect.

Consider another such illustration.[24] Suppose a culture developed the idea that the best way to respect the dead was by eating their raw, putrefied corpses. In that culture, it really would be a (socially constructed) fact that failing to eat the dead expressed disrespect, while eating rotting raw flesh would express respect. But suppose that eating raw, putrefied corpses tends to make people sick. In fact, it does: the Fore tribe of Papua New Guinea used to suffer from fatal prion infections as a result of its former practice of eating the dead (a practice that they regarded as showing respect for their dead). In that case, the culture would have excellent reasons to eliminate its practice and modify its semiotics. (That's just what the Fore did; when they realized their code was destructive, the Fore changed it.) Languages and social practices are not necessarily equal in their utility. This way of expressing respect would tend to make people sick and kill them. The interpretative practice of equating the eating of rotting flesh with showing respect is thus a destructive, bad practice. The people in that culture have strong moral grounds to change. The culture's semiotics about what it takes to express respect is itself morally defective.

Or consider that in some cultures, women are expected to undergo genital mutilation. Such mutilation marks fidelity and respect for the group, or fidelity and respect for religion. Many versions of this practice (such as clitoridectomies or infibulation), however, are extremely harmful. In those cases, the cultures in question have strong grounds to revise the semiotics they impute to genital mutilation.

Let us turn this kind of reasoning back onto the issue of epistocracy. Suppose for the sake of argument that epistocracy would produce more just outcomes than would democracy. That would give us compelling grounds for revising the meaning we attach to voting rights. It would mean that our cultural semiotics—our tendency to attach special meaning to equal voting rights—hurts us. Just as the Fore tribe of Papua New Guinea had compelling reasons to change the meaning it attached to eating the dead, so we would have compelling reasons to change the meaning we attach to the right to vote. If epistocracy works better than democracy, then we should stop viewing the right to vote as a badge of equal status, and instead regard it as having no more symbolic power than a hunting or plumbing license.

In my view, the choice between democracy and epistocracy is not about semiotics. Whichever system works better—producing more just outcomes as well as better protecting civil and economic rights—is better. If it turns out that empirically, epistocracy works better, then we should not take our cultural practice of signaling respect through the right to vote for granted. Instead, we should revise this practice, and regard the right to vote no differently from how we regard any other licensed rights, such as the right to drive or practice medicine. After all, substantive justice is at stake. To refuse to do so, to maintain the semiotics of voting rights at the expense of substantive justice, would itself be morally wrong.

The unequal distribution of power on the basis of competence seems elitist, but it is not inherently more elitist than the unequal distribution of plumbing or hairdressing licenses. Comparing voting rights to hairdressing licenses might seem jarring. But that is only because most people view political power as majestic while they regard plumbing as lower-status work. Again, that is just how people happen to think. People don't have to think that way. I, for one, don't think that way, and the rest of you could be like me.

Rawls argued that we cannot treat envy as a moral emotion.[25] Envy threatens to turn positive-sum games into zero-sum games or worse. If we focus on how well we do compared to others rather than how well we are doing in absolute terms, then we will choose policies that bring everyone down as opposed to policies that lift everyone up. Rawls thinks that when it comes to wealth and income, we should not be obsessed with relative status.

Unlike wealth, political power is in some sense a zero-sum game. One person can gain in voting power only if another person loses. Still, even in a democracy, voters have infinitesimal voting power. If it turns out that epistocracy delivers substantially more just or better consequences than democracy, then we should apply Rawls's insight about envy to political status. Status envy is not a moral emotion. We should not yield to it at the expense of our well-being or other concerns of justice.

INSULT TO DISADVANTAGED GROUPS

One variation of the semiotic argument holds that epistocracy is insulting not because it imbues individuals with unequal power but rather because it will distribute power unequally among different demographic groups. Restricted suffrage epistocracy signals disrespect to whatever groups end up having less political power.

This argument relies on the fact that political knowledge and economic literacy are not evenly spread among all demographic groups. As I mentioned in chapter 2, high-income middle-aged men do about 2.5 times better than low-income young black women on surveys of basic political knowledge.[26] Other attempts to measure political knowledge, including more advanced knowledge of economics or the social sciences, produce similar results.

POLITICS IS NOT A POEM   **133**

Now one worry about this is that it will cause epistocracy to advance disproportionately the interests of the already advantaged. I am less worried about this than many democrats, because such concerns seem to assume that people vote in their self-interest, the disadvantaged know enough about politics to choose policies that promote their interests, and if the disadvantaged vote, politicians will respond to them as much as they respond to the advantaged. I think these assumptions are mistaken. Even if I am wrong and these assumptions are right, this is a worry not about the semiotics of epistocracy but instead about its expected consequences. I'll examine this issue further in chapter 8.

So suppose that if the United States transitioned to a restricted suffrage epistocracy, disadvantaged minority women would be much less likely to qualify for voter licenses than privileged white men. Suppose also, for the sake of argument, that because the voting public is now better informed as a whole, this epistocracy would produce better, more substantively just results than it would as a democracy. Some people believe that this epistocracy remains objectionable because it sends the message that minority women's opinions count for less.

But let us be clear about what is going on. Suppose an evil demon appears before the president and says, "I will force you to follow the policy preferences—as determined by majority voting—of either ten thousand randomly selected rich white middle-aged men, or ten thousand randomly selected poor young black women. You must choose now which group you will obey. I will reveal their policy preferences to you only after you choose." In this case, I would recommend that the president take the advice of the rich white men over the poor black women. A fortiori, I think the president would act unjustly—would violate their fiduciary duties to the public—were they to choose otherwise. (I'll present an argument to that effect in chapter 6.)

Yet this is not because I think white men are morally superior, have greater intrinsic dignity, have more valuable lives, or that their interests count for more. Rather, I am engaging in rational statistical discrimination. There is ample and persistent evidence that right now, rich white men know more about politics than poor black women. There is also ample evidence that policy preferences depend on information—that high-information voters have systematically different policy preferences from low-information voters, and that low-information voters make systematic errors.[27] There is also overwhelming evidence that people do not form their ideologies on the basis of self-interest, and that when voting in large groups, people choose what they consider the national interest versus their self-interest.

In comparison, medical licensing in the United States also systematically leads to underrepresentation by blacks. (Blacks make up 13.1 percent of the US population but only 3.8 percent of medical doctors.)[28] Yet while many people believe underrepresentation is a problem, few think this shows that medical licensing *inherently* humiliates blacks or insults their dignity. The problem is not with medical licensing itself. Rather, there are underlying and historical injustices that reduce the chance that blacks will become doctors. It is these injustices that give grounds to feel insulted, not the disparate results from medical licensing. It is these underlying injustices that need to be rectified, not the fact of medical licensing. (That said, to be clear, I am taking no stance here for or against affirmative action programs in medical schools.)

Similarly, voter licensing would lead, at least at first, to systematic underrepresentation by blacks and the poor. (In fact, even under universal suffrage, including in compulsory voting regimes, blacks and the poor are much less likely to vote than are whites or the rich.)[29] But part of the reason voter licensing would disproportionately exclude blacks and the poor is that they are already mistreated. For instance, the United States wages a drug war that ghettoizes inner cities and destroys families. It shuffles many minorities into overcrowded, dysfunctional schools. It has criminal policies that all but ensure that blacks grow up accustomed to the idea that young black men go to jail. The United States polices blacks in a more adversarial and violent way than it polices whites. It imposes a string of licensing and zoning requirements that make it disproportionately difficult for blacks to start businesses. And so on. This country treats blacks in deeply unjust ways. So as with medical licensing, disproportionate voting power would not in and of itself create injustice; it would be a symptom or result of underlying injustices. If it turns out that poor minorities overwhelmingly disqualify as voters under an epistocracy, this does not automatically demonstrate that epistocracy sends a racist or classist message. Rather, it shows us that there is some underlying injustice in that society, and we should try to fix that underlying injustice. (Again, if someone responds that democracy is needed to fix that underlying injustice, they are making a consequentialist, not a semiotic, argument for democracy.)

DEMOCRACY AND SELF-EXPRESSION

Since we're on the topic of the expressive value of democracy, let's consider one final argument for why possessing the rights to vote and run for office might be seen as valuable, or why people ought to have the right to vote and run for office. This claim holds that the political liberties are important means of self-expression. Call this the expression argument:

1. Generally, it is valuable to each citizen for that citizen to be able to express their opinions about what their country is doing, what values should be promoted, what changes should be made, and so on.
2. The political liberties are a valuable means for a citizen to express their opinion on these matters.
3. Therefore, in general, the political liberties are valuable to each citizen.

The expression argument suffers from many of the same flaws as the other arguments I've considered over the past two chapters. Exercising the political liberties is not a good way to express oneself. There are much better alternatives.[30]

The political liberties are ineffective ways to communicate our attitudes to others. A vote is not an expressive instrument. It's like a piano with only four keys and that breaks after playing one note. I might add that the strings tend to be out of tune and rusty.

In the last US presidential election, I voted for a certain candidate, regarding him as the lesser of two warmongering, corporatist, paternalistic, plutocratic evils. A colleague voted for that same candidate, regarding him as a truly positive change he could believe in.

Suppose someone else voted for that same candidate because they wanted to fit in with their friends. Suppose a fourth person cynically voted for that candidate because they wanted to hasten their country's demise. What did any of our votes express to others? Just by knowing whom someone voted for, you cannot infer what someone meant to express.

When I reveal to others how I voted, we know how they are likely to take it. If they agree with my vote, they'll tend to think I'm a good person, and if they disagree, they'll tend to think I'm selfish, bad, stupid, or evil (see chapter 2). So my vote doesn't easily communicate what I want it to communicate to others.

Or suppose I run for office. What does that communicate? I might claim that I want to change the world for the better, but every politician says that. Regardless of my communicative intentions, running for office tends to communicate that I am power and status hungry.

Given this, exercising the political liberties is ineffective if we want to communicate with others. Still, sometimes we simply want to express our attitudes to ourselves as opposed to others. In private, the heartbroken boy might delete photographs of his recent ex-girlfriend. The point here is to express finality to himself and perform a closing ritual to help him move on. Or in private, a person might paint their room black and red, thereby expressing fidelity to the Marxist revolution to come. I might wear a Slayer T-shirt even on a day when I don't bother to leave the house; in doing so, I express my commitment to awesome thrash metal. No doubt some people use their votes this way. So while the political liberties have little value in expressing our attitudes to others, they have some value in expressing our attitudes to ourselves.

Still, we have many other better outlets for self-expression. Even if someone wants to communicate their political attitudes to themselves, they can usually best do so without exercising the political liberties. The citizen, say, could donate money to the candidate, write a poem, or build and burn an effigy. And if someone wants to communicate with others, then writing letters, joining online forums, creating websites, making YouTube videos, and the like, are much more effective means of communicating than voting or running for office.

Furthermore, even if a vote were a good way of expressing oneself, it's unclear why this would be good reason to imbue people with a right to vote. The problem is that a vote is a form of expression that *exerts power over others*. When we empower large groups of people to vote, we thereby give them the ability to express themselves, perhaps, but these forms of expression can harm others or directly produce unjust political outcomes.

Imagine a large group of artists said, "We want to express Christian existentialist angst over divine absence in the face of suffering. To do this, we wish to create a sculpture or installation in which we nail live children to the floor, with food and water just out of reach. We'll watch them suffer and die, and then reflect on their predicament is a metaphor for our own." We have every reason to forbid the artist from making such an art installation—however sublime the finished product might be—because this mode of self-expression harms people or violates their rights. The artists have the right to express themselves, but not in this way.

Or imagine a person said, "I want to express my commitment to justice. To do so, I need to be an absolute king in order that I can unilaterally impose just outcomes on all without opposition. Where's my crown?" We'd think this request is absurd; even if this person has a compelling interest in expressing his commitment to justice, it's not a reason to give them *all* the political power. But if not, why would it be reason to give them *any* political power?

I'm skeptical that voting rights are a worthwhile form of self-expression. But I'm even more skeptical that we should imbue people with such rights *because* those rights are a form of self-expression. People should have a right to express themselves and their commitment to justice. The solution here is the traditional liberal solution, though: we give each person an extensive right of free speech. The right to free speech creates a sphere of personal autonomy in which individual people have control rights over themselves.

Yet suppose I'm wrong about that. Even if we grant for the sake of argument that each person ought to have a right to vote because it is an avenue of self-expression, it takes additional work to show that they ought to have an *equal* right to vote. In one form of epistocracy, ignorant voters might have one vote each, while qualified voters might get, say, ten votes each. In this case, the ignorant voters would as individuals have less expressive power than the qualified voters. Since individual votes count for so little, it's hard to see why this is a significant injustice or impediment to self-expression.

As political philosopher Ben Saunders remarks, "When it comes to political power . . . each person's share is so small that to insist on strict equality would be more like arguing over the crumbs of a cake than insisting on equal slices."[31] In an epistocracy in which everyone had at least one vote, but some people had more than one, that would mean that some people had a poor form of self-expression, while others had a slightly less poor form of self-expression.

Remember, my view is that we should choose epistocracy over democracy just in case epistocracy produces better-quality government as well as more substantively just and good outcomes. It seems implausible to hold that in order to make sure everyone has a weak and ineffective form of self-expression, we should choose to suffer from worse-quality government and worse outcomes. If democrats want to find something inherent to democratic procedures that can trump a commitment to producing the best possible outcomes, this is not it.

CONCLUSION

Epistocracy sends some clear messages: people are not by virtue of birth or residency alone presumed competent to make high-stakes political decisions that will be imposed by force on other citizens; the citizenry as a whole, as a collective body, is not presumed competent either. But it's not clear why we should presume otherwise. For any plausible account of competence, it is really an open empirical question whether democracies are competent in any absolute sense. It is also an empirical question whether democracies are more competent than certain untried alternatives to democracy, although we are quite sure that democracies are usually more competent than many alternatives we have tried.

Sending the message that the electorate would probably be more reliable without than with you may feel insulting. But if it is done for the right reason—to secure better and more just outcomes—and if the message is correct, then it should not be insulting. People should get over it or study more.

Epistocracy is inherently elitist the way that plumbing or medical licensing schemes are inherently elitist. If epistocracy turns out to have worse consequences than democracy, or if it is objectionable on other nonsemiotic grounds, then by all means, let us view it as expressing disrespect. Otherwise, we should stop using the right to vote as a badge of honor.

When we ask what makes a hammer good, we judge it by how well it functions. When we ask what makes a poem good, we often judge it by what it symbolizes and expresses. When we judge what makes a person good, we frequently say that people are valuable as ends in themselves. As I see it, political institutions are more like hammers than persons or poems. Institutions are tools. Institutions that help us live together in peace and prosperity are good. Institutions that, compared to the alternatives, hinder us in doing so, give us little reason to support them, regardless of what they symbolize.

At this point, we've seen that many of the major arguments for holding that political participation and political rights are inherently good for you, as an individual, fail. We've also seen that most of the major proceduralist arguments for democracy don't succeed. It might be that certain types of government, such as theocracy, should be ruled out on proceduralist grounds, but we don't seem to have proceduralist reasons to prefer democracy to epistocracy. If not, then the choice between the two is merely instrumental. In the next chapter, I turn to contending that if epistocracy "works" better, then we should be epistocrats. If epistocracy and democracy work equally well, then either system is fine.

CHAPTER 6

THE RIGHT TO COMPETENT GOVERNMENT

Democracy with unconditional universal suffrage grants political power in a promiscuous way. When hobbits and hooligans vote, they exercise political power over others, and this cries out for justification. It needs to be justified against alternative systems—in particular, against epistocratic systems that try to reduce the damage hobbits and hooligans might do.

I can point to the average voter and reasonably ask, "Why should *that person* have any degree of power over me?" I can similarly turn to the electorate as a whole and inquire, "Who made *those people* my *boss?*" As we saw in chapter 2, most of them have little sense of what's going on. Why should I be subject to the rule of hobbits and hooligans?

In chapter 1, I introduced two basic theories about how to distribute political power. Proceduralists say that some ways of distributing power are either intrinsically unjust or intrinsically just. Instrumentalists say that we should (or at least *may*) distribute political power in whatever manner best produces just outcomes, where such outcomes are defined independently of the procedure that produced them. I said that in my view, the choice between democracy and epistocracy is purely instrumental. Over the past few chapters, I've debunked a number of proceduralist arguments against epistocracy and on behalf of democracy. I've also provided some empirical evidence that democratic electorates tend to act, on the whole, in incompetent ways.

A democrat, however, could in principle just accept everything I've argued for so far, but then remark, "Sure, democracies are not intrinsically just, and epistocracies are not intrinsically unjust. Let me even agree for the sake of argument that epistocracies even outperform democracies. But even if so, that doesn't show that we're *required* to choose epistocracy over democracy. After all, maybe justice simply requires that we choose a political system that's *good enough*. Why think we have to pick the *best-* or even *better*-performing system? That's a demanding view, and you haven't yet defended it."

The hypothetical democrat has a point. In our daily lives, we aren't generally required to maximize the good. An economist might add that while political competence is important, presumably there will be diminishing marginal returns and increasing marginal costs as we push for ever more competent and better-performing political decision-making methods. Resources, time, and effort spent on trying to produce more effective or competent government are resources, time, and effort not spent on other valuable things. From a cost-benefit analysis perspective, the *most competent* government probably might not be worth the price we would have to pay for it.

This chapter responds to these worries. I won't argue for the stronger instrumentalist claim that we are required to use the most competent political system. Instead, I will argue for the weaker instrumentalist claim that it is presumptively unjust to use an incompetent political decision-making system when there is a more competent one available. In the end, my final argument for epistocracy is effectively this:

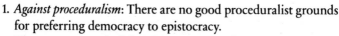

1. *Against proceduralism*: There are no good proceduralist grounds for preferring democracy to epistocracy.
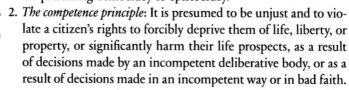
2. *The competence principle*: It is presumed to be unjust and to violate a citizen's rights to forcibly deprive them of life, liberty, or property, or significantly harm their life prospects, as a result of decisions made by an incompetent deliberative body, or as a result of decisions made in an incompetent way or in bad faith.

Political decisions are presumed legitimate and authoritative only when produced by competent political bodies in a competent way and in good faith.

3. *Corollary of the competence principle*: Presumptively, we ought to replace an incompetent political decision-making method with a more competent one.

4. *Comparative institutional claims*: Universal suffrage tends to produce incompetent decisions, while certain forms of epistocracies are likely to produce more competent decisions.

5. *Conclusion*: We should probably replace democracy with certain forms of epistocracy.

Over the past few chapters, I've mostly argued for the first and fourth premises. I'll argue for the second and third ones in this chapter. In this and following two chapters, I'll supply more reasons in favor of the fourth premise.

DEMOCRACY AND POLITICAL INCOMPETENCE

Most of my fellow citizens are incompetent, ignorant, irrational, and morally unreasonable about politics. Despite that, they hold political power over me. These people can staff offices of great power and wield the coercive authority of the state against me. They can force me to do things I do not wish to do or have no good reason to do. They wield their power in ways that they cannot justify, and impose policies on me that they would not support if they were informed or processed political information in a rational way.

At least at first glance, it seems that as an innocent person, I should not have to tolerate that. Just as it would be wrong to force me to go under the knife of an incompetent surgeon or sail with an incompetent ship captain, it seems wrong to force me to submit to the decisions of incompetent voters. People who exercise power over me—including other voters—should do so in a competent and morally reasonable way. Otherwise, as a matter of justice, they ought to be forbidden from exercising power over me, or there ought to be robust institutions in place that protect me from their incompetence. Or so I will contend.

In this chapter, I argue that citizens have at least a presumptive right to have a competent decision-making body, in a competent way, exercise any political power held over them. They ought not be subject to incompetently or capriciously made high-stakes political decisions.

In realistic circumstances, universal suffrage will often violate this presumptive right. Current democracies are to that extent unjust. The only reason to put up with democracy, I will argue, is if we cannot find a way to make epistocracy work better.

THREE INTUITION PUMPS

Before moving on to my main argument, I want to present three "half" ones. These are meant to pump your intuitions. My goal here is to show that people seem inclined to make exceptions on behalf of democracy that they wouldn't make elsewhere; they tend to hold democratic bodies to lower moral standards than they hold others.

How Do We Respond to Pollution?

Most of my readers and fellow philosophers believe that the government not only may but instead *must* regulate carbon emissions. Their basic assertion is that pollution is a collective action problem. On an individual basis, any one of us can pollute to our heart's content, and it would have no real impact. But if we *all* pollute to our hearts' content, the results can be catastrophic.

The problem is that as individuals, we have little reason to change our behavior. Consider some of my behaviors. I fly over twenty times per year. I drive a twin-turbo sports sedan, which I generally leave in Sport or Sport+ mode for maximal acceleration. I play electric guitar through a high-wattage tube amp rather than acoustic guitar. I leave the air conditioner on in my house all summer. I almost never shut off any of my three computers. Out of the goodness of my heart, I might reduce my energy usage, but what good would it do? My individual impact is so small that such sacrifices would make no difference. I would suffer, but it wouldn't help.

This line of reasoning applies to each of us. As individuals, none of us have much incentive or reason to pollute less, even though we all want everyone to pollute less. Unilateral reductions in consumption have purely symbolic value.

Therefore, most of my colleagues conclude, we should license the government to regulate pollution levels. Government can solve our collective action problem. Call this kind of reasoning the public goods argument for environmental protection.

As we saw in chapter 2, we face something similar to this collective action problem when it comes to voting. It's not precisely the same: if I were the only voter, my vote would make all the difference, while if I were the only polluter, my pollution would still make little difference. But it's similar enough: given that there are so many other voters, for each of us, our individual votes make no difference. We have every incentive to free ride on others' efforts, externalize the cost of our biases onto others, and pollute democracy with our uninformed, misinformed, or irrational votes.

If the argument for regulating air pollution is sound, why not regulate votes as well? Why does the public goods argument justify regulating air pollution, but doesn't justify regulating voting pollution? Why is it legitimate to regulate pollution to protect us from ourselves, yet not legitimate to regulate voting to protect us from ourselves? In chapters 4 and 5, I examined a series of deontological arguments that tried to show that voting rights are different, but none of these arguments succeeded. So these questions remain open.

Is King Carl Acting Unjustly?

Imagine that the unfortunate kingdom of Bungleland suffers under the rule of King Carl the Incompetent. For the most part, King Carl means well. But as his epithet implies, King Carl is incompetent.

A good king would have a strong grasp of history, sociology, economics, and moral philosophy—all subjects needed to understand which policies secure social justice and promote the common good. Despite his ignorance, Carl has strong opinions about all these subjects. He does not form his political beliefs and policy preferences after examining evidence. Instead, he tends to hold political beliefs that he finds flattering. He chooses beliefs and courses of action that reinforce his self-image. Often, Carl just chooses in the heat of the moment, based on his gut feelings. He pays little attention to the consequences of his actions. Carl takes credit for any good that happens during his reign, but blames bad results on his political enemies. He has no clue whether he's making things better or worse.

Bungleland is a constitutional monarchy. By law, Carl must respect basic liberal rights, such as the right to free speech and the right of immunity to arbitrary search and seizure. And for the most part, Carl does respect these rights. For the most part, Bungleland enjoys the rule of law.

Still, King Carl retains expansive discretionary power inside these constitutional limits. He may choose economic, environmental, educational, land use, and foreign policies. He appoints nearly every position in government. Carl may start wars, change property regimes, set central bank interest rates, impose tariffs and trade restrictions, issue industrial and commercial regulations, transfer wealth from one person to another, create licenses and restrictions on entry into professions, tax at whatever level he prefers, choose public school curricula, legalize or criminalize drugs, decide which people may enter or leave the kingdom, determine the penalties for breaking the law, and much more. Moreover, sometimes he exceeds the authority granted to him by his country's constitution, and much of the time, he gets away with it.

Carl's subjects bear the burden of his mistakes. His subjects face profligate spending, high debt, foolish underregulation in some places, and foolish overregulation in others. They suffer through symbolic politics; Carl frequently chooses counterproductive policies because, in his mind, imposing those policies shows his commitment to noble goals. Carl's subjects live with lower economic opportunities, higher crime, higher prices, and greater injustice than they would under a competent ruler. His decisions can deprive citizens (and foreigners) of opportunity, liberty, property, and even life.

Now ask, Is Bungleland a *just* regime? One might think it's obviously not—after all, Bungleland is a monarchy. Monarchies tend to imbue a king with political power just because they gestated in the right womb at the right time. That is, it seems like a silly way to distribute political power. And so most modern readers conclude that monarchies are inherently unjust. Suppose they are right. Now ask, Is that the *only* problem with Bungleland?

Consider, in contrast, Rivendell, ruled by Lord Elrond the Wise. Elrond always chooses what's best for his subjects. He uses all available information. He knows all there is to know about the social sciences. Elrond consults all rational and reasonable points of view. And he always makes decisions in a rational, reasonable way, free of bias and caprice. You might believe that monarchies are inherently unjust, regardless of how well they perform, and so even Lord Elrond's rule is unjust. Perhaps you are right. But even if we grant that Lord Elrond's rule is unjust, it looks like Carl's rule is worse and even more unjust. Here the difference is not in the *kind* of regime—they are both hereditary monarchies. Instead, the difference lies in *how* Elrond and Carl make their decisions, and how those decisions affect their subjects.

Consider some real-life examples. Caligula, Nero, and Antonius Pius were all emperors of Rome. If you think monarchy is inherently unjust, then you must conclude that they each ruled unjustly simply by virtue of being monarchs. But even if that's so, they aren't equally unjust. Caligula and Nero were wicked and evil men, and their subjects suffered greatly from their depraved decisions. Antonius Pius brought his subjects peace and prosperity, and instituted reforms that further protected and promoted his subjects' civil liberties. The way Caligula and Nero made decisions was unjust, while the way Antonius Pius made them was comparatively good and just.

Bungleland is unjust not merely because it is a kingdom or the wrong form of government. The fact that the king makes decisions *badly* is an additional injustice. He doesn't use his power wisely. He owes his subjects a duty of care. Their lives and livelihoods are in his hands, and his recklessness is a danger to them all.

Now imagine things change in Bungleland. King Carl dies, but before his death, he converts his kingdom into a democracy. Yet suppose that the more things change, the more things stay the same. As a collective body, the voters of Bungleland are no better—no wiser, no more rational, no less capricious—than King Carl. Suppose that the majority of voters in Bungleland are hobbits and hooligans, while only minority are vulcans. Instead of one incompetent ruler, Bunglelanders now have many.

What then? Would replacing King Carl with an equally incompetent democratic majority *sanctify* incompetent decision making? Or would the incompetent decision making impinge on the democratic majority's right to rule? Again, in chapters 4 and 5, I examined a wide range of deontological arguments that tried to demonstrate there is an inherent difference between incompetent Carl and an incompetent majority, but these arguments did not work. Thus, these questions remain open.

Why Don't We Let Six-Year-Olds Vote?

Why don't we let little kids vote? Why not let a first grader, a fifth grader, or at least a high school junior vote? There seem to be three basic reasons:

Membership: Little kids are not yet full members of society, so they don't *deserve* a vote.

Dependence: Little kids will just vote however their parents tell them to vote, so giving them a vote is just giving their parents an extra vote.

Incompetence: Little kids don't know enough to vote well.

Most people regard each of these reasons as sufficient to justify restricting the suffrage. That is, even if two out of the three concerns were shown to be false, most people would think the remaining issues would still be enough to stop kids from voting.

With that, let's consider the third complaint. There is a simple argument against letting high school juniors (or younger students) vote: their votes affect all us. A voter chooses for everyone, not just themselves. We might worry that most sixteen-year-olds lack the wisdom or knowledge to cast smart votes. Since politicians tend to give voters what they want, lowering the voting age would produce lower-quality government. We forbid them from voting because we want to protect ourselves from them.

While many people accept this argument, it has implications they aren't inclined to accept. If ignorance is a sufficient reason to exclude youths from voting, it should be sufficient reason to exclude large swaths of the voting public.

As I discussed in chapter 2, political knowledge is not evenly spread among all groups. If you think that the demographic group called "sixteen- and seventeen-year-olds" is too ignorant to vote, then you should also be in favor of excluding low-income earners and black people from voting, since on the whole, their levels of political knowledge are comparable. Consider the following two statements:

- Most people between the ages of fourteen and eighteen are too ignorant to vote well, although some are well informed. Nevertheless, we should ignore individual differences and just prohibit everyone from this demographic group from voting.
- Most poor black women are too ignorant to vote well, although some are well informed. We nevertheless should ignore individual differences and simply prohibit everyone from this demographic group from voting.

Most people accept the first notion but recoil at the second. They favor discriminating against some demographic groups, but not others, even though their grounds for discriminating against one applies just as well to the others.

Here's an alternative idea: instead of just discriminating against all children under age eighteen, instead of treating them all the same and assuming they're all incompetent, why not permit them to vote provided they can demonstrate a sufficiently high level of political competence? For instance, why not grant them the right to vote if they could pass the civics test portion of the US citizenship exam. (As I'll explain in the next chapter, most of the information on tests like these isn't useful for being a competent voter, but a person who can pass that test probably has more of the knowledge that is useful.)

But there's a problem. If we conclude this is a reasonable standard for a sixteen-year-old to meet, many adults of voting age would fail to meet it. It seems arbitrary to merely assume everyone under age eighteen is incompetent yet everyone over eighteen is competent. It seems unjust or at least morally arbitrary to deprive competent, wise sixteen-year-olds of the right to vote simply because they are members of a demographic group that is, as a whole, not particularly competent, when we would not thereby be willing to discriminate against other demographic groups with similar levels of political ignorance. We know, for example, that rich white men tend to have high levels of basic political knowledge, while poor black women tend to have low levels, but we wouldn't think that this would justify a rule that says poor black women can't vote, while rich white men can.

So instead of engaging in age discrimination, as modern democracies all do, why not subject *everyone* to a voter competence exam? Why not say that by default, regardless of age, everyone starts off with zero votes, but a person can acquire a right to vote provided they can demonstrate competence? Interestingly, none of the deontological arguments in chapters 4 or 5 addressed these questions at all. Most democrats just assume that only adults should have the right to vote, and they don't reflect on why they think it permissible to exclude children from voting.[1]

A PRESUMPTIVE CONDITION OF THE RIGHT TO RULE

My thesis in this chapter is that competence and good faith are at least *presumptive conditions* of the right to rule. I'll start by explaining what I mean by *the right to rule*, and what it means for competence to be a presumptive condition of this right.

A government is said to have the right to rule over a particular geographic area, over a particular set of people, when the following conditions obtain:

- It is morally permissible for it to create and enforce laws, rules, policies, and regulations for those people in that area.
- Certain people (citizens, residents, visitors, etc.) have moral obligations to abide by the laws, rules, policies, and regulations of the government, *because* the government issued those rules.[2]

When the first condition obtains, a government is said to be legitimate. When the second condition obtains, a government is said to have authority.[3]

By definition, a government is legitimate just in case it is permissible for that government to stand and to create, issue, and coercively enforce rules. By definition, a government is authoritative (or "has authority") over certain people just in case those people have a moral duty to obey that government's laws, edicts, and commands. Legitimacy is the thing that it supposed to make it okay for the police to arrest you. Authority is the thing that is supposed to make it wrong for you to resist them when they try to arrest you. In short, *legitimacy* refers to the moral permission to coerce, while *authority* refers to a moral power that induces in others a duty to submit and obey.[4]

Note that these are just the definitions of the terms. In defining them, I take no stance on whether any governments are or could be legitimate or authoritative, nor have I said anything substantive yet about what, if anything, would make governments legitimate or authoritative. An anarchist and a statist can both agree that a state has legitimacy just in case it may permissibly create and enforce rules, although the anarchist and statist disagree about whether any states are in fact legitimate. Two different statists can agree that a state has legitimacy just in case it may permissibly create and enforce rules, but then disagree about exactly what it takes for a state to be legitimate.

Importantly, for a government to have authority, it must be able to *create* obligations where there were none, or at least create an additional source of obligation. By definition, if government has authority over a person, then when the government commands that person to do something, they have a moral duty to do it because the government says so. So consider that I have a preexisting moral duty not to rape. My government also forbids me to rape. Yet the reason I must not rape is not because my government forbids me to rape. Even if the government gave me a "license to rape," I would still have a duty not to rape. The government did not create my moral duty not to rape, and it lacks the power to relieve me of that duty.

On the other hand, my government also commands me to pay it various taxes. Here, if I have a duty to pay, this duty exists only because my government created it. If the government rescinded the command, the duty to pay would disappear.

I argue below that a presumptive condition of the right to rule is that political decisions must be made competently by competent bodies, or those decisions are otherwise presumed illegitimate and nonauthoritative. Presumptive conditions are similar to but weaker than necessary conditions. Having some property P is a necessary condition for having some property Q when the failure to have P makes it impossible to have Q. In contrast, having P is a presumptive condition for having Q when the failure to have P indicates the failure to have Q, unless defeated or outweighed by countervailing conditions. Presumptive conditions are defeasible; necessary conditions are not.

For my purposes in this book, I need only argue for the relatively weak claim that competence and good faith are at least presumptive conditions of the right to rule. To claim that they are necessary conditions would impose a greater argumentative burden on me than I need to defend my thesis.

I will sometimes talk about people having a right not to be subject to incompetent governments that rule in bad faith. Here again, I mean only to assert that this is a presumptive versus an absolute right. For the purposes of this book, I remain agnostic about whether this right is stronger than a presumptive right. Again, the reason I don't take a stronger stance is that my argument doesn't require it. In philosophy, we use the least controversial and weakest premise we need to get the job done. One doesn't argue "always" when "generally" will do, and one doesn't maintain "this is wrong no matter what" when "this is presumed wrong unless there's a good reason to do it" will do.

THE RIGHT NOT TO BE SUBJECT TO AN INCOMPETENT, BAD FAITH JURY

Before talking about democracy, let's start by thinking about what it would take for juries to be legitimate and have authority. Most people believe that defendants have a right to a competent jury that acts in good faith. Let's take a look at *why* defendants might have such a right.

Imagine there are five different juries, each of which hears a complicated capital murder trial. Imagine each jury suffers from some defect, and then consider whether it seems justifiable to impose the jury's decision on the defendant.

The first jury is *ignorant*. During the trial, these jurors ignore the evidence presented to them. When asked to deliberate, they refuse to read the transcript. Instead, they flip a coin and find the defendant guilty of first-degree murder. After the trial, they admit they decided the case in ignorance.

The second jury is *irrational*. Its members pay attention to the evidence presented at the trial. These jurors, however, evaluate the evidence in cognitively biased, nonscientific, or even antiscientific ways. Perhaps they subscribe to bizarre conspiracy theories. Perhaps they decide on the basis of wishful thinking. Maybe they just routinely miscalculate the weight of evidence, coming to the opposite conclusion of what the evidence supports. They find the defendant guilty. After the trial, they describe to us their thought processes, such that it is obvious they processed the evidence irrationally.

The third jury is *impaired*. The jurors here try to pay attention to the evidence and process the information scientifically, but they are simply not competent to do so. Perhaps they are cognitively impaired or the case is too complicated for their mental capacities. They find the defendant guilty. After the trial, they admit that, try as they might, they did not understand the case.

The fourth jury is *immoral*. These jurors pay attention to the evidence and evaluate it in a scientific, rational way. Yet they decide to find the defendant guilty because the defendant is black, Jewish, Republican, or whatnot, and they dislike people like that. Or suppose they believe the defendant is innocent, but find them guilty merely because they like to see innocent people suffer. After the trial, they admit that this is how they decided that case.

The fifth jury is *corrupt*. The jurors pay attention to evidence and evaluate it rationally. Nevertheless, they find the defendant guilty because someone paid them each ten thousand dollars to do so. After the trial, we learn that such bribery occurred.

Now ask, May we *enforce* the juries' decisions in these cases? Should the defendant submit to their authority?

It seems not. In each case, the jury acts badly, and everyone knows it. Intuitively, it seems that these jury decisions lack authority and legitimacy. If a defendant knew they had been subject to one of these juries, they would have no moral obligation to regard their decisions as authoritative. That the jury found the defendant guilty provides in itself no reason for them to accept punishment. (Of course, if the defendant did in fact commit the crimes, they would have independent reasons for submitting to the punishment.)

It would also be unjust for a government to enforce those decisions. The defendant is presumed free until conclusive reasons arise for interfering with their liberty. That any of one these juries found them guilty offers no such reason. The defendant is presumed free unless deprived of their freedom by due process. In this case, they did not receive due process.

In the United States, the law to some extent follows these moral judgments. If a defendant is found guilty, but it is later discovered that the jury acted incompetently or with prejudice in certain ways, then the defendant can appeal.[5] In addition, the presiding judge can override the jury's guilty verdict on the spot if they believe that no reasonable jury could have arrived at that verdict. Judges rarely do so, but in principle, they can.

What explains our moral judgments in these cases? In a jury trial, the following features obtain:

- The jury is charged with making a morally momentous decision, as it must decide how to apply principles of justice. It is the vehicle by which justice is to be delivered. It has special duties to administer justice.
- The jury's decision can greatly affect the defendant's and others' life prospects, and it can deprive the defendant of life, liberty, and/ or property.
- The jury is part of a system that claims sole jurisdiction to decide the case. That is, the system claims a monopoly on decision-making power, and expects the defendant and others to accept and abide by the decision.
- The jury's decision will be imposed, involuntarily, by force or threats of force.

These seem to be good grounds for holding that juries have strong duties toward defendants, and also that the jury's legitimacy and authority depends on its discharging these duties.[6]

The four features above are grounds for accepting the competence principle. As applied to juries, the competence principle holds the following:

Defendants and other citizens have a right that jury decisions should be made by competent people, who make their decisions competently and in good faith. It is unjust, and violates a citizen's rights, to forcibly deprive a citizen of life, liberty, or property, or significantly harm their life prospects, as a result of decisions made by an incompetent jury, or decisions made incompetently or in bad faith.

One justification for the competence principle is that it is unjust to expose people to undue risk. In the cases above, the jurists are acting negligently toward the defendant. From the defendant's point of view, a jury's decision is momentous and the outcome is imposed involuntarily. In those kinds of cases, a jury has an obligation to take adequate care in making its decisions.

To see why, consider some parallel cases. Suppose I have severe bronchitis. My physician consults a witch doctor for treatment advice. The witch doctor burns some animal fat, then tosses in some alphabet soup, and reads the patterns of letters. By chance, the letters spell out a drug, which my physician then prescribes to me. Regardless of whether the drug ends up being the right (e.g., prednisone) or wrong one (e.g., moxonidine), the physician has done something wrong. The physician used a highly unreliable decision method to arrive at their prescription. Using this method puts me at serious risk of harm. If the physician had the power to *force* me to take the drug (just as juries have the power to force their decisions on defendants), this would be intolerable.

The competence principle implies the following, *pro tanto*:

- In order to sit as a jury, the jury as a collective body must not have bad epistemic and moral character.
- And even if a jury is competent overall, if a particular decision is made incompetently or in bad faith, that decision should not be enforced, and defendants have no duty to submit to that decision.

In short, the competence principle requires each jury decision to be made competently by a competent group. Let's further unpack just what this means.

Regarding the first condition: Suppose most juries are competent, but the particular jury that decided this trial is not. We could not justify enforcing this particular jury's decision simply by pointing out that most *other* juries are competent. That's irrelevant. We cannot deprive a defendant of liberty, property, or life on the basis of an incompetent decision just because *other* juries are competent. Imagine saying, "Sure, we know *your* jury was bribed or insane, but all the other juries in the world do a great job. So the decision stands."

Regarding the second condition: Suppose this particular jury is usually competent, but was incompetent in this specific case. Suppose the same panel of jurors hears a hundred cases. It decides ninety-nine cases in a rational, well-informed, and morally reasonable way, but decides one last case in an irrational, ignorant, misinformed, and/ or morally unreasonable way. Suppose they find the defendant in this last case guilty. We could not say to this defendant, "Sure, the jury was incompetent in your case, but it was competent in the other cases. Thus, we will enforce its decision and you must submit to it." The defendant could object, "It sure is nice that those jurors did such a good job with all those *other* trials, but this is *my* life and *my* freedom you're talking about. The jury decided *my* case in an incompetent and unreasonable way." The defendant's objection seems to me to be decisive.

The competence principle does not claim that juries have authority and legitimacy only when they make *correct* decisions. Instead, it claims that juries lack authority and legitimacy when they reach answers in unacceptable ways, regardless of whether their answers are correct or not. The competence principle does not disqualify jury decisions on the basis of their substantive content. It disqualifies jurors based on their bad moral or epistemic character, and disqualifies individual jury decisions based on the kind of reasoning (or lack thereof) the jury used to arrive at its decision.

GENERALIZING THE COMPETENCE PRINCIPLE

The competence principle appears to have a broad scope of application. There doesn't seem to be any reason to think it applies only to juries. Individual government agents, branches, bureaucracies, and administrations along with the government as a whole can also deprive citizens of life, liberty, and property. Like juries, they have the power to cause great harm. Like juries, they also claim sole jurisdiction and the right to rule. And like juries, they impose their decisions on (potentially) innocent people who do not consent to these decisions.

If a police officer, judge, politician, bureaucracy, or legislative body makes a capricious, irrational, or malicious decision, a citizen cannot just walk away.[7] Government decisions tend to have these crucial features:

- Governments are charged with making morally momentous decisions, as they must decide how to both apply principles of justice and shape many of the basic institutions of society. They are one of the main vehicles through which justice is supposed to be established.
- Government decisions tend to be of major significance. They can significantly harm citizens' life prospects, and deprive them of life, liberty, and property.
- Governments claim sole jurisdiction for making certain kinds of decisions over certain people within a geographic area. Governments expect people to accept and abide by their decisions.
- The outcomes of decisions are imposed involuntarily through violence and threats of violence.

Governments do more than choose melodies for national anthems and flag colors. They make policies and choose courses of action that can have momentous and even disastrous consequences for citizens. If the Federal Reserve, for example, pursues deflationary monetary policies while the US government imposes high trade barriers, this can push a recession into a deep depression. If military leaders inflate or misrepresent military intelligence, we might fight a costly, destructive, and inhumane war.

In light of the four features just noted, citizens have at least as strong grounds as defendants to expect competence from government officials and decision makers as a matter of right. This can be expressed in a generalized form of the competence principle:

It is presumed to be unjust, and to violate a citizen's rights, to forcibly deprive a citizen of life, liberty, or property, or to significantly harm their life prospects, as a result of decisions made by an incompetent deliberative body, or decisions made in an incompetent way or in bad faith. Political decisions are presumed legitimate and authoritative only when produced by competent political bodies in a competent way and in good faith.

Presumptively, just as defendants have a right not to be subject to incompetent jury trials, innocent people have a right not to be subject to incompetently made political decisions. If the legitimacy and authority of jury decisions at least presumptively depend on competence and good faith, then so do the legitimacy and authority of all government decisions. If the legitimacy and authority of the jury system as a whole depends on juries typically being reliable and acting in good faith, then we should say the same about other government branches, administrations, and practices.

We have, in some respects, even stronger grounds for demanding competence and good faith from other governmental decision makers than we do from juries. After all, there is a philosophical puzzle about how to describe the rights of defendants. Many people on trial have in fact committed the crimes they are charged with, and it is tempting to say that they thus deserve punishment or may have already forfeited some of their rights. The defendants know that some of their rights have been forfeited, so for them to demand competence is just to demand that juries take care in determining what the defendants themselves already know. Some philosophers might therefore claim that the jury does not necessarily owe the defendant competence and good faith. Instead, the jury has a fiduciary duty to their fellow citizens to administer justice competently and in good faith. Others might contend that even if the defendant is guilty, they retain a moral right of due process that the law should instantiate. Still others might insist that the competence principle should be understood as a prophylactic against government abuse.

At any rate, while there is a puzzle about how to portray the rights of possibly guilty defendants, we have no such challenge when thinking about the rights of citizens. Most citizens are innocent and have forfeited none of their rights. They retain the strong liberal presumption against coercive interference of any kind. They retain the strong presumption that evils not be visited on them. As such, the average citizen is in a stronger position than the average defendant to demand competence.[8]

APPLYING THE COMPETENCE PRINCIPLE TO THE ELECTORATE

On its face, the competence principle applies equally well to the electorate as to juries. Consider these five hypothetical electorates:

Ignorant electorate: The majority of voters pay no attention to the details of the election or the issues at stake. During the election, they choose a particular candidate at random.

Irrational electorate: The majority pays some attention to the details of the election and the issues at stake. At the same time, they vote not on the basis of evidence but rather on the basis of wishful thinking and various disreputable social scientific theories they happen to believe without justification.

Impaired electorate: The majority pays attention to the details of the election and the issues at stake. Most of the discussion nevertheless is beyond their level of comprehension, requiring more intelligence than they in fact have. Still, they choose one candidate over the others, with no real clue what effect that will have.

Immoral electorate: Out of racism, the majority chooses a white candidate over a black one. Or, out of superficiality, they choose the better-looking candidate.

Corrupt electorate: The majority of voters choose a policy in their own self-interest, even though the policy severely harms or has a serious risk of imposing harm on the minority.

Suppose, in each of these cases, the majority does not represent everyone in society. For example, there might be some well-informed, rational, and morally reasonable minority voters, or innocent nonvoters such as children or resident aliens. If so, then majority voters have done something deeply unjust: they have imposed a ruler (and whatever policies come from that ruler) on innocent people without having adequate grounds for that decision.

There are a few points to remember here. First, as I discussed in chapter 2, if voters tend to be ignorant, irrational, or morally unreasonable, this not only tends to result in bad choices at the polls but also to make it so that the candidates on the ballot are of bad quality. The quality of the candidate pool itself depends significantly on the quality of the electorate. Second, as I explored in the introduction, we can't just say that the "electorate is only hurting itself." Political decisions are imposed on everyone, including dissenting voters, nonvoters, innocent children, immigrants, and foreigners.

Just as defendants have at least a presumptive right not to be exposed to bad juries, the governed have at least a presumptive right not to be exposed to undue risk in the selection of policy or of the rulers who will make policy. When elections are decided on the basis of unreliable epistemic procedures or unreasonable moral attitudes, this exposes the governed to an undue risk of serious harm. Since the governed are *forced* to comply with the decisions of the electorate, negligent decision making is intolerable. The electorate has an obligation to the governed not to expose them to undue risk.

In democracies, the ultimate holders of power are voters. If voters are systematically incompetent, as a collective entity, the consequences can be dire. We should not understate the damage bad voting can do. Bad voting can be and has been disastrous. Even if in the United States or United Kingdom disastrous candidates rarely have a chance of winning, we should not forget that many disastrous candidates have been elected to power in other parts of the world. The voters who put the National Socialists in power in Germany in 1932 cannot be held responsible for everything their government did. But much of what their government did was foreseeable by any reasonably well-informed person, and so their supporters were blameworthy. More recently, Venezuelan and Greek citizens are blameworthy for supporting politicians with terrible ideas about economic policy.

It's crucial to remember that the competence principle applies to *individual* political decisions. With that in mind, we need to distinguish between the following:

Electoral decisions: Whom or what the electorate chooses during the election.

Postelectoral decisions: What elected officials, bureaucrats, judges, and other government officials do after the election.

The competence principle says that every individual high-stakes political decision ought to be made competently and in good faith by what is generally a competent decision-making body. It might turn out that in modern democracies, because voters are systematically incompetent, most electoral decisions violate the competence principle. Yet despite that, it may also turn out that many postelectoral decisions are made competently. If so, then the competence principle says that the (incompetent) electoral decisions are unjust, but it does not thereby condemn any of the competently made postelectoral decisions. The competence principle doesn't imply any sort of "contamination theory." That is, it doesn't follow that if a prior or upstream decision violates the competence principle, all subsequent or downstream decisions are for that reason invalidated.

As an illustration, imagine that as a matter of fact, your Aunt Betty would be the best possible president. But suppose no one knows this or has any reason to believe it. Aunt Betty leads a quiet, nonpolitical life, and there is no publicly available evidence that she would make a good president. Suppose that radio personality Howard Stern organizes a campaign to get Betty elected, purely as a giant practical joke. (Stern and everyone else thinks Betty would be a bad president, but they don't care. They think supporting her is funny.) Imagine Stern is successful; Betty ends up winning, even though all her supporters believe she'll be incompetent. Fortuitously, though, Betty turns out to be the best president ever.

In this case, the competence principle says that what the voters did was wrong, but it doesn't thereby condemn any of Betty's decisions as president. The decision to make her president was unjust, although it fortuitously turned out to have good consequences, but her subsequent decisions as president are not rendered unjust.

If that seems puzzling to you, compare this again to a medical case. Suppose you go to a medical doctor. They use improper methods to diagnose you. They open a can of alphabet soup and dump it on the floor. The letters spell out "CANCER," and so they conclude you have cancer and send you to the Cancer Treatment Centers of America (CTCA). Fortuitously, you do in fact have cancer, and the CTCA is the best place for you to go. The CTCA provides excellent treatment, and you are cured. In this case, it seems that what your original doctor did was wrong—they violated their duty of care toward you. Although the original doctor acted badly, it doesn't follow that anything the CTCA did was wrong or in some way contaminated by the first doctor's bad decision-making method. Their treatment decisions were made competently, with appropriate care and good faith.

Hence, to be clear, I am not arguing that if the electorate makes a series of incompetent decisions during the election, everything a democratic government does between then and the next election is incompetent, unjust, or in violation of the competence principle. Despite incompetent voting at the polls, we might still get many good policies after the election.

In the next chapter, I'll examine a range of reasons to think that democracies often produce good results even though the electorate is incompetent. Although most voters are ignorant and irrational, it may turn out that many or even most postelectoral decisions made in modern representative democracies comply with the competence principle.

Some democratic theorists contend that the electorate as a whole tends to be competent even though most individual voters are incompetent. In chapter 7, I'll show that these arguments fail. There are more promising claims on behalf of democratic competence, however. In particular, there's good reason to think that democracies tend to make good decisions in large part because the electorate does not get in its way. Politicians, bureaucracies, and judges frequently ignore or override voters' expressed preferences. High-information voters appear to have disproportionate influence when compared to low-information voters, and this may reduce some of the potential harms from voter incompetence. Not everything that happens in government is a direct or indirect result of voters' behavior.[9]

Still, voting does make a difference. In general, the lower the epistemic and moral quality of the electorate, the worse governmental policies will tend to be. Whom the voters select as a leader does make a significant difference.

This concludes the basic argument for the competence principle. When high-stakes decisions are imposed on innocent people, the competence principle requires every individual decision to be made competently and reasonably by competent, reasonable people. It applies not merely to jury decisions but also to any significant decision made by those holding political power.

WHAT COUNTS AS COMPETENCE?

I've maintained that people have a presumptive right not to have incompetently made high-stakes decisions forced on them, but I have not yet tried to outline a theory of what exactly counts as competence. In political philosophy, we don't attempt to settle a debate unless we have to. As far as I can tell, for my argument to go through, I need rely only on relatively uncontroversial platitudes about competence. It's not clear I need to defend a precise theory of political competence. After all, even if it's difficult to determine where precisely to draw the line between political competence and incompetence, it may be easy to show that democratic voters as a whole are on the wrong side of that line.

To demonstrate why, I'll draw on the related literature on competence in medical ethics. One of the major issues in medical ethics is whether patients are competent to make decisions for themselves. Doctors are supposed to allow patients to decide for themselves what treatments to pursue, and may overrule patients' expressed decisions only if the patient is incompetent. Jillian Craigie says that the "standard criteria for competence" are as follows:

- Patients must be aware of the relevant facts.
- They must understand the relevant facts.
- Patients must appreciate the relevance of those facts for their own particular case.
- Patients must be able to reason about those facts in an appropriate way.[10]

People will reasonably dispute how to fill in all the details of these four criteria, but in the abstract they seem unobjectionable. Indeed, these four criteria appear to be the same ones we'd use to assess competence over any matter, not just medical decisions.

We'd apply these same criteria to assessing whether a doctor was competent to treat you. A doctor must be aware of the relevant facts.

We wouldn't say a doctor is competent to treat you if they know nothing about your medical history or symptoms. The doctor must also *understand* the facts. Suppose you experience severe shortness of breath. You tell your doctor you have asthma, and they respond, "OK, got it. So there's this condition called asthma, and you have it. I don't personally know what asthma is, but it sounds bad. Is it?" This doctor is not competent to help you. A doctor must also be able to appreciate the relevance of the facts for your case. Suppose you tell a doctor that your stool is a bright fuchsia, and you're worried about whether you have internal bleeding. Imagine you also tell the doctor that you've eaten nothing but red Jell-O and beets for the past three days. The doctor should see that this might explain why your stool is red. Finally, a doctor must be able to reason about your case in an appropriate manner. Suppose the doctor understands all this, but decides to give you an MRI after consulting a Ouija board. Again, the doctor acted incompetently.

Or suppose you hired a plumber to fix your clogged pipes. What counts as a competent plumber? To know exactly what makes a plumber competent, you'd have to know plumbing. I presume plumbers disagree about some hard cases—say, whether certain apprentice plumbers qualify as competent or not. Still, the abstract criteria for assessing plumbing competence are simple. We expect a competent plumber to be aware of the facts of the case at hand, understand what those facts mean, understand how to apply those facts to determine what to do, and reason about the facts in an appropriately rational way. So if a plumber saw that your pipes were clogged and concluded that they needed to mow your grass in order to fix the clog, they'd be incompetent. If they understood that the pipe was filled with hair, but then had no idea why this would stop water from going through, they'd be incompetent. If they thought the best response to the clog was to pray for the plumbing gods to intervene, the plumber would be incompetent. And so on.

We'd use these same four criteria to determine what makes a jury competent. A jury must be aware of the relevant facts. So, for instance, if the jurors didn't know that the defendant was left handed, but the victim appeared to have been stabbed by the attacker's right hand, then the jurors aren't likely competent to decide the case. They must understand the facts. If, for example, the jurors didn't understand what *handedness* means, then they aren't likely competent to decide the case. They must understand the relevance of those facts for the case. So if jurors knew the aforementioned facts, but didn't realize that the fact that the victim was stabbed by a right hand casts doubt on whether the defendant attacked the victim, they aren't competent to decide the case. The defendants must also be able to reason in an appropriate way. If the weight of the evidence suggests there is strong doubt that the defendant is guilty, but the jurors find them guilty just because they just want *someone* to be punished, then they acted incompetently.

In chapters 2 and 3, I examined at great length facts about what voters know and don't know, about why and how they form political beliefs, about how they respond to new information, and about how they make decisions. In light of that, it looks like the electorate is straightforwardly incompetent. Candidates run on policy platforms and policy bents. Most voters are ignorant or worse about the facts. They lack the knowledge of basic civics, recent history, candidate platforms, what powers different offices have, and the social science needed to assess candidates' performance or proposals. They don't know who the incumbents or challengers are, what the incumbents or challengers want to do, what they have the power to do, and what is likely to happen if these candidates get their way. Most voters make decisions about politics in irrational, capricious ways.

Now some might say that democracies perform better than many other systems. Indeed, they tend to do so. Democracies tend to have peaceful transitions of power, tend not to engage in the mass murder of civilians, and rarely experience famines. That might make them better than autocracies, but that doesn't suffice to show that in most elections, the electorate behaves competently.

After all, suppose I describe two medical doctors to you. One of them is a hack who wants to help their patients, but who regularly prescribes them the wrong medicine. The other is a jerk who doesn't care about their patients, regularly takes advantage of them, and even murders them when they feel like it. The first doctor might be better overall than the second, yet that doesn't suffice to make them competent.

A moderate position on democratic competence might hold that voters should do the following:

- Voters should act on widely available, good information, if not always the best information available anywhere.
- They should avoid mass superstition and systematic error.
- They should evaluate information in a moderately rational, unbiased way—if not with the perfection of a vulcan, at least with the degree of rationality a first-year college student brings to thinking about introductory organic chemistry.
- Voters should be aware of their limits, and thus always look for more and better information on any high-stakes decision.

As we've seen, most voters fail to live up to even this moderate set of criteria. Most voters overestimate themselves. They either don't seek out information or only seek out information that reinforces whatever beliefs they already hold for nonrational reasons. Collectively, they do have mass superstitions and make systematic errors. And finally, voters don't know how little they know.

It also may be that the reason democracies outperform autocracies is not because the electorate is competent but instead because the electorate's power is greatly limited. I'll discuss this point further in the next chapter.

COMPETENCE IN CONTEXT

So far, I have argued that universal suffrage, as practiced in contemporary democracies, tends to violate the competence principle. I have not yet made any positive policy proposals in light of this point.

The competence principle is not the sole one by which to judge the distribution of political power. There may be other deontological principles restricting or determining the allocation of power. Some ways of distributing power will tend to produce better (including more just) political outcomes than others. Presumably the consequences of different allocations of power matter as well.

Theories of legitimacy and authority generally comprise two kinds of principles. They have principles of disqualification—*disqualifiers,* for short—which articulate grounds against either distributing power in certain ways or allowing the scope of power to extend in certain ways. They also have principles of qualification—*qualifiers*, for short—which articulate grounds on behalf of either distributing power in certain ways or allowing the scope of power to extend in certain ways. Sometimes a principle serves as both a disqualifier and qualifier.

The competence principle is a disqualifier. It does not justify imbuing anyone with power. Rather, it provides grounds for not allowing certain people or political bodies to hold power, and against allowing certain decisions to be enforced. To know exactly what we should do, in light of the competence principle, we need a complete theory of government legitimacy and authority. We need to know what other principles regulate the use of power. I am not trying to articulate a full theory of legitimacy and authority here, because that goes beyond the scope of the book. Instead, I am simply arguing in this chapter that you should add the competence principle to your theory of legitimacy and authority, whatever that theory is. (In previous chapters, I've contended you should subtract a number of prodemocracy or antiepistocracy principles from your theory, whatever that theory is.)

To comply with the competence principle, a political system may need to modify any of the following:

Scale of government: Like firms and markets, governments have economies and diseconomies of scale. A body competent to govern three million people might be incompetent to govern three hundred million. If a government is too big or too small in this sense, it may have to split up into smaller governments or join together with another government.

Scope of government: The scope of government concerns the issues or areas government has the right to regulate. Libertarians advocate a minor scope of government; they think government should keep its hands off most things. Totalitarians advocate an extensive scope of government; they think the government should have its hands in everything. In principle, we might want government to perform certain tasks or control certain affairs. If a government turns out to be systematically incompetent to perform those tasks or control those affairs, however, then citizens have a moral right to a more limited government that leaves those issues alone. So, for instance, since governments are incompetent to set prices, they are forbidden to do so.

Timing of government: The timing of government concerns the speed at which government decisions are made, both in terms of how quickly the government responds to a problem and how quickly government deliberation proceeds. Governments may be required to speed up or slow down their decision making.

Form of government: The form of government concerns who rules and how political power is distributed. (For example, is a government a monarchy or democracy? Does it have a presidential or parliamentary system? Does it use proportional, Condorcet, or first-past-the-post voting rules?) Governments may need to restrict or modify who holds political power, or may need to create (or eliminate) certain checks or balances within government.

The competence principle forbids incompetence, but by itself it does not tell us just how we must achieve competence. The best way to comply with the competence principle depends on our other concerns, including other principles of legitimacy, authority, justice, efficiency, stability, and so on. It will also rely on empirical facts that might vary from culture to culture or state to state.

EXAMPLE APPLICATIONS OF THE COMPETENCE PRINCIPLE

In this section, I outline some applications of the competence principle. Each of these applications depends not just on the competence principle itself but also on additional claims about sociology, economics, or political psychology. Thus, if any of the following examples are bad policy, it need not be because the competence principle is mistaken; it is because these additional claims are wrong.

The Scale of Government

Larger countries are often multiethnic and multilingual ones, composed of many different nationalities. For various reasons, this seems to lead to lower-quality government on average. Economists Alberto

Alesina, Enrico Spolaore, and Romain Wacziarg summarize some of the literature on this question:

> The costs of heterogeneity in the population have been well documented, especially for the case in which ethnolinguistic fragmentation is used as a proxy for heterogeneity in preferences. Easterly and Levine (1997), La Porta et al. (1999) and Alesina et al. (2003) showed that ethnolinguistic fractionalization is inversely related to economic success and various measures of quality of government, economic freedom and democracy.[11]

The basic idea here is that well-functioning governments rely on mutual trust among citizens. Yet ethnic and linguistic diversity lead to decreased trust, which in turn causes voters (and in turn politicians) to have greater mutual distrust and conflict, which in turn leads to worse political outcomes. In some cases, countries might do better to break up into smaller, less diverse countries. Now the competence principle says that citizens are presumptively entitled not to be subject to incompetent decisions or decisions made in bad faith. This means that, at least presumptively, if breaking a country apart is needed to ensure political competence and good faith, then citizens have a right to this split.

The Scope of Government

Consider Stephen Nathanson's famous paper "Should We Execute Those Who Deserve to Die?"[12] Nathanson assumes for the sake of argument that some people (e.g., certain murderers) deserve to die. He says although they should die, that does not mean the state may execute them. According to Nathanson, jurors, prosecutors, judges, and others make decisions about the death penalty in arbitrary and racist ways. They thus are cognitively and morally incompetent when they decide whom to kill, and this incompetence disqualifies them from having permission to kill. That a person deserves a punishment is not sufficient for a government to have the right to punish them; the government must also make decisions about punishment in an acceptable way. Nathanson's argument in effect is an application of the competence principle. If he is right that US jurors, prosecutors, and judges make racist and arbitrary decisions about the death penalty, then the competence principle presumptively forbids them from making such decisions.

Here is another illustration of how the competence principle could constrain the scope of government. Democratic governments could set commodity prices by legal fiat. That is, instead of having prices emerge from market processes, we could directly set prices after reasoned deliberation. Economists contend that for a wide range of cases, emergent methods of social construction are not only smarter and faster than direct methods but direct methods are inadequate. Economists hold that political systems are incompetent to set prices because they cannot acquire the needed information.[13]

If economists are correct that governments are incompetent at setting prices, then the competence principle presumptively forbids governments from doing so. The economic reasoning against price controls is old, and no economically literate person now advocates price controls (except in unusual circumstances). Notice, however, that the competence principle adds extra normative weight to the old economic argument. Price controls are not merely imprudent, wasteful, and inefficient, as an economist might say. The competence principle adds that they are also *immoral* and violate citizens' rights. The competence principle implies that individual citizens have the moral authority to demand that their governments refrain from setting prices. Governments have no permission to set and enforce prices, and citizens are not bound to respect or adhere to price controls.

The Timing of Government

James Madison probably was the principal author of the US Constitution, and was of course the principal author of the *Federalist Papers*. Madison famously advocates a system of checks and balances, and famously wants politics to be an adversarial system in which if any factions arise, they find their power constrained by rival factions.

Most people interpret Madison as advocating all this because he had severe reservations about majority rule. On this common interpretation, the system of checks and balances is meant to require, in effect, a supermajority to support a piece of legislation before it can pass into law.

Political theorist Greg Weiner disagrees. In his recent book *Madison's Metronome*, Weiner extensively catalogs Madison's various arguments and positions on questions of majority rule and constitutionalism.[14] Weiner claims that Madison wanted a system of checks and balances not primarily to reduce factionalism or majority rule but instead to *slow down* the process of political decision making. According to Weiner, Madison held that democratic bodies are prone to hotheadedness and fits of passion. This hotheadedness impedes their ability to make sound, rational decisions. Madison wanted the legislative process to be convoluted in order to prevent impulsive decisions.

As an analogy, suppose a twelve-year-old wants to pierce their ears. Their parents might say, "We're not opposed to you doing this, but we want to make sure you really want your ears pierced, and aren't just doing it spur of the moment or in response to peer pressure. So if you still want to get your ears pieced in six months, you can." In Weiner's view, Madison views the Constitution as playing the role of the parents here.

The Form of Government

On average, democratic governments tend to perform better than monarchies, oligarchies, dictatorships, and traditional aristocracies. In light of the discussion in chapters 2 and 3, we have plenty to reason to believe that democracy systematically violates the competence principle. (We'll examine some attempts to resist this conclusion in the next chapter.)

Suppose it turned out that some version of epistocracy satisfies the competence principle, while democracy systematically violates it. The competence principle then presumptively disqualifies democracy. Since the competence principle is a disqualifier, not a qualifier, it does not thereby tell us that epistocracy is just, legitimate, or authoritative. But in previous chapters, I've already shown that a number of arguments against epistocracy or on behalf of democracy fail.

At this point, we have a strong presumptive argument against democracy and on behalf of epistocracy. There are two major challenges to this presumptive argument. First, some democratic theorists contend that democratic decisions tend to be competent as a whole even though the majority of voters are not competent. I'll explore such arguments in the next chapter. Further, whether we should choose epistocracy over democracy depends on whether we can actually instantiate epistocracy in a way that works better than democracy. In chapter 8, I'll look more closely at this question.

CHAPTER 7

IS DEMOCRACY COMPETENT?

In chapters 2 and 3, we saw that most democratic citizens are hobbits or hooligans. Voters are for the most part ignorant, irrational, and misinformed, but nice. While voters vote for what they perceive to be the national interest, the most straightforward reading of the evidence suggests voters as a whole are incompetent. They support bad policies (or politicians who support bad policies), which they would not support if they were better informed and processed that information in a rational way.

Perhaps this seemingly straightforward conclusion is mistaken. It's at least theoretically possible that the democratic electorate is competent as a collective whole even if the overwhelming majority of the individuals within that body are incompetent at politics. Sometimes intelligence is an emergent feature of a decision-making system. That is, sometimes a decision-making system can be competent even if all or most of the individuals within that system are incompetent as individuals.

So to take the best-understood example of emergent collective wisdom, market prices emerge from individual actions, and these prices quickly and efficiently coordinate the activities of billions of people, even though individual agents on the market know hardly anything, and even though no individual or group of experts could themselves plan a large-scale economy. More specifically, no single human being has the knowledge or ability to make a number 2 pencil from scratch (including growing the tree, making the saw that cuts it down, producing the truck that takes it to the sawmill, making the paint, etc.), and yet the market produces them cheaply and efficiently.[1] As individuals, people are too dumb to make pencils by themselves, but in a market economy, as a collective, they're excellent at it.

It's at least possible that democracies are like the market in this way. It might be that collective decision making by the dumb many produces smart results. It's even possible that decision making by an enormous number of badly informed voters outperforms collective decision making by a smaller number of better-informed ones. It's at least possible that some form democracy would always make smarter decisions than the best version of epistocracy.

In the attempt to demonstrate that competence is an emergent feature of democratic decision making, political theorists frequently cite three mathematical theorems:

> *Miracle of aggregation theorem*: If errors in an enormous democracy are randomly distributed, then as long as there is a minority of well-informed voters, a democracy made up almost entirely of ignorant voters will perform just as well in epistemic terms as a democracy made up entirely of well-informed voters.[2]
>
> *Condorcet's jury theorem*: If voters are independent, and if the average voter is sufficiently well motivated and more likely than not to be correct, then as a democracy becomes larger and larger, the probability that the demos will get the right answer approaches 1.[3]
>
> *Hong-Page theorem*: Under the right conditions, cognitive diversity among the participants in a collective decision-making process better contributes to that process producing right outcomes than increasing the participants' individual reliability or ability.[4]

All three of these theorems can be used to produce an *epistemic defense* of democracy. An epistemic defense of democracy tries to show that democracy produces smart or at least smart enough decisions.

In this chapter, I first argue that none of these theorems succeed in proving that actual democracies are competent. The theorems show that democracy can be smart only if certain conditions are met. But in each case, I maintain, the conditions are not met. The Hong-Page and miracle of aggregation theorems are mathematical curiosities yet tell us little about real-world politics. Condorcet's jury theorem, far from being a prop for democracy, is more of an ax one might use to chop democracy down.

That being said, democracies do better than we might expect, given how misinformed and irrational voters are. In the final few sections of this chapter, I'll outline a few reasons why democracies seem to systematically outperform what might be expected of them. Alas, one plausible explanation for why democracies do better than we might expect is that they do *not* cater as much to voters as most democrats want them to do; democratic politics allows politicians, bureaucrats, and others to do things most voters oppose. Even if democracies tend to make good decisions *after the election*, though, this will probably leave my main argument for epistocracy intact. After all, it still looks like the electorate systematically violates the competence principle during the election, even if elected leaders, bureaucrats, and others are less likely to violate the competence principle after the election.

A PRIORI PROOFS VERSUS EMPIRICAL REALITIES

Many of the leading epistemic defenses of democracy are a priori and theoretical, while epistemic critiques of democracy tend to be a posteriori or empirical.[5] Each of the three epistemic defenses of democracy I listed above has the same format. Each involves a mathematical theorem or model showing that if certain conditions are met, then democratic decision procedures must produce good outcomes. In contrast, work on political ignorance, such as that by Somin, Caplan, Michael X. Delli Carpini and Scott Keeter, or Althaus, tends to be empirical. The worry is usually this: citizens have low levels of knowledge, and as a collective, they can be shown to make systematic errors. They can be shown to make choices and support policies they would not make were they better informed.

It's hard to overstate the importance of critiques based on systematic error. If one can demonstrate that citizens are systematically mistaken, this is bad news for all three a priori defenses of democratic intelligence. If citizens are systematically mistaken, then by definition their errors are not randomly distributed, and so the so-called miracle of aggregation does not occur. If they are systematically mistaken, then Condorcet's jury theorem condemns rather than defends democracy. (It would then imply that democracies always make the wrong choice.) If citizens are systematically mistaken, it follows that citizens do *not* have cognitive diversity—they instead share the same incorrect model of the world—and so the Hong-Page theorem does not apply. It's thus vital to all three theorems that citizens are not systematically in error.

Again, not all defenses of democracy rely on such theorems. In the final sections of this chapter, I'll describe some epistemic defenses of democracy that might succeed even if voters are in systematic error. Interestingly, what most of these defenses have in common is the idea that what the majority wants during an election does not matter that much; after the election takes place, government agents tend not to do what the median voter or majority want.

Some political theorists who rely on these a priori theorems readily admit that their defenses of democracy are a priori versus empirical. Landemore, for instance, says,

> The third characteristic of the epistemic claim presented in this book is that it is theoretical and a priori rather than empirical. I thus rely on models and theorems to support my case for democracy, rather than on case studies of empirical evidence. . . . I am interested primarily in the *ideal* of democratic decision-making.[6]

Critics of democracy claim that as matter of fact, real democracies make systematic errors. Landemore needs to respond to critics on their own terms. She needs to explain why they have not, in fact, demonstrated that democracies make systematic errors, which means she must attempt to refute their empirical arguments using better empirical evidence. Thus, the question for epistemic democrats is not what mathematical models would show to be the case under stipulated and unrealistic conditions but instead whether actual or possible democratic decision making is adequately modeled by the theorems. If not, then these theorems are just mathematical curiosities.

Landemore herself readily admits that a demonstration of systematic error would doom her argument for democracy:

> The main problem with the optimistic conclusions about group intelligence that I have derived in the previous chapter is that in some way or another they rely on the assumption that there is a symmetrical distribution (random or otherwise) of errors around the right answer (Miracle of Aggregation) or that errors are negatively correlated (Hong and Page's account).[7]

If these assumptions are both false, then her reasoning fails. Similar remarks apply to Condorcet's jury theorem.

THE MIRACLE OF AGGREGATION

Many political theorists and philosophers believe in the miracle of aggregation. The miracle of aggregation holds that large democracies with only a tiny percentage of informed voters perform just as well as democracies made up entirely of informed voters.

The proof of the theorem appears simple. Suppose there are two candidates, Abe and Bob. Suppose Abe is better than Bob. Now suppose that 98 percent of the voters are completely ignorant. When they vote, because they're ignorant, they'll have no reason to prefer Abe to Bob or Bob to Abe. So when they vote, they'll vote at random. It will be like flipping a coin. As long as the voting public is enormous, 50 percent of the ignorant votes will vote for Abe, and 50 percent will vote for Bob. All the ignorant voters will just cancel each other out. Now suppose the other 2 percent of the voters are well informed, and so know that Abe is better than Bob. They'll all vote for Abe. Thus, in the final tally, Abe will get 51 percent of the votes (all the informed votes plus half the ignorant ones) while Bob will get 49 percent of the votes (none of the informed votes, but half the ignorant ones). Abe will win.

The miracle of aggregation theorem holds only if the uninformed voters vote randomly, with their votes centered around the right answer. As I discussed in chapter 2, empirical research shows real-life voters are not like that. The real-life voters whom we call ignorant do not have random preferences. Rather, they have systematic preferences and make systematic errors.[8] Well- and badly informed citizens also have systematically different policy preferences.[9] As people (regardless of their race, income, gender, or other demographic factors) become more informed, they tend to favor overall less government intervention and control of the economy, although they do not become libertarians. They are more in favor of free trade and less in favor of protectionism. They are more pro-choice. They favor using tax increases to offset the deficit and debt. They favor less punitive and harsh measures on crime. They are less hawkish on military policy, even though they favor other forms of intervention. They are more accepting of affirmative action and less supportive of prayer in public schools. They are more supportive of market solutions to health care problems. They are less moralistic in law; they don't want government to impose morality on the population. And so on. In contrast, as people become less informed, they become more in favor of protectionism, abortion restrictions, harsh penalties on crime, doing nothing to fix the debt, hawkish intervention, and so on. Again, remember that these results *control* for differing demographics between low- and high-information voters. Ignorant voters do not vote randomly.

Not only do ignorant voters have systematic as opposed to random political preferences, they also have systematic biases, such as biases to select more attractive over less attractive candidates, or vote for names that sound right rather than wrong. Also, because of the Dunning-Kruger effect, politically incompetent citizens are systematically bad at identifying who is more competent than they are.[10] They cannot identify the most competent political candidates, nor can they identify which pundits are the best to turn to for advice.

In the real world, so-called ignorant voters are not completely ignorant. Even though most voters cannot identify the incumbent, as a whole, low-information voters are biased to select the incumbent over the challenger. As Somin concludes concerning the research on whether ignorant voters vote randomly, "A recent attempt to test the [miracle of aggregation] on samples drawn from six recent presidential elections (1972–1992) found that, controlling for various background characteristics of voters, poor information produces an average aggregate bias of 5 percent in favor of the incumbent."[11] Unless the percentage of high-information voters is high, a 5 percent bias is enough stop the miracle of aggregation from occurring.

Yet another problem is that voters are followers. Suppose early in the political process, some relatively uninformed voters randomly settle on supporting a particular candidate. When other uninformed voters see this, they in turn are more likely to support that candidate. Ignorance can compound rather than cancel out.[12] But let's not overstate this. The people who pay attention to politics first—the ones who tend to select the candidates who make it on the final ballot—tend to be high-information hooligans as opposed to low-information hobbits. Hooligans may be biased, but at least they know something. In the US presidential elections, high-information voters select candidates during the primaries. During the main election, a higher number of low-information voters then participate. The good news, perhaps, is that high-information voters tend to have more power over the US presidential election than one might antecedently expect, but this isn't good news for the miracle of aggregation theorem. After all, the low-information voters still don't appear to vote in harmless random ways; they tend to follow what the high-information primary voters want.

Althaus has a separate statistical argument for the claim that there are systematic errors:

> In order for random errors to sum to zero, they must be scaled in standardized form with a mean of zero. While the expected value of standardized random error is zero, the expected value of unstandardized random error is equal to the midpoint of the range of possible responses. . . . Random errors do not, strictly speaking, cancel out. . . . These random errors . . . continue to influence the location of means and modes as well as the shape of marginal percentages.[13]

Random voting will tend to fall along what statisticians call a normal distribution. Smart voting will also tend to fall along a normal distribution. But these distributions will have different peaks. What the mean and median random voters want will often be different from what the mean and median smart voters want. Even on a simple left-and-right scale, random voting will tend to shift the balance of public opinion one way or another. The more random voting there is, the worse the effect.

It does not appear that low-information voters vote randomly. They have significant systematic errors, beliefs, and biases. If so, then the miracle of aggregation doesn't happen.

CONDORCET'S JURY THEOREM

Another popular epistemic defense of democracy relies on Condorcet's jury theorem.[14] According to Condorcet's jury theorem, if certain conditions are met, then a democratic majority has a near-certain probability of making the correct choice.

Condorcet's jury theorem claims that "on a dichotomous choice, individuals who all have the same level of competence (or probability of being correct) above 0.5, can make collective decisions under majority rule with a competence that approaches 1 (infallibility) as either the size of the group or individual competence goes up."[15] If voters are deciding between two candidates or policies under majority rule procedure, and are on average more likely than not to make the right choice, then as the number of voters increases, the electorate is all but certain to make the right choice.[16] Thus, even if individual voters are on average just slightly more likely than chance to make the right choice, Condorcet's jury theorem says that an electorate of only ten thousand voters is close to certain to make the correct choice.

Whether Condorcet's jury theorem tells us anything at all about democracy depends on whether democratic voting meets a number of conditions. For instance, voters have to be sufficiently independent of one another—they cannot just be copying each other's votes. I suspect these conditions are not met, and so I think the theorem can be used neither to defend nor criticize democracy.[17]

That's ideologically inconvenient for me, though, since one of my goals is to criticize democratic decision making. After all, Condorcet's jury theorem applies as a *defense* of democracy only if a number of assumptions hold. By far the most important assumption is that voters are on average more competent than incompetent. That is, Condorcet's jury theorem can be used to defend democracy only if voters are on average at least slightly more likely to be right than wrong. Condorcet's jury theorem can be used to defend democracy only if individual citizens on average are better than chance. If average voter competence is *lower* than 0.5, then the probability that the majority will make the right choice approaches 0, while the probability that the majority will make the wrong choice approaches 1. That is, if voters are on average slightly more likely to be wrong than right, then as the number of voters increases, the electorate is all but certain to make the *wrong* choice. It's therefore essential to anyone who defends democracy using Condorcet's jury theorem that they know individual voter competence is greater than 0.5 rather than less than 0.5. Otherwise Condorcet's jury theorem implies that democracy is bad.

Again, I am not sure Condorcet's jury theorem tells us anything at all about actual democracy, because I am unsure whether the theorem's other assumptions hold. Yet as we've seen over the past few chapters, there is strong evidence that voters are in systematic error and their average reliability is less than 0.5. So if Condorcet's jury theorem does apply to real-life democracies, it is more plausibly used as a critique of democracy, not a defense. One striking feature of contemporary democratic theorists who invoke Condorcet's jury theorem is that they almost never attempt to show that voters are more reliable than chance.

LANDEMORE'S APPLICATION OF THE HONG-PAGE THEOREM

Sometimes two less smart heads are better than one smart head. Consider this: a typical economics professor might know more than any one of the third-year PhD students in their program, but the PhD students in aggregate probably know more than the professor. If there were some way to aggregate the students' collective knowledge into a single decision, the students as a collective might be more reliable as a source of economic wisdom than the professor by themselves.

Somin summarizes the idea here:

> Some scholars argue that aggregation can work especially well if participants have diverse views and abilities. When a large and diverse group seeks a solution to a problem, it can often make better decisions than a smaller, more expert group because it can pool its diverse collective knowledge which, in the aggregate, is greater than that of the smaller group.[18]

Somin and I both accept this abstract point. We nevertheless are both skeptical about whether this can be used to show that democracy tends to be smarter than any available form of epistocracy, or even whether democracy tends to be smart enough to count as competent.

Lu Hong and Scott Page developed a mathematical theorem in which they showed that, under the right conditions, aggregating a large number of diverse perspectives can produce smarter decisions than relying on a small number of expert but less diverse perspectives. The theorem is quite technical, but we can translate it into common English. The Hong-Page theorem says that under the right conditions, cognitive diversity among the participants in a collective decision-making process better contributes to that process producing right outcomes than increasing the participants' individual reliability or ability. These conditions include the following:

- The participants must have genuinely diverse models of the world.
- The participants must have sufficiently complex models of the world.
- They must agree on what the problem is and what would count as a solution.
- The participants must all be trying to solve the problem together.
- And they must be willing to learn from others and take advantage of other participants' knowledge.[19]

Recently, mathematician Abigail Thompson has argued that the proof of the Hong-Page theorem suffers from "essential and irreparable errors." She notes that the "proof" of the Hong-Page theorem rests on a triviality, "has no mathematic interest and little content," and Hong-Page's computational experiment is erroneous.[20] Indeed, she claims to have found seven fatal flaws, each of which is individually sufficient to show the theorem is mistaken or unproven, or tells us nothing about "diversity." I won't review her technical critique here, but I alert readers that the Hong-Page theorem might rest on a mistake. If so, that's of course devastating for democratic theorists (such as Landemore) who try to use it to defend democracy. That said, in the spirit of charity, I will assume the theorem is correct here, but instead just argue that even if it is, it cannot be used to defend most realistic democratic decisions, and it presents no serious challenge to epistocrats.

Landemore's recent book *Democratic Reason* tries to use the Hong-Page theorem to demonstrate that democracies are smart. (Note: If Thompson's critique of the Hong-Page theorem is correct, then Landemore's book is fatally flawed.) She has an ambitious thesis. She intends to show that democracy outsmarts epistocracy—that the rule of the dumb many usually beats out the rule of the smart few. As she sums up her thesis, "For most political problems, and under conditions conducive to proper deliberation and proper use of majority rule, a democratic procedure is likely to be a better decision procedure than any nondemocratic procedure, such as a council of experts or a benevolent dictator."[21] By "better" here, she means that democracies are likely to *outperform* nondemocracies, producing better *outcomes*, where such outcomes are measured independently of the procedure itself. Notice also that Landemore says "any" nondemocratic procedure; this is what makes her thesis so ambitious. She's arguing that even *mild* forms of epistocracy—say, an epistocracy that excluded only the bottom 5 percent of citizens from voting—perform worse than full democracies with universal suffrage.

While Landemore draws on a wide range of theoretical literature, in my view her argument fails, as I'll explain over the next few sections.

WHY HAVE *EVERYONE* VOTE?

Two heads are sometimes better than one, but that does not mean that *all* the heads are always better than some of them. This seems to be Landemore's essential problem. As far as I can tell, Landemore is much more optimistic about the Hong-Page theorem's ability to defend democracy than is Page himself. That doesn't necessarily mean that Landemore is wrong. Sometimes people who devise a theorem don't recognize the real power of it. Yet when we see why Page didn't himself draw the same conclusions as Landemore, we'll see some grounds to suspect she's overextending the theorem.

Page says there is value in cognitive diversity. *Cognitive diversity* means including diverse perspectives ("ways of representing situations and problems"), diverse interpretations ("ways of categorizing or partitioning perspectives"), diverse heuristics ("ways of generating solutions to problems"), and diverse predictive models ("ways of inferring cause and effect").[22] The Hong-Page theorem says that when it comes to making accurate predictions, increasing the amount of cognitive diversity among decision makers is as important as increasing the predictive power of any subset of them.[23] That is, sophistication and cognitive diversity are equally good.[24]

But Page himself explains that crowds are not always wise. Crowds can make bad, even mad decisions, either when there are systematic biases, or when a tendency toward conformity in deliberation leads to less accuracy and diversity. So, for instance, Page says that if individuals are unduly influenced by charismatic others whose ideas are inaccurate, then group accuracy will be poor.[25] We should thus ask, Are real-life voters influenced by charisma and political spectacle, or are they instead dispassionate, rational truth seekers not so easily beguiled?

Page holds that increasing diversity can be a bad thing when people's predictive powers are poor. Page claims that for the Hong-Page theorem to take hold, the individual decision makers must be fairly sophisticated, if not as sophisticated as experts. Page's modest conclusion is that having many diverse and good predictors tends to be more successful than having just a few excellent ones.[26] Page says in a lecture, "If we don't get collective wisdom, it's going to be because either people lack sophistication—that's the garbage in, garbage out—or they lack diversity." He adds that people need not just diverse information but diverse and good "models," too, or methods to interpret that information.[27] He writes: "For democracy to work, people need good predictive models. And often, the problems may be too difficult or too complex for that to be the case."[28] Page doesn't argue that having many diverse but stupid predictors always works better than having fewer, smarter, but less diverse predictors. On Page's account, highly unsophisticated but diverse crowds do not make good predictions.

It is thus important for Landemore to try to prove that the average or typical citizen is sufficiently sophisticated about politics. But as we saw in chapter 2, the evidence tends to show that most citizens are highly unsophisticated about politics, possessing little of what Page or Landemore would call a mental model. Many of them are hobbits.

It's a puzzle, therefore, why Landemore interprets the Hong-Page theorem as implying it's best to have *all* adult citizens participate. The Hong-Page theorem is supposed to tell us that diversity is good, but it doesn't imply that it's literally best to have every single citizen vote, or even to have most of them vote. The theorem instead says that two heads are frequently better than one, that five million are usually better than two, but sometimes two hundred million are much worse than five million.

As far as I can tell, Landemore never actually tries to show that democracy beats all forms of epistocracy. At most she attempts to demonstrate that democracy with universal suffrage beats out forms of epistocracy in which only a tiny number of citizens are allowed to vote. But that isn't enough to generate her conclusion. Landemore never seriously considers whether a limited form of epistocracy—say, one in which the most ignorant or unsophisticated 5 percent of citizens are excluded from voting—would outperform democracy with universal voting. There's nothing in the Hong-Page theorem that says universal participation always beats more limited participation.

An epistocrat could accept the Hong-Page theorem (though Thompson's critique makes me think not), but not conclude that we should have democracy instead of epistocracy. Instead, it would imply that we should have an epistocracy with a large and diverse group of epistocratic voters. The Hong-Page theorem could be one reason to favor having larger versus smaller epistocratic bodies.

Many heads are sometimes better than fewer heads, yet that doesn't mean that many heads are always better than fewer heads. To return to my earlier point, a collection of third-year economics

PhD students might collectively know more about economics than one star professor, although that star professor might easily know more about economics than an entire high school. The US public as a whole makes systematic mistakes about economics, including most of the mistakes Smith warned us not to make back in 1776.

Landemore asserts, on the basis of the Hong-Page theorem, that she prefers the rule of the many over the rule of the few. But that's a misleading way of putting it. Most epistocrats also want the rule of the many. What Landemore really prefers is the rule of everybody over the rule of the many-but-not-quite-everybody.

ARE VOTERS TRYING TO SOLVE THE PROBLEM?

One further worry about Landemore's use of the Hong-Page theorem is that it assumes individual decision makers have identified a problem, and are each trying to solve that problem. The Hong-Page theorem assumes individual decision makers agree on what the problem is, and are each dedicated to solving that problem.

Throughout her book, Landemore says that voters and political deliberators are analogous to a group of people trying to find their way out of a maze together. In the maze case, everyone agrees on what the goal is: they should exit the maze. Everyone agrees on what counts as exiting the maze; it's not as though once they make it out, half would continue to believe they're still stuck in the maze. Everyone is also prepared to listen to what others have to say about the maze, and then interpret others' testimony in a rational and unbiased way.

This does not appear to be analogous to how real-world deliberation proceeds. As we saw in chapter 3, even carefully controlled laboratory experiments in political deliberation don't usually sound much like Landemore's example. The world is much messier than that. While most voters want to promote the common good, they do not agree on what the common good is, what the main problems facing their country are, or what the relative ranking of those problems may be. Even if common goals have been achieved, many continue to dispute whether the goals have in fact been achieved. Americans in the early 1990s, for example, wanted crime rates to go down. Over the next twenty years, crime rates did go down dramatically, but few Americans know this. Americans in fact mistakenly think gun crimes are up.[29] (In contrast, in Landemore's maze analogy, no one continues to think they're stuck in the maze once they find their way out.) In a modern democracy, citizens may agree that "things should be better," but they disagree on what it means for things to get better and just what it would take to show things are better. Moreover, many citizens vote simply to express their dissatisfaction or display fidelity to their favorite group. They are not actively engaged in problem solving; they are not like the people in the maze. Finally, as we saw in chapters 2 and 3, citizens are *terrible* at listening to each other, unlike the people in Landemore's maze example.

Landemore also frequently tries to defend democracy by treating democratic deliberation as if it were like the deliberation of the jurors in the film *Twelve Angry Men*. Yet there are major differences between how the fictional jurors and actual democratic citizens behave. The fictional jurors spend ample time debating, considering the information available to them and the import of that information, listening to and formulating arguments, considering opposing viewpoints, and trying to see things from multiple perspectives. They do so because they know that their individual votes count a great deal, and they know that their collective decision will have a major impact on someone else's life. But as was noted in chapter 2, real-life voters act as if their individual votes don't matter. Most citizens don't invest the effort to be informed or rational about politics. They deliberate in biased and counterproductive ways.

In response to these kinds of complaints, Landemore just says that she is working with "democracy as an ideal type."[30] She responds to empirical critiques of democratic behavior by retreating to ideal theory. Landemore contends that real-life democracies aren't sufficiently democratic, as the people do not behave the way she thinks they ought to behave. Democracy would be smart, she claims, if only people took it seriously, deliberated the right way, considered information the right way, tried to solve problems as a collective, and so on. That's like saying that democracy would be smart, and smarter than epistocracy, if only citizens acted like the jurors from *Twelve Angry Men* rather than acting the way they in fact do. It's like saying that frats would be great if only they behaved the way they are supposed to rather than the way they do.

In chapter 3, I discussed how many deliberative democrats claim that democratic deliberation would educate and ennoble citizens. The available empirical evidence, however, more strongly supports the view that democratic deliberation tends to stultify and corrupt us. In response, many deliberative democrats could retreat to ideal theory. They could respond that deliberation would ennoble us, if only we did it the right way. I pointed out that such reasoning seems analogous to claiming that frat houses would tend educate and ennoble their brothers, if only their brothers used fraternity life the right way. Landemore doesn't want her epistemic defense of democracy to amount to that. An epistocrat can just agree, "Sure, ideal democracy sounds great. But in the real world with real people, we should replace democracy with epistocracy."

IGNORANCE AND MISINFORMATION

The deepest problem for Landemore, though (if we charitably assume Thompson's critique is mistaken), is the evidence of systematic error. If citizens make systematic mistakes, it follows that they are not sufficiently diverse, and so the Hong-Page theorem does not apply. Yet as shown in chapter 2, citizens do in fact make many systematic errors about crucial issues.

In response, Landemore notes that many simple gauges of voters' political knowledge test information that may not be relevant for political decision making. So, for instance, few Americans can name all the Supreme Court justices off the top of their heads. But it is unlikely that having this information would matter in most elections.

Nevertheless, many mistakes in basic information do matter. For example, most Americans believe that the budget for foreign aid is too high. Americans' mean estimate, however, is that foreign aid takes up 28 percent of the total federal budget, when in fact it is closer to 1 percent.[31] Americans also systematically overestimate the *amount* spent, not just the proportion of the budget dedicated to foreign aid. (The modal and mean guesses are also far higher than the real number.) Similarly, Americans systematically underestimate how much money is spent on defense and welfare. Or consider the fact that that more than half of white Americans believe that US whites and blacks earn the same amount of money, when in fact the median white person earns about twice as much.[32] It seems likely this kind of systematic misinformation would affect the quality of voters' decision making. It would affect how they would choose to allocate resources or what they'd want politicians to prioritize.

Suppose you had low standards for what counts as informed voting. You do not ask voters to know anything about economics or political science. You do not ask them to be able to identify the consequences of the policies they support. You do not ask them to be able to explain their ideology—if they even have one—or defend it from objections. You simply say to voters, "If you're on the Left, vote for the left-wing party. If you're on the Right, vote for the right-wing party. That's all I ask."

It seems that the bottom 25 percent of voters cannot even follow this advice. As I discussed in chapter 2, the bottom 25 percent are not just ignorant. They know *less than* nothing. And since voters tend to know more than nonvoters, we have reason to suspect that the bottom 25 percent of current nonvoters are even worse.

Again, it remains unclear why the Hong-Page theorem should be used as an argument for universal suffrage with high rates of participation rather than for mass abstention or epistocracy. Even if the Hong-Page theorem tells us it's good to have many pretty smart heads versus only a few super smart minds, that doesn't mean democracy makes better decisions with the worst citizens' input than without it.

SYSTEMATIC ERROR, AS SHOWN BY THE ENLIGHTENED PREFERENCES METHOD

Indeed, there may be even more systematic error than there seems at first glance. If we just survey citizens about basic, easily verifiable facts, we find that many of them are mistaken, but what about less easily verifiable beliefs, such beliefs about economics?

Recall, as mentioned in chapter 2, that Althaus wanted to measure how citizens' knowledge affected their policy preferences. The idea is that if we survey tens of thousands of voters, collecting as much demographic information about them as we can, while simultaneously gathering information about what they know and what their policy preferences are, then we can determine how political knowledge influences voters' preferences. We can then determine how political knowledge affects policy preferences, while correcting for any biases that might be introduced by demographics. Using this information, we can estimate what the US voting population *would* prefer if it had perfect political knowledge.

Recall, as chapter 2 noted, that Althaus finds that poorly informed people have systematically different preferences from well-informed people. Gilens and Caplan, among others, find similar results using different data.

On its face, this research defeats Landemore's argument. It looks like the Hong-Page theorem doesn't hold for real-life democracies. People aren't sufficiently diverse, and instead have systematic political preferences—preferences that get expressed through politics, and would change systematically if they were better informed. Worse, the poorly informed outnumber the informed.

Landemore's response to this problem is puzzling. She admits that demonstrations of systematic error would invalidate her use of the Hong-Page theorem. But in response to Althaus's work, she asserts that just because the well informed have different policy preferences than the badly informed, this does not entail logically that the well informed are right.[33] It's possible that the badly informed are right and the well informed are wrong.

Still, no one claims it's a matter of logical necessity that the well informed are right and the poorly informed are wrong. The argument instead goes like this:

1. Much of the basic, objective political knowledge tested by political scientists such as Althaus is not in itself (for the most part) strictly speaking necessary or relevant to make good political decisions or form sound, justified political beliefs. So, for instance, you don't need to be able to name the president of Georgia to be a good voter in the United States.

2. Yet certain social scientific knowledge is necessary and relevant to make good political decisions as well as form sound, justified

political beliefs. If you don't understand basic economics, your opinions about economic policy are probably unjustified.

3. It turns out, empirically, that high scores on tests of political knowledge are correlated with systematically different political beliefs than low scores, and this difference is not explained by demographics. This presents a conundrum that demands explanation.

4. If the three premises above are correct, the *best explanation* is that political knowledge of the sort tested by Althaus, while for the most part not in itself relevant to hard political questions, is positively correlated with the kind of social scientific knowledge that is relevant and necessary to form sound and justified political beliefs.

5. If this last premise holds, then the country's enlightened preferences, as Althaus measures them, are *more likely* to be correct than the country's actual, unenlightened preferences.

6. Therefore, the electorate's enlightened preferences are more likely to be correct than the country's actual, unenlightened preferences, and the electorate is likely to be in systematic error.

In short, the argument here is probabilistic. It's an abductive rather than a deductive argument. On its face it seems powerful. It appears to be powerful evidence that US democracy wouldn't do what it does if only Americans knew better.

If this abductive argument is successful, it's fatal to Landemore's argument. It means that the democratic process makes systematic mistakes. We could improve on democracy by shifting to an episto-cratic system of "government by simulated oracle," which I will describe in further detail in chapter 8.

Althaus's reasoning is strengthened if other people get similar results using the same method with different data sets on different questions. Thus, Caplan's *Myth of the Rational Voter* strengthens Althaus's case, just as Althaus strengthens Caplan's. It's especially interesting, then, that Althaus's and Caplan's enlightened publics end up having the same opinions about economics.

Caplan's work, if correct, is also fatal to Landemore's thesis. Landemore seems to characterize Caplan's argument in an uncharitable and inaccurate way. So, for instance, she says in response to Caplan that "the question of who knows best and what the right answers are is a priori locked in and determined. The economists know better—their answers are the right ones—and thus any deviation from their position must be measured as bias."[34] But Caplan does not take it for granted that whenever economists and laypeople disagree, this shows laypeople are wrong. Instead, Caplan, like Althaus, is making a probabilistic, abductive argument. As Caplan writes, "My empirical approach does not rule out the possibility that the public is right; neither does it rule out the possibility that the experts are wrong. Its key assumption is simply that after controlling for a long list of possible confounding variables, any *remaining* lay-expert belief gaps are evidence of public bias."[35]

Caplan borrows Althaus's enlightened preferences method, but uses different data. He finds that the lay public and economists have systematically different beliefs about the economy. For the issues he studies, he usually finds that the lay public agrees that X, while economists agree that Y. He also finds that these differences in beliefs are not explained by demographics. Caplan is careful to note when economists agree about matters that are not explained by their background ideologies. So, for instance, left-wing, right-wing, moderate, and libertarian economists all support free trade. It's not their overall ideologies that are at work here but rather the fact that they understand and accept mainstream economics.

Caplan isn't asserting that as a matter of logic, economists must know best. He's instead saying that when economists and laypeople systematically disagree about economic issues, and when this disagreement is not explained by demographic factors or any noncognitive biases we can measure, it's more likely that the economists than the laypeople are right. It's worth noting, too, that Caplan largely confines himself to the low-hanging fruit of microeconomics rather than disputed issues in macroeconomic theory.

Caplan studies whether the voting public is literate in economics, but as Landemore might note, economics isn't everything. Many political issues that involve economics go beyond mere economics, and many issues don't involve economics at all. That said, though, it's clear that *most* issues in most major elections require economic knowledge.

Take the issue of immigration. Most Americans are anti-immigration—they favor increasing rather than decreasing immigration restrictions. When asked in 1996 why the economy isn't doing as well as it might, the average American views "too much immigration: as somewhere between a 'minor reason' and a 'major reason.'"[36]

Now consider what economists think about immigration. First, in 1996, economists disagreed with the average American—they denied that immigration is holding the country back.[37] Second, the consensus among published economic work on immigration seems to be that the restriction introduced by mostly closed borders on labor mobility is the single most inefficient thing governments do. Scholarly articles in economics estimate, on average, that the deadweight loss of immigration restrictions is around 100 percent of world product. That is, gross world product should be about $160 trillion, but immigration restrictions cut this to a mere $80 trillion.[38] Moreover, the people who suffer the most from these deadweight losses are the most vulnerable in the world.

While doubling world economic output isn't everything, it swamps most things on the political agenda. But voters get the answer *wrong*. Their other worries about immigration are equally wrong, too. Even if free immigration would double gross world product, the average voter might worry that it would lead to more crime or would depress domestic workers' wages. Here again, however, the average voter would be wrong as far as the evidence goes. Empirical studies tend to show that immigrants are less likely to commit crime than are natives, and other empirical studies demonstrate that immigration boosts most domestic workers' wages while generally only hurting the wages of high school dropouts.[39] (Again, basic economics is relevant here: since the gain to the winners is vastly higher than the loss to the losers, we can just compensate the losers and make everyone a winner.)

Landemore says that Caplan overestimates how much experts know. In defense of this claim, she cites psychologist Philip Tetlock's famous studies on expert prediction. In *Expert Political Judgment*, Tetlock asked almost nearly three hundred purported experts to make nearly thirty thousand predictions.[40] As Landemore characterizes Tetlock's results, Tetlock finds that—on the questions he studied—political experts were no better than "laypeople" at making predictions, and were often worse.[41]

Yet just as Landemore seems to overextend the Hong-Page theorem, she seems to do the same in relation to Tetlock's work. Caplan wonders,

> Is my confidence in experts completely misplaced? I think not. Tetlock's sample suffers from severe selection bias. *He deliberately asked* [his test subjects] *relatively difficult and controversial questions.* As his methodological appendix explains, questions had to "Pass the 'don't bother me too often with dumb questions' test." Dumb according to whom? The implicit answer is "Dumb according to the typical expert in the field." What Tetlock really shows is that experts are overconfident if you exclude the questions where they have reached a solid consensus.[42]

Landemore seems to misunderstand Tetlock's book. Tetlock does not show, and does not see himself as showing, that experts are no better than laypeople or average voters. After all, Tetlock didn't study laypeople or average voters at all. Tetlock's laypeople, against whom the so-called experts were compared, were Berkeley undergraduate students—that is, some of the smartest and most educated people on earth. Tetlock was testing the cognitive hyperelites against the cognitive superelites.

Beyond that, Tetlock only tested experts on what the experts themselves regard as the "hard" questions—questions for which there is considerable controversy. So, going back to economics, there is a wide range of controversy in economics (e.g., should we use monetary or fiscal policy to fix a recession?), but there is also a wide range of agreed-on views, such as that we should have free trade and avoid price controls. The voting public gets the easy questions—econ 101—wrong.

Tetlock's book is not a vindication of the wisdom of crowds. As Caplan further explains, "There is only one major instance in which Tetlock compares the accuracy of experts to the accuracy of laymen. The result: the laymen (undergraduate Berkeley psychology majors— quite elite in absolute terms) were far inferior not only to experts but also to chimps [i.e., random guessing]."[43] In short, Tetlock demonstrates that experts are terrible at making predictions on what they themselves regard as the hard questions, but that Berkeley undergraduates are even worse.

All that aside, if one wants to interpret Tetlock's result as saying that both experts and laypeople do worse than chimps on most issues, I don't see why, pace Landemore, that vindicates democracy. Instead, it suggests we advocate chimp-ocracy.

EMPIRICAL EVIDENCE INSTEAD OF A PRIORI PROOFS

In chapters 2 and 3, I examined at significant length the empirical work on voter ignorance, misinformation, and irrationality. This work shows that the mean, median, and modal voters know little, and worse, on many major issues most voters know less than nothing.

One way to rescue democracy from that critique would be to show that democracies tend to make smart decisions as collectives even if the majority of voters are incompetent. The miracle of aggregation, Condorcet's jury theorem, and the Hong-Page theorem (in Landemore's hands) were all intended to demonstrate just that. Unfortunately for democrats, though, these theorems cannot be used to defend democracy. It's not that empirical evidence gives us presumptive reasons to doubt democracy, but the three theorems *outweigh* the empirical evidence and instead tell us to trust democracy. The empirical evidence not only gives us presumptive reasons to doubt democracy but also tells us at the same time that the three theorems *don't apply* to real-life democracies. Or, more precisely, it tells us that the Hong-Page and miracle of aggregation theorems don't apply, yet that if Condorcet's jury theorem applies to real-life democracies, then this means that real-life democracies are all but certain to be wrong in every decision they make. Epistemic democrats who rely on these three theorems are mistaken.

A much more promising route for epistemic democrats is to defend democracy on empirical grounds. Right now, for the most part, democracies are better places to live than the nondemocracies. Democracies do not allow mass famine.[44] Many scholars believe that democracies tend not to make war against one another, although some dispute this theory.[45] Democracies are systematically more likely than existing monarchies, oligarchies, and one-party governments to recognize as well as protect civil and economic liberties.[46] While I think democracies systematically underperform, they perform wonderfully when compared to most historical alternatives. In the next few sections, I'll consider some empirical accounts of why democracies might tend to produce good results on the whole, even if most voters are ignorant or misinformed. I'll then explain why these points, even if correct, don't suffice to save democracy.

DO POLITICAL PARTIES REDUCE THE EPISTEMIC DEMANDS ON VOTERS?

In modern democracies, most candidates join political parties. Political parties run on general ideologies and policy platforms. Individual candidates may have their own idiosyncrasies and preferences, but they have a strong tendency to fall in line and do what the party wants.

Many political scientists think party systems reduce the epistemic burdens of voting. Voters can get by reasonably well by treating all Republicans and Democrats as two homogeneous groups. In an election, instead of learning what this particular Republican and Democratic want to do, I can treat the candidates as standard Republicans and Democrats, and vote accordingly. This kind of statistical discrimination leads to mistakes on an individual basis, but on a macro level, with 535 members of Congress, these individual mistakes are likely to cancel out. The party system thus provides voters with a "cognitive shortcut"; it allows them to act as if they were reasonably well informed.

There's much to be said for this line of reasoning. So long as voters tend to have reasonably accurate stereotypes of what policies the two major political parties tend to prefer, then voters as a whole can perform well by relying on such stereotypes.

That said, we should be careful to avoid overstating just how much of a shortcut parties supply. First, as highlighted in chapter 2, many voters and many more nonvoters fail to have a reasonable understanding of what different political parties want to do. Many voters lack a stereotype for the major parties, and many have their stereotypes backward.

Second, as I also discussed in chapter 2, to vote well, it's not enough to have a general idea of a candidate or party's policy preferences. One must also know whether the candidates are likely to be able to impose their favored policies, and whether the policies are likely to result in good or bad consequences. This requires tremendous social scientific knowledge—knowledge that most voters lack.

Third, as also examined in chapter 2, voters tend to become hooligans for one party or the other. They tend to evaluate information about the parties in a biased way. Thus, even when new evidence comes in that indicates they should switch sides, they tend to stick to their current party.

Fourth, as Somin complains, "An implicit assumption of the party identification shortcut literature is that voters need only have sufficient political knowledge to choose between the two options available in the election."[47] The implicit assumption is all that matters is that voters use shortcuts to choose between the candidates who happen to be on the ballot. But as Somin complains, and as I've complained elsewhere, the quality of the candidates who make it on the ballot depends in large part on the quality of the electorate.[48] Political parties choose candidates whom they believe will appeal to typical voters. Voters are systematically ignorant, incompetent, and misinformed, and as we saw in chapter 2, this systematically changes their policy preferences. If voters were better informed, they would have different political preferences. If political candidates face a more knowledgeable electorate, they would have different policy platforms. In short, it's true that the party system makes it easier for low-information voters to choose among the candidates presented to them, but at the same time, because voters are badly informed, the quality of the candidates is much lower than it otherwise would be.

DOES DEMOCRACY WORK WELL BECAUSE IT DOESN'T WORK?

Given how little voters know and how badly they process information, it's not surprising that democracies frequently choose bad policies. But given how little voters know and how badly they process information, it's surprising democracies don't perform even worse than they do.

For a long time, the dominant model of how politicians respond to voter preferences was the median voter theorem. Imagine that voters are normally distributed along a one-dimensional issue space, from, say, the Far Left, to the moderate, to the Far Right. Suppose extreme leftist Lefty Lucy and extreme right-winger Righty Rory run for office. The leftists want Lucy, while the right-wingers want Rory. People in the middle of the distribution may be indifferent to the two of them. Rory, however, could win more voters by moving a bit to the Left. As she does so, right-wingers are unlikely to abandon her—they still prefer her to Lucy—while the moderate voters come to prefer her to Lucy. To gain votes, Lucy will do something similar: she'll move more to the right. They both can capture more votes by moving toward the middle. Now apply this logic again: both Lucy and Rory can gain more votes by moving closer to the middle. In the end, they'll represent the position of the median voter. It's thus not surprising that candidates in any given electoral district are ideologically quite similar and tend to be moderate (as compared to voters in that district).

Political scientists have long thought the median voter theorem is too simple (as I've described it) and admits of certain qualifications, but Gilens has recently provided strong evidence that it may be quite far off. Instead of responding to the median voter's preferences, politicians might be responding to the preferences of *richer* voters.

Recently, Gilens measured how responsive different presidents have been to different groups of voters. He finds that when voters at the ninetieth, fiftieth, and tenth percentiles of income disagree about policy, presidents are about six times more responsive to the policy preferences of the rich than the poor.[49] To Gilens's surprise, George W. Bush, whom his colleagues and mine are inclined to portray as a tool of the wealthy, was *more* likely to side with the poor on policy issues than any recent president, including Kennedy, Johnson, or Obama.

Gilens is in some ways horrified by results like these, but he admits there's an upside. Voters at the ninetieth percentile of income tend to be significantly better informed than voters at the fiftieth or tenth percentile, and this information changes their policy preferences. As I discussed in chapter 2, Gilens finds that high-information Democrats have systematically different policy preferences from low-information Democrats. High-income Democrats tend to have high degrees of political knowledge, while poor Democrats tend to be ignorant or misinformed. Poor Democrats approved more strongly of invading Iraq in 2003. They more strongly favor the Patriot Act, invasions of civil liberty, torture, protectionism, and restricting abortion rights and access to birth control. They are less tolerant of homosexuals and more opposed to gay rights.[50]

For an instrumentalist like me, Gilens's results are reason to celebrate. It means that democracy works better than it otherwise would, because it doesn't exactly work. Democracy is supposed to give every individual citizen equal voice, but it doesn't. For whatever reason, smarter and better-informed voters, with more enlightened policy preferences, are better represented, with their preferences better realized, than less informed voters with less enlightened preferences. Smarter and better-informed voters are more likely to get their way.

Gilens hypothesizes, although he doesn't quite prove, that the reason higher-income voters have more power is that they *donate* more to political campaigns.[51] Sure, rich citizens are slightly more likely to vote than poor citizens, but politicians are on average about six times more likely to side with the rich than the poor. The rich donate to campaigns about six times more than the poor do.

I'm unsure whether Gilens's hypothesis is correct. First, there is a large literature that seems to show that campaign contributions make little difference in political outcomes.[52] High-income voters, being high-information voters, are also probably much better at retrospective voting than average or low-income voters, and so politicians have a stronger incentive to please them than they do others. I won't attempt to prove this alternative hypothesis here. But it's worth noting that if Gilens is correct that high-income voters have more power because they donate more, then certain campaign finance reforms could produce worse-quality government by making politicians more responsive to average voters' unenlightened policy preferences versus the more enlightened policy preferences of higher-income voters. It may be that higher-income voters are buying power, but in this way they seem to be buying better government for all.

The majority of citizens in modern democracies are ignorant and irrational, supporting policies and candidates they would not support were they better informed. Nevertheless, most democracies tend to make reasonably good decisions, compared to dictatorships, oligarchies, monarchies, and one-party states. They also tend to make better decisions than we might expect in light of how ignorant and irrational citizens are, although part of the reason for this seems to be that better-informed citizens exercise a disproportionate share of political power and can get away with doing things the majority opposes.

OTHER MEDIATING FACTORS: HOW SMART IS DEMOCRACY, ALL THINGS CONSIDERED?

Voters elect politicians with certain ideological or policy bents, and hence make it more likely that laws, regulations, and policies fitting those bents will be implemented. But the path between an election and law or regulation being passed is complicated. It's not as though during an election we just ask voters to choose from a catalog of possible laws and whatever the majority picks is immediately enacted. Instead, there is a wide range of political bodies and administrative procedures that mediate between what the majority of the moment appears to want during the election and what laws and rules actually get passed. Many empirically minded democratic theorists, such as Ian Shapiro or Danny Oppenheimer, argue that one reason democracy works better than we might expect is for reasons like this. Sure, the voting public is largely irrational, but the voting public doesn't just get what it wants.

Consider some such mediating factors:

- Modern democracies allow a wide range of avenues for political contestation. If groups of citizens take a serious interest in some topic, they can apply significant pressure to politicians. Often, they can sway public opinion to their side. (Witness, for example, the recent switch in US public opinion about gay marriage.)
- Large government bureaucracies, including the military, have a life of their own. They do not simply follow presidential or

congressional orders but instead frequently set their own agendas as well as act independently or in defiance of oversight from elected officials. Similar remarks apply to the judiciary.

- The design of the political process—with checks and balances, frequent elections, and so on—tends to prevent political instability.[53]
- While voters are badly informed, politicians are much better informed, and many are reasonably well motivated. They make deals with one another and compromise, or they hold fast and prevent the other side from unilaterally imposing its will. As a result, political outcomes tend to be relatively moderate and conservative, in the sense that changes from the status quo come gradually.
- Political parties have significant power to shape the political agenda as well as make decisions independently of voters' desires, opinions, and wishes. Since most voters are ignorant, they are unlikely to know what the parties have done, and thus are unlikely to punish them for imposing laws the voters wouldn't like if only they knew about them.

Each of these mediating factors tends to reduce the power of the majority of the moment during the election and instead place greater power in the hands of more informed citizens. In that sense, there are epistocratic checks within a democratic system.

There is an impressive body of empirical literature in political science showing how such factors mediate between what voters seem to want during an election and what actually gets done. What democracies do is not simply a function of voter preferences.

The competence principle requires that every high-stakes political decision be made competently and in good faith by what is generally a competent body. But as I explained in the last chapter, I am not making the following argument:

1. During the typical election in a modern democracy, the electorate as a whole violates the competence principle.
2. Therefore, everything a typical modern democracy does runs afoul of the competence principle. Every decision at every level is unjust, illegitimate, and nonauthoritative.

The second premise doesn't follow from first, and it's based on a misunderstanding of the competence principle. The competence principle looks at each decision independently. It doesn't hold that if an upstream decision is made incompetently, then every downstream decision is thereby considered or rendered incompetent, bad, or unjust.

This chapter is titled "Is Democracy Competent?" That question is too simple. Instead, perhaps democracies are incompetent at some things and competent at others. It may be that certain political decision makers are competent while others are incompetent.

We've seen that there is strong evidence that the electorate, during an election, is systematically incompetent, making electoral decisions out of ignorance and irrationality. The mediating factors in the list above may suffice to show that despite this, many of the decisions democratic governments make are made competently. Again, the competence principle applies to every individual decision. As such, the competence principle might well condemn the typical election, even if it does not thereby condemn everything or even most of what democracies do after the elections have passed.

Given that so many factors mediate between what voters prefer during an election and what governments actually do, one might then wonder whether the competence principle even applies to electoral decisions. I'll answer this objection in the abstract, in the form of a dilemma. The competence principle applies only to *high-stakes* decisions—decisions that can tend to cause significant harm to people, or deprive them of life, liberty, or property. It doesn't apply to low-stakes decisions, such as what the national anthem or flag colors will be. Now ask, In light of all these mediating factors, do electoral decisions count as high stakes or not? There are two possibilities:

Most elections are still high stakes. On this view, even though many factors mediate between what voters want and what governments do, voters still have enough power (in most elections) such that their decisions count as high stakes. If so, then, in light of the empirical evidence on voter and electoral behavior I've examined over the course of this book, we should conclude that most electorates violate the competence principle. If it turns out that certain forms of epistocratic decision-making methods would perform better, then we ought to replace democracy with epistocracy. We should use epistocratic not democratic elections. (This assumes, of course, that the benefits of epistocracy exceed the costs of transitioning from democracy to epistocracy.)

Most electoral decisions are not high stakes. On this view, the various mediating factors are so significant that we can't meaningfully call elections high stakes. If not, then the competence principle doesn't apply to them, and it doesn't matter from a moral point of view that electorates tend to make such decisions incompetently.

So, which is it, the first or second possibility? Do elections matter or not? This is a big question. In a sense, thousands of political scientists have devoted their careers to trying to answer this question. I don't want to do a hundred-page review of the empirical literature on all the various mediating factors here. I read this literature as showing that most major elections remain high stakes, if not as high stakes as a naive fifth grader might think. Elections of officeholders do not directly decide policy, but they significantly change the probability that different policies will be implemented. If I'm right, then we have presumptive grounds to view democratic elections with universal equal suffrage as unjust, even though this doesn't mean every decision every democratic government agent makes is therefore unjust.

Suppose I'm wrong. Suppose possibility two turns out to be correct and elections don't really matter. Suppose that the postelectoral mediating factors are so significant that the typical parliamentary, congressional, or presidential election doesn't qualify as high stakes. If so, then the competence principle doesn't apply to these elections, and the facts about voter behavior explored in chapters 2 and 3 don't give us reason to prefer epistocracy to democracy.

Yet if the second possibility is correct—if elections don't really matter—this should be little solace to most democrats. After all, think of their major reasons for preferring democracy to epistocracy. Most of their arguments rely in some way on the view that elections matter, that elections empower groups of voters, that elections with universal suffrage are necessary to make sure that governments respond appropriately to citizens' interests, and so on. But if possibility two is correct, they'll have a hard time making such arguments. Possibility two says that it's only the postelectoral stuff that matters. If so, then it's unclear why a democrat would prefer democratic elections (with universal equal suffrage) to epistocracies (which in some way have unequal suffrage). After all, the proceduralist arguments for democracy (reviewed in chapters 4 and 5) don't succeed. Possibility two, combined with the failure of the proceduralist arguments, implies that there's no reason to prefer epistocratic to democratic elections or vice versa.

In short, if the first possibility is correct, then the competence principle gives us presumptive grounds to favor epistocracy over democracy. If the second possibility is correct, then the choice between democracy and epistocracy is something of a toss-up—in effect, it just doesn't matter which one we pick. Either way, my argument so far in this book puts democrats in an uncomfortable position. They should at this point either presumptively favor epistocracy over democracy or be indifferent. When I say, "Let's try epistocracy!" you should either be with me or at least not against me, depending on whether you think the facts support possibility one or two. With that, let's take a look at some possible forms of epistocracy.

CHAPTER 8

THE RULE OF THE KNOWERS

In chapter 1, I asked, What kind of value does democracy have, if any? Some people think democracy is valuable the way a painting is—we should value it for what it expresses or symbolizes. Others think we should value democracy the way we value a person, as an end in itself. But as we saw over the past few chapters, arguments for these conclusions don't work. This leaves us with a final option. Perhaps democracy is valuable the way a hammer is valuable. It's nothing more than a useful tool. As we have seen over the past few chapters, though, it's a flawed tool. We should ask if there is an even better hammer.

This chapter explores ways we might experiment with various forms of epistocracy. I begin by describing various mistakes philosophers tend to make when they theorize about institutions, in part to clarify just what the question is, in part to warn critics of epistocracy not to make these mistakes, and in part to discipline myself to avoid making these mistakes myself. I then explain how various forms of epistocracy might go, and what some of the problems of implementing epistocracy might be.

THE BIG PRETTY PIG CONTEST

Political scientist Michael Munger has a thought experiment that exposes a common mistake people make when reasoning about institutions. Imagine the state fair decides to hold a "Big Pretty Pig" contest. There end up being only two entries. While there are lots of big pigs and plenty of pretty pigs, few pigs are both big and pretty. The judge takes a long look at the first pig and exclaims, "My God, that's one ugly pig! You know what, let's just give the prize to the second one."

The judge's mistake is clear. The second pig might be even uglier.

It's an obvious mistake, but many economists, political scientists, and philosophers make this same mistake when they judge institutions. They complain about how ugly some institutions are in practice and then say we should go with their favored alternatives instead. But they fail to examine whether their favored alternatives are even uglier. So, for instance, a left liberal might identify a market failure and propose that we empower government to solve the problem, but fail to consider whether government failure in this area might be even worse than the market failure. Or a libertarian might identify a government failure and propose we leave the issue to the market, but fail to consider whether leaving it to the market might be even worse.

I intend to avoid this mistake. Over the past few chapters, I've shown that democracy is an ugly pig. But even if real-world democracy is uglier than we realized, that doesn't automatically mean that epistocracy will be prettier. We need to look at this second pig.

There's a problem, however: I don't have a second pig to look at. In effect, I'm recommending we genetically engineer a second pig. It's hard to know whether epistocracy would be better, because we have not really tried it. Some governments have had epistocratic elements in the past, but not of the exact sort I advocate here. When I argue that epistocracy could do better than democracy, I have to speculate more than I would like to. That said, we can speculate in an informed way. We have data about citizens' knowledge and competence. We have significant knowledge of how institutions work and how people respond to incentives. We have significant evidence of which kinds of institutions tend to encourage corruption and which tend to reduce it. Still, it's easy to expose the pathologies of democracy; it's harder to design institutions that would improve on it.

Democrats might think this is a decisive objection to my argument. Yet they should consider that in the seventeenth century, their prodemocracy forbears also had to speculate about whether democracy would really be superior to monarchy. Three hundred years ago, early advocates of democracy were forced to speculate that democracy would turn out to be superior to monarchy. They didn't have enough historical examples to know for sure. They had reasonable hypotheses. But there were also reasonable worries that democracy would be an even bigger mess than monarchy—indeed, even today, some democracies are worse than some monarchies.

THE PERFECT PIG

This brings up a different kind of problem. Consider the following two sets of questions:

> *Question 1*: What kind of political regime would be morally best if people were motivated by a nearly perfect sense of justice and were fully competent to play whatever role they have in society, if institutions always work as intended, and if there were favorable background conditions?
>
> *Question 2*: What kind of political regime will best tend to promote and protect important moral values (such as justice and prosperity) given that people's willingness and ability to comply are imperfect, people are sometimes incompetent and corrupt, institutions are not guaranteed to work as intended, and background conditions can be unfavorable?

Question 1 asks what kind of regime would be better under ideal conditions, while question 2 asks what kind of regime would be better in realistic conditions. It's important we keep these questions separate, and don't jump back and forth between them in a careless way.

There's no reason to presume these questions will have the same answer. Different conditions call for different tools. Suppose we asked engineers to design jets on the assumption that all pilots are perfectly competent and all skies will be perfectly safe. In that case, engineers might not bother to install any safety measures. But in the real world, engineers have compelling reason, even a duty, not to build jets like that. In the same way, if people were unfailingly good and just, we would design institutions differently. We probably wouldn't need a government at all.[1] Or if we did, we'd need few checks and balances. We would have reason to entrust government with a great deal more power than we do if people are corrupted or can be corrupted by power.

Suppose I said, "Democracy has many pathologies. Let's imagine a form of monarchy with an all-wise, all-benevolent king. That would be better than real-world democracy! Therefore, monarchy is better than democracy." You'd see right through that argument. Sure, ideal monarchy might be better than real-world democracy. But that leaves open whether ideal monarchy is better or worse than ideal democracy, or whether real-world monarchy is better or worse than real-world democracy. Ideal monarchy lacks the problems of real-world democracy, but that gives us no reason to try to instantiate monarchy here and now. Ideal monarchy isn't a live option for us.

In a similar vein, I want to avoid saying, "Let's imagine a form of epistocracy in which all-wise, all-benevolent epistocrats rule. That would be better than real-life democracy." Indeed it would, yet ideal epistocracy isn't a live option. We instead should ask, Given what we know about political behavior, including what we know about rent seeking, corruption, and abuses of power, which is likely to deliver better results, some form of epistocracy or some form of democracy?

Both systems will work better in some places than others. Because of cultural and other differences, democratic institutions work better in New Zealand and Denmark than they do in the United States or France, which in turn do better than Russia, Venezuela, or Iraq. I'd expect something similar would hold true of epistocracy. Both systems will suffer abuse, scandal, and government failure. In the real world, both pigs will be ugly. Realistically, epistocracies will still feature the rule of hooligans rather than vulcans, although epistocratic hooligans may be more vulcan-like than in democracy. Fair enough. But since there are no proceduralist grounds to prefer democracy to epistocracy, and since democracy seems to violate the competence principle, if epistocracy (warts and all) works better than democracy—that is, produces more substantively just outcomes—let's go with epistocracy. Let's go with the prettier (or less ugly) pig, whatever that turns out to be.

FORMS OF EPISTOCRACY

Below I'll describe a number of possible forms of epistocracy. A political system is epistocratic to the extent it distributes political power in proportion to knowledge or competence, as a matter of law or policy. This distribution has to be de jure, not merely de facto. Suppose a democracy with universal suffrage always elected the most competent people to run the government. While the most competent people would end up holding office, this system would still be a democracy, because by law it distributes fundamental political power equally. In contrast, in an epistocracy, the law does not equally distribute basic political power.

Many forms of epistocracy worth considering have some of the same institutions we find in democracies. Epistocracies might have parliaments, contested elections, free political speech open to all, many of the contestatory and deliberative forums that neorepublicans and deliberative democrats favor, and so on.[2] These epistocracies might retain many of the institutions, decision-making methods, procedures, and rules that we find in the best-functioning versions of democracy. The major difference between epistocracy and democracy is that people do not, by default, have an equal right to vote or run for office.

VALUES-ONLY VOTING

Christiano proposes we instantiate a sort of halfway point between standard democracy and epistocracy. He begins by noting that it's unrealistic to expect voters to have sufficient social scientific knowledge to make good choices at the polls:

> It is hard to see how citizens can satisfy any even moderate standards for beliefs about how best to achieve their political aims. Knowledge of means requires an immense amount of social science and knowledge of particular facts. For citizens to have this kind of knowledge generally would require that we abandon the division of labor in society.[3]

Christiano believes the typical citizen is competent to deliberate about and choose the appropriate aims of government. For citizens to know the best means for achieving those aims, however, they would have to become experts in sociology, economics, and political science. They are not competent to make such determinations.[4] Christiano's proposed solution is to create a division of *political* labor: "Citizens are charged with the task of defining the *aims* the society is to pursue while legislators are charged with the tasks of implementing and devising the *means* to those aims through the making of legislation."[5]

Christiano argues, and I agree, that this regime qualifies as a type of democracy. Fundamental political power is still spread evenly among citizens. Under Christiano's proposal, the legislators have only instrumental authority. They are administrators more than leaders.

As an analogy, consider the relationship of a yacht owner to the yacht's captain. The owner tells the captain where to go, but the captain does the actual sailing. While the captain knows how to steer the boat and the owner does not, the owner is in charge. The owner can fire the captain, and as such the captain serves the owner. Christiano might contend that in the same way, under his proposal the legislators serve the democratic electorate. While the legislators set laws that the democratic body must follow, the democratic body told the legislator what direction these laws must go in.

Christiano acknowledges that there are serious worries about implementing this kind of system. Right now we allow citizens to choose not just the ends of government but also to a significant degree the means. Potential legislators and political parties run platforms that contain aims as well as policies meant to realize these aims. Christiano worries (as I do) that citizens don't know enough to vote on the means. Yet as Christiano recognizes, if they lack the social scientific knowledge needed to choose among different candidates' policy platforms, they will presumably also lack the social scientific knowledge needed to determine whether the legislators have competently and faithfully chosen policies that will realize citizens' aims.

In the case of a yacht owner and ship captain, the owner can at least tell whether the captain has gotten them to their preferred destination. They can at least determine whether they are in Bermuda or

Haiti, even if they won't know whether a better captain could have gotten them there faster. But there's no parallel here for democracy. To know whether legislators did a good job trying to realize the electorates' aims, the electorate will need to have the social scientific knowledge that Christiano says they lack. Furthermore, if citizens become accustomed to outsourcing the choice of means entirely to legislators, they might become even worse at evaluating means than they already are.

Imagine citizens pick the Full Employment Party, whose sole goal is to reduce unemployment as much as possible. Four years later, suppose unemployment has in fact doubled. Has the Full Employment Party done a bad job? Not necessarily. Perhaps it did the best anyone could do under highly unfavorable circumstances. Perhaps any other set of policies would have resulted in even worse unemployment. To evaluate whether the Full Employment Party did its job, citizens need a tremendous amount of social scientific knowledge—knowledge that most citizens lack. Or they would have to identify experts who can evaluate whether the Full Employment Party did its job. But if citizens were good at sorting through expert evaluations, we wouldn't need to follow Christiano's proposal in the first place.

Christiano devotes considerable space to the attempt to overcome these objections. Whether he succeeds is not my concern here, because I want to press the problem further than he would. My question is, Why suppose that citizens are competent even to vote on aims or purely normative issues? The problems examined in previous chapters—severe cognitive biases, political hooliganism, and the lack of incentive to think rationally about politics—apply to normative as much as empirical considerations.

Moreover, Christiano and I have both seen firsthand thousands of times that many people cannot think clearly about values even when they have a strong incentive to do so. Christiano, for instance, used to teach large introductory political philosophy classes at his university. Although the standards for these introductory classes are low, and even though students' grades are at stake, many students cannot muster even a rudimentary understanding of the most basic issues in political philosophy. Yet these students—many of whom will fail out of college—are among the intellectual elite in the United States.

Finally, it's unclear how much we can disentangle normative and empirical considerations. Perhaps we can debate or rationally form beliefs about the most abstract or general principles of justice without needing any significant social scientific knowledge. (Whether this is so is heavily disputed in contemporary political philosophy.)[6] But in the scenario Christiano proposes, political parties run on real platforms, such as protecting the environment versus economic growth. We would need to know something about the possible trade-offs and opportunity costs of such goals before we can form reasonable views of what our aims should be. Once again, this requires tremendous social scientific knowledge—knowledge that most citizens lack.

RESTRICTED SUFFRAGE AND PLURAL VOTING

Driving imposes risk on innocent bystanders. For that reason, in the United States (and most other countries), a person must earn the right to drive. In any given state, every person of age has to pass an exam demonstrating basic driving competence. Every person—rich or poor, black or white—takes the same exam, though of course some people have a better chance of passing than others.

Unlike individual bad drivers, individual bad voters make no difference. But as a group, they can impose serious risk on innocent bystanders. A restricted suffrage epistocracy—or what I've previously called an elite electoral system—responds to this problem by restricting political power to citizens who demonstrate a basic level of knowledge.[7] Everyone begins as an equal in this system. By default, no one is entitled or permitted to exercise any degree of political power. They have extensive civil liberties to exercise political speech, publish political ideas, protest, and so on, but not to vote. Nonetheless, just as in most parts of the United States one cannot become a judge without having demonstrated some basic level of legal knowledge (for instance, by getting a law degree), an elite electoral system requires citizens to earn a license to vote (and perhaps also to run for office).

One form of restricted suffrage epistocracy requires potential voters to pass a voter qualification exam. This exam would be open to all citizens regardless of their demographic background. The exam would screen out citizens who are badly misinformed or ignorant about the election, or who lack basic social scientific knowledge. The United States, for example, might use the questions on the ANES. Alternatively, the United States might require citizens to pass the citizenship exam, or score a three or higher on the Advanced Placement economics and political science exams. Alternatively, the test might be entirely nonideological. We might simply require potential voters to solve a number of logic and mathematics puzzles, or be able to identify 60 percent of the world's countries on a map. In this case, the exam would not directly test knowledge but things that might be positively correlated with political knowledge.

It's probably impossible to design an exam that would precisely test the knowledge needed for any particular election. After all, what's at stake and thus what knowledge is needed varies from election to election. Also, what counts as relevant knowledge is reasonably disputed. That's not to deny that there's a truth of the matter about what knowledge is relevant. The point is that we have to rely on real people with their own agendas and ideologies to design as well as implement any such test.

To keep the test objective and nonideological, we might limit it to basic facts and fundamental, largely uncontested social scientific claims. Much of this knowledge is strictly speaking irrelevant to any given election. For instance, almost nothing in the US citizenship exam is needed to be a good voter.[8] Still, at least right now, a person who possesses this knowledge is much more likely to have the kind of knowledge that is relevant. As we saw in previous chapters, citizens who know the answers to basic civics questions, say, tend to have political opinions that more closely match what economists of all ideological stripes believe. That said, it might be that if we made voting rights conditional on passing such exams, this correlation would diminish or disappear. There are currently some Americans who possess a high degree of political and social scientific knowledge, and hence score well on the citizenship exam. But if we used the citizenship exam to determine who could vote, people might "cram for the exam," learning just the basic facts on the test and nothing else, and so the exam would stop being a proxy for background social scientific knowledge. It might be that effective voter qualification exams need to test basic social scientific knowledge, such as introductory micro-economics and introductory political science.

To encourage the poor and disadvantaged to become good voters, governments could offer incentives to citizens who can pass the exam and acquire the right to vote. For instance, the government might offer a prize: anyone who qualifies to vote gets a thousand-dollar tax credit.

Alternatively, a restricted suffrage regime could allow anyone who passes an exam to vote for free. It might then allow those who fail the exam be permitted to vote, but only if they pay a penalty of two thousand dollars. In the same way, the US government imposes a "gas guzzler" tax on automobiles with low gas mileage.

In a restricted suffrage regime, citizens have either one or zero votes. Another version of epistocracy allows for an even greater disparity in voting power. Under a plural voting regime, as proposed by Mill, each citizen has by default one vote. (Though the default could instead be zero.) By performing certain actions, passing certain exams, or otherwise demonstrating competence and knowledge, a citizen could acquire more votes. Mill wanted to distribute additional votes to citizens who had certain academic degrees. We might decide that everyone gets one vote at age sixteen, five more votes if they graduate high school, five more votes if they get a bachelor's degree, and five more for a graduate degree. Alternatively, we could grant every citizen one vote at age sixteen, but then grant citizens ten more votes if they can pass the voter qualification exam.

I've heard laypeople object that restricted suffrage and plural voting systems create a class of "philosopher kings with absolute power." But that's not even close to an accurate characterization. As I discussed at great length in previous chapters, individual voters in modern democracies have infinitesimal power. Saunders jokes that "when it comes to political power . . . each person's share is so small that to insist on strict equality would be more like arguing over the crumbs of a cake than insisting on equal slices."[9] In a plural voting or restricted suffrage regime, the typical voter has only infinitesimal power. So, for example, if the United States were to restrict voting rights to only the top 10 percent most competent of the adult population, the remaining voters would still have less voting power than the average voter in Canada or Australia. If Australia were to limit voting rights only to its top 10 percent most competent voters, these individual voters would still typically have much less than a one-in-ten-million chance of breaking a tie in an election.

THE ENFRANCHISEMENT LOTTERY

In *Democracy and Disenfranchisement*, López-Guerra defends an epistocratic system he calls the "enfranchisement lottery." Here is how López-Guerra describes the system:

> The enfranchisement lottery consists of two devices. First, there would be a sortition to disenfranchise the vast majority of the population. Prior to every election, all but a random sample of the public would be excluded. I call this device the *exclusionary sortition* because it merely tells us who will *not* be entitled to vote in a given contest. Indeed, those who survive the sortition (the *pre-voters*) would not be automatically enfranchised. Like everyone in the larger group from which they are drawn, pre-voters would be assumed to be insufficiently competent to vote. This is where the second device comes in. To finally become enfranchised and vote, pre-voters would gather in relatively small groups to participate in a *competence-building process* carefully designed to optimize their knowledge about the alternatives on the ballot.[10]

Under López-Guerra's scheme, by default, no one has the right to vote. Everyone starts on an equal footing in that way. A lottery selects a random but representative subset of citizens. Only these citizens may earn the right to vote in the coming election (which will take place shortly). The purpose of the lottery is to ensure that the voting populace is likely to be identical in demographics to the populace at large. Finally, these citizens engage in various deliberative forums with one another, and are asked to study party platforms and the like.

López-Guerra says his system is significantly different from all the other epistocratic systems that philosophers and political economists have entertained. Most epistocratic systems try to screen for the most competent voters or, alternatively, screen out the least competent ones. His proposed system is meant to *breed* the most competent voters.[11]

There's much to be said on behalf of López-Guerra's favored form of epistocracy. In particular, it avoids the "demographic objection" to epistocracy, which I'll look at below. That said, I worry, in light of the facts about voter psychology and deliberation that I discussed in chapters 2 and 3, that breeding competent voters is significantly harder and more likely to fail than *selecting* for them. López-Guerra is much more sanguine about deliberative democracy's ability to produce good voters than I am. Furthermore, he seems to have lower standards for competence than I do. I think good voting requires knowledge not just about what candidates want to do and are likely to be able to do but also social scientific knowledge about how their preferred policies are likely to work. I doubt a couple days of deliberation can impart that knowledge—after a semester's worth of study, most undergraduates still don't understand, say, basic microeconomics.

López-Guerra acknowledges that his competence-building process "increases the risk of manipulation and agenda control."[12] His response to this concern seems right to me. Sure, he says, in many places or cases it may be abused, and if so, that could be a reason not to do it. But we should just do comparative institutional analysis. If in some places the enfranchisement lottery (with whatever abuses it might suffer) works better than democracy (with all its problems), let's use the enfranchisement lottery.[13] If in other places, democracy works better, let's use that. In the end, López-Guerra's view is like mine: pick the least ugly pig.

UNIVERSAL SUFFRAGE WITH EPISTOCRATIC VETO

Consider instead a hybrid political system called *universal suffrage with epistocratic veto*. This system has the same political bodies and institutions we find in contemporary democracies. It has unrestricted, equal universal suffrage. All citizens have equal rights to run for office and vote. The fair value of these political liberties is guaranteed.

Yet the system also has an *epistocratic council*, a formally epistocratic deliberative body. Membership in the epistocratic council is potentially open to all members of society. Citizens may join the epistocratic council only by passing rigorous competency exams, in which they demonstrate strong background knowledge in the social sciences and political philosophy. Admission to the council may also require some sort of character check—for instance, felons or government employees (who have conflicts of interest) might be excluded. (I don't actually favor stripping felons of voting rights; I only suggest this is a possible variation.)

This epistocratic council has no power to *make law*. It cannot appoint anyone to any office, nor can it issue any decrees or regulations. It cannot instantiate any coercive regulations or rules on citizens. But it has power to *unmake law*. The epistocratic council can *thwart* others' political decisions, but cannot make new decisions itself. It can *stop* political action, but cannot initiate it. It can *veto* any (or almost any) political decisions made by the general electorate or its representatives, on the grounds that the decisions were malicious, incompetent, or unreasonable. It might be empowered, for example, to decide that the electorate chose the president out of paranoia, and then veto that decision. This would require a new election or some sort of new action from the electorate or its representatives. Just as judges in jury trials can overturn jury convictions when the judges believe the jury acted incompetently or maliciously, so an epistocratic council can overturn a democratic decision.

There are many possible ways to fill in the details, some of which will be more defensible than others. The system might have just one council, for instance, or it might have multiple councils at different levels of government. The system might have a large council with millions of members. Or it could be small, but have its members randomly drawn from all citizens who meet the competency requirement. Councils could meet regularly, or they might conduct their veto powers through some alternative means. Councils might require a simple majority or supermajority vote to overturn democratic legislation. Democratic bodies might able to overturn vetoes with supermajority decisions, or they might not.

It is possible that in universal suffrage with epistocratic veto, there will be heavy gridlock. The epistocratic council can only veto bad decisions as well as incompetently made laws and rules. It can stop incompetently made laws from coming into existence, but cannot thereby guarantee that competently made laws will come into existence. Universal suffrage with epistocratic veto allows for a cycle in which the democratic legislature continually passes laws, only to have such laws vetoed by the epistocratic council. The council cannot force the general electorate or its representatives to act competently when making laws and rules.

That said, in some cases gridlock can increase the competence of political decision making. After all, hasty decision making is one source of democratic incompetence. As Weiner has argued, following Madison, democracies often make bad decisions in the heat of the moment.[14] Gridlock slows downs decision making. It helps passions subside and cool heads prevail. As noted in chapter 2, people suffer from action bias—that is, the tendency to act even when one lacks sufficient information to act. Because of this action bias, democracies have a tendency to do too much rather than too little. Thus, gridlock can at least sometimes improve overall decision making.

Epistocrats worry that the median voter under universal suffrage is misinformed and irrational about politics. Given this, under universal suffrage the winning candidates will be those who appeal to misinformed voters. Yet universal suffrage with epistocratic veto could have all winning candidates screened by an epistocratic council. These councils could routinely veto the worst candidates. This may cause gridlock, but it may also force the general electorate to educate themselves and produce better candidates. By eliminating bad candidates from holding office, universal suffrage with epistocratic veto might produce more competently made legislation and rules. The epistocratic council might not need to oversee all day-to-day legislation, though it retains the right to veto any such legislation. There are different ways to institutionalize this system, and some will perform much better than others.

There are some ways in which universal suffrage with epistocratic veto may perform better than epistocracy with restricted suffrage. Plural voting and restricted suffrage regimes are "front-end" solutions: they try to comply with the competence principle by restricting the rights to vote and run for office. Universal suffrage with epistocratic veto can have both front- and back-end solutions. The epistocratic council could veto bad elections, but also veto bad legislation, regulations, and executive orders.

Universal suffrage with epistocratic veto may enjoy more *perceived* legitimacy than restricted suffrage or plural voting epistocracy. As uncomfortable as people might be with an epistocratic council vetoing their democratically made decisions, they would probably be even less comfortable with allowing an epistocratic council to simply make all the decisions without them. A democracy with an epistocratic council would probably be more stable over time than a full-fledged epistocracy. Lopéz-Guerra points out that "disfranchisement, if it is perceived as unfair, can become the reason for the escalation of conflict during hardship."[15] Epistocracy with restricted suffrage does not enfranchise everyone. Universal suffrage with epistocratic veto, in contrast, enfranchises everyone, but it puts a check on their power.

IS UNIVERSAL SUFFRAGE WITH EPISTOCRATIC VETO ACTUALLY DEMOCRATIC?

Universal suffrage with epistocratic veto might not technically be a form of epistocracy. It's a borderline case. I'll argue here that it's no less undemocratic than judicial review. Many democrats think judicial review is incompatible with democracy, but most do not.[16] Most democrats believe it is permissible to imbue some political body with the power to veto laws that are unconstitutional or violate citizens' basic rights. They also believe it is acceptable to have *competency* requirements to serve in courts. The US Supreme Court is a kind of epistocratic council.

Most believe that a democracy can institutionalize judicial review without thereby being transformed into a nondemocracy. Liberals often maintain that because the judiciary (or whatever body performs the judicial review function) is subject to oversight along with checks and balances from other branches of government, judicial review is both democratic and consistent with liberal legitimacy. While the judiciary can veto or thwart the power of the electorate or other branches of government, it is not completely independent. The rights that the judiciary is charged to protect may be limited to whatever rights are enshrined in a democratically approved constitution.

Given that most democrats consider judicial review to be compatible with democracy, one might hold that epistocratic veto is also compatible with democracy because it is analogous to judicial review:

1. Universal suffrage with judicial review is compatible with democracy.
2. In judicial review, a cognitively elite body is democratically authorized to veto the political decisions of other bodies, including the general electorate.
3. In universal suffrage with epistocratic veto, the epistocratic council, a cognitively elite body, could be democratically authorized to veto the political decisions of other bodies, including the general electorate.
4. Therefore, the epistocratic council and judicial review are analogous.
5. Moreover, if judicial review is compatible with democracy, so is an epistocratic council.
6. As such, an epistocratic council is compatible with democracy.

Granted, the first premise is itself controversial. There are many philosophers and political theorists who think judicial review is inherently undemocratic, and hence cannot be justified.[17] They may be right. My point here is simply that if you regard judicial review as democratic, then you might also reasonably regard epistocratic veto as democratic.

Note that the analogy argument does not assert that epistocratic veto is *justified* for the same reasons that judicial review is justified. I do not claim that philosophers' arguments in favor of judicial review also commit them to accepting epistocratic veto. The analogy argument simply contends that epistocratic veto is similar enough to judicial review that if the latter is consistent with democracy, so is the former.

Let's take a closer look at premises two and three. The power of judicial review is usually held and exercised by a court. Courts are cognitively elite deliberative bodies whose members have special qualifications. Often courts have strict educational requirements—only citizens with sufficient legal education are eligible to hold the positions. Generally, judges are not directly elected. Their qualifications are set and controlled democratically, though, and judges are frequently appointed through a representative democratic process. Courts with the power of judicial review have the power to thwart or override the decisions and power of other bodies, including the electorate. Courts are generally charged with upholding constitutional essentials, which are set democratically. They may even be charged with defending rights even if such rights are not explicitly enumerated. Finally, when courts veto the decisions of the electorate or their representatives, the electorate or their representatives can reverse the veto with a supermajority decision. (In the United States, for example, if a court decides a law is unconstitutional, a supermajority can change the Constitution, after a long amendment process.)

This is analogous to a system of universal suffrage with epistocratic veto. We can imagine that an otherwise-normal democracy creates a cognitively elite deliberative body with explicit qualifications. For instance, it may make the epistocratic council open to all citizens (with potentially hundreds of millions of members), provided they first pass a competency exam. Or it may require additional credentials, such as character references, university degrees, background checks, and the like. Members of the epistocratic council might not be directly elected, but they are subject to democratic oversight. The democracy imbues an epistocratic council with the power to thwart or override the decisions and power of other bodies, including the electorate itself. (A democracy might even enshrine the right to a competent government in a bill of rights in its constitution.) We might also imagine that the electorate or its representatives retain the power to overturn or reverse the council's veto, provided it can produce a sufficiently large supermajority.

Universal suffrage with epistocratic veto seems to capture what is desirable about epistocracy without itself being an epistocracy. It also captures much of what is desirable about democracy while providing a check against democratic irrationality and incompetence.

GOVERNMENT BY SIMULATED ORACLE

Suppose that for any issue in politics, Pythia the Oracle is wiser, better motivated, and more knowledgeable than any of us. In fact, she is wiser, better motivated, and more knowledgeable than *all* of us, collectively. No matter what voting or deliberative procedure the rest of us use, she is more reliable. So imagine we have two options:

A. We ask Pythia what to do, and then do it.
B. We deliberate or vote among ourselves about what to do, and then do it.

Pythia is not omniscient and can make mistakes. But by hypothesis, option A is superior to option B. Whenever we disagree with Pythia, she is more likely to be right. We should in general defer to her opinion. If we disagree with her, we're probably wrong. If we don't defer to Pythia—if we don't do what she says we should—then we substitute a less reliable decision procedure in place of a more reliable one. We increase the probability of arriving at harmful and unjust policies. If we persist in holding our opinions, we'd better have excellent grounds for thinking this is one of the special cases where we're right and she's wrong.

In the real world, we have no such oracle. But what if we could build one? More specifically, what if we could *simulate* this oracle?

As I mentioned in chapters 2 and 7, social scientists such as Althaus have shown that we can estimate what the electorate would prefer if only it were well informed. We can administer surveys that track citizens' political preferences and demographic characteristics, while testing their basic objective political knowledge. Once we have this information, we can simulate what would happen if the electorate's demographics remained unchanged, but all citizens were able to get perfect scores on tests of objective political knowledge. We can determine, with a strong degree of confidence, what "We the People" would want if only "We the People" understood what we are talking about.

Suppose the United States had a referendum on whether to allow significantly more immigrants into the country. Knowing whether this is a good idea requires tremendous social scientific knowledge. One needs to know how immigration tends to affect crime rates, domestic wages, immigrants' welfare, economic growth, tax revenues, welfare expenditures, and the like. Most Americans lack this knowledge; in fact, as I mentioned in chapter 6, our evidence is that they're systematically mistaken.

But we might have a referendum on this issue using the enlightened preference method. Every citizen is allowed to vote to express their political preferences. As citizens vote, we collect their anonymously coded demographic information. While expressing their opinions, they must also take a publicly approved exam on objective political knowledge, basic history, and social sciences. All these data will be made public, so that any news source or policy center can analyze it. We can then—on the basis of publicly available data and methods that any social scientist can check—simulate what the voting public would want if it were fully informed. Whatever the enlightened public says, goes.

We could use something similar for deciding elections. Suppose there is a range of candidates from various political parties. We can ask citizens to provide their anonymously coded demographic information and then take a test of basic objective political knowledge. They then rank the candidates from most to least favored. Using these data, we can determine how the public would rank the candidates if the public were fully informed. Whatever candidates ranks the highest, wins.

WHO DECIDES WHAT COUNTS AS COMPETENCE?

An epistocracy tries to apportion power according to real expertise. On almost any issue, some people are objectively more competent than others. It's not merely a matter of opinion that Albert Einstein understood physics better than the average person, that my plumber understands plumbing better than I do, or that Chong understands political psychology better than my mom does. Sure, there are hard cases, but many (or perhaps most) comparisons are easy.

Many democrats agree. Estlund asserts that "removing the right issues from democratic control and turning them over to the right experts would lead to better political decisions, and more justice and prosperity."[18] He accepts that well-run epistocracies would probably perform better than well-run democracies, and agrees that some citizens have more moral-political expertise than others.[19] Estlund even says it would be unreasonable to deny that some know more than others. It would be unreasonable to believe that all people are in fact equally competent to rule.

Of course, there's a problem here: people disagree about both who knows more than others and who the experts are. As Estlund complains, "The trick is knowing . . . which experts to rely on for which issues." He adds, "Any *particular* person or group who might be put forward as such an expert would be subject to . . . controversy."[20]

The fact that something is controversial doesn't mean that there's no truth to the matter. Nor does it mean that we don't know what the truth is. People dispute all sorts of things—evolutionary biology, microeconomics, or the Monty Hall problem—that some of us know.

The problem is that in the real world, we're going to have to put the task of deciding who counts as competent in someone's hands. That person might themselves be incompetent to decide who counts as competent, or might use this power in bad faith.

In the real world, I'd expect there to be a political battle to control what goes on any voter qualification exam. Just as congresspeople now gerrymander districts to help ensure they'll win, they might try to control the exam for their own benefit. In the United States, the Democratic Party has an incentive to make the exam easy, while the Republicans have an incentive to make the exam moderately hard, but not too hard. No doubt any such exam will be subject to abuse, just as democratic procedures are abused in the real world. The question is just how badly abused the system would be.

Imagine I'm right that the choice between democracy and epistocracy is instrumental, not procedural. If so, then the question is this: In any given society, would epistocracy, with whatever degree of abuse and government failure it would have in that society, perform better than democracy, with whatever degree of abuse and government failure it would have in that society? If the answer is "yes," then I favor epistocracy for that society. If epistocracy, warts and all, performs at all better than democracy, warts and all, than we should have epistocracy. I'm not arguing, and need not argue, that epistocracy will be wart free.

So, for instance, Estlund complains that during the Jim Crow era, governments deprived blacks of the rights to vote by requiring them to pass nearly impossible literacy tests.[21] Governments claimed these tests had an epistocratic purpose, when in fact they only had a racist purpose. These tests were administered in bad faith. They were designed to be impossible to pass, and whites were not required to take them. The fact that governments used to hide their racism beneath an epistocratic disguise does not show us that epistocratic exams are inherently objectionable. Similarly, if it turned out that medical licenses—which nominally are supposed to protect consumers from incompetent practitioners—used to be distributed in racist ways, or that medical exams used to be administered in a racist way, that would not prove that medical licensing is inherently objectionable. Instead, the question we would need to ask about any such exam is just how badly it would be abused today, and what the effects of such abuse would be.

The competence principle can be stated as a slogan. *Power: use it well or lose it.* When a government tends to be incompetent to govern certain issues, it loses any right to govern those issues. I have not argued that democracies are incompetent to decide all decisions or that all actions democratic governments undertake are incompetent. The evidence suggests that the electorate is competent at some issues and bad at others. The competence principle only forbids democratic decision making in the latter cases.

Democracies might themselves be competent to adjudicate the nature of political competence. Perhaps citizens have sufficient knowledge and rationality to choose among competing conceptions of political competence. Democratic decision making might itself be a fair and reliable way of adjudicating what counts as competence. If so, then we might use a democratic decision method to choose a legal conception of political competence, and then use that conception to decide who is allowed to vote. From the viewpoint of most democrats, this will seem like an insidious result. If the facts turn out the right way, democracies will be permitted or even required to use democratic procedures to establish a kind of epistocracy.

The average citizen could produce a *reasonable* concrete theory of competence. Most citizens have good and reasonable intuitions about political competence. The average citizen can give a reasonable account of the difference between a good and bad juror, between a well-informed and ignorant voter, between an incompetent and competent member of parliament, or between a competent and incompetent district attorney. If we asked democracy to try to operationalize the competence principle by delivering a legal definition of political competence, it would probably deliver a pretty good, reasonable answer—that is, an answer within the range of acceptable views. So if we're asking how to design a voter qualification test, why not let democracy decide?

This might seem like a strange move to make. One might object that if citizens are competent to decide what counts as competence, why aren't they thereby competent to choose good candidates for office?

The answer is that it's much easier for citizens to articulate a concrete view of political competence than to identify and vote for competent candidates. The average citizen is probably able to produce a good theory of political competence, even though they may be incompetent at applying their theory.[22] Even heavily biased and ideological voters can describe what makes a candidate good. The empirical literature on voter irrationality and ignorance does not say that voters have bad standards but rather that they are bad at *applying* their reasonable standards.[23]

There is nothing unusual about this. In parallel, almost anyone can give an excellent concrete account of what would make someone a good romantic partner. I asked my eight-year-old son what makes someone a good husband or wife, and he gave about as good an answer as I've read in any psychology journal. Despite it being easy to identify *standards* for what makes someone a good or bad partner, many of us continue to have bad relationships. We have bad relationships not because we have unreasonable beliefs about what makes someone a good partner but instead because we are bad at applying our standards to real people.

This seems to describe voters, too. Voters know senators should not be blamed for weather. Yet when voters actually vote, they tend to punish incumbents for bad weather, even though they know senators are not to blame.[24] Voters know that politicians are not to blame for international events beyond their control. Yet when voters actually vote, they actually do punish incumbents for international events beyond their control.[25] Voters know that good-looking candidates aren't thereby better candidates, but nevertheless they tend to vote for the better-looking ones.[26] Also, voters know corrupt liars should not be made president, but they often have difficulty determining which candidates are corrupt liars. Voters are more trustworthy and reliable in being asked what makes someone a good candidate than in being asked to identify actual good candidates. They are better at articulating standards than they are at applying them.

Questions about competence are easy. Questions about economic policy or foreign policy are much harder. They require specialized knowledge and at times academic training. As we saw in previous chapters, citizens make systematic mistakes on these kinds of issues. So there is good reason to hold democracy is incompetent to decide certain economic and political policies, and yet could be competent to decide what counts as competence.

There are many different democratic methods for choosing a conception of political competence. The legislature could submit a range of candidate legal conceptions of competence to a public referendum. Or citizens could form a competence council, which in turn would produce a legal definition of competence. Or the government might employ deliberative polling. That is, it could randomly select a few hundred citizens, ask them to deliberate on the nature of competence, and then produce a concrete account of political competence. Alternatively, a democracy might imitate the medieval Venetian system for selecting the doge (Venice's lifetime leader). The Venetian system alternated between using sortition (selection by lottery) and voting.[27]

THE DEMOGRAPHIC OBJECTION

As noted in chapter 2, political knowledge is not evenly dispersed among all demographic groups. Whites on average know more than blacks, people in the Northeast know more than people in the South, men know more than women, middle-aged people know more than the young or old, and high-income people know more than the poor. In general, people who are already advantaged are much better informed than the disadvantaged. Most poor black women, as of right now at least, would fail even a mild voter qualification exam.

This leads to what we might call the demographic objection to epistocracy:

Under any realistic epistocratic system, people who belong to certain already-advantaged groups are likely to acquire more power than people who belong to certain disadvantaged groups. An epistocracy is thus likely to have unfair policies that serve the interests of the advantaged rather than those of the disadvantaged.

This sounds like a strong objection. I think there's a grain of truth in it, but it's not as powerful as it appears at first glance. (Note also that López-Guerra's enfranchisement lottery avoids the objection altogether.)

First, keep in mind that even in democracies, certain groups do better than others, and governments serve some interests better than others. So the demographic objection should be understood as arguing not that real-world epistocracies will fail to be perfectly just—of course they will fail—but rather that they will be *worse* than democracies, at least in this one respect.

But that said, this objection relies on a number of questionable assumptions. It seems, for starters, to presuppose that voters will each vote for their self-interest or for those of whatever group they belong to. But as already discussed in chapter 2, that's false. Most voters vote for what they perceive to be the national common good. If only a tiny number of citizens were able to vote—say, a hundred—I'd expect them to vote in selfish ways. Yet so long as in an epistocratic system thousands or more citizens have the right to vote, the evidence indicates they will likely vote sociotropically.[28]

Second, it assumes that the disadvantaged citizens—the citizens who will have less power in an epistocratic regime—know how to vote in ways that promote their own interests. That's probably false, as mentioned in chapter 2. These voters might know what kinds of *outcomes* would serve their interests, but unless they have tremendous social scientific knowledge, they are unlikely to know how to vote for politicians or policies that will produce these favored outcomes.

One might assert that so long as many members of a group vote, politicians will produce policies that serve their interests, even if these are not the policies the groups favor, and even if the people in those groups lack the knowledge needed to evaluate whether politicians are helping or hurting them. If this contention were true, then I'd be all in favor of democracy—it would mean that democratic ignorance is basically harmless. But politicians tend to give citizens what they want as opposed to what's good for them.

If the United States were to start using a voter qualification exam right now, such as an exam that *I* got to design, I'd expect that the people who pass the exam would be disproportionately white, upper-middle- to upper-class, educated, employed males. The problem here isn't that I'm racist, sexist, or classist. My moral credentials are of course impeccable, and on implicit bias tests, I score many standard deviations lower than the average person. Instead, the problem would be that there are underlying injustices and social problems that tend to make it so that some groups are more likely to be knowledgeable than others. My view is that rather than insist everyone vote, we should *fix* those underlying injustices. Let's treat the disease, not the symptoms. As we saw in previous chapters, low- and high-information voters have systematically different policy preferences, including preferences for how to deal with these underlying injustices. In the United States, excluding the bottom 80 percent of white voters from voting might be just what poor blacks need.

ON THE CONSERVATIVE ARGUMENT FOR DEMOCRACY

Whether we should prefer epistocracy to democracy is in part an empirical question, which I am not fully able to answer. We can study how badly voters behave, and thus determine potential improvements that epistocracy could produce. But we are not sure how well any epistocratic measures would actually work. There are good reasons to think epistocracy would produce better results than democracy with universal suffrage, yet there are reasons to worry it will not.

Consider, by analogy, how weak the case was for democracy as of the mid-1790s. The French Revolution was supposed to replace what was clearly an unjust regime with a better one. In the end, the result was disaster. It led to war, mass tyranny, chaos, mass executions, and ultimately the rise of Napoleon. Although Louis XVI's reign was unjust and ineffective, the French might have done better putting up with it than trying to replace it with something better.

English politician Edmund Burke wrote a famous set of letters reflecting on what went wrong. He worried that people are imperfect, and there are limits on how much justice we can hope to achieve. He complained that human beings aren't smart enough to remake society from scratch. Burke thought that the failures of the French Revolution showed us that many institutions and practices that seem unjust on philosophical reflection turn out to serve useful purpose. This purpose is obscured to us, and we don't discover it until we've destroyed the institutions. By then it's too late. Society and civilization are fragile. Society is held together not by reason but rather by irrational beliefs and superstitions, including irrational beliefs in authority and patriotism.

These kinds of ideas are now often called *Burkean conservativism*. The basic thought is that we must be extremely cautious when making radical changes to existing institutions. Society is complex—more complex than our simple theories can handle—and our attempts to fix things frequently have deleterious unintended consequences. There is a presumption in favor of preexisting social institutions. These institutions may seem unjust, but they at least have a history of working as well as they do. Moreover, existing legal and political institutions have evolved over generations—they have, in effect, adapted. Just as we should be wary of interfering with an ecosystem, the Burkean conservative thinks we should be wary of replacing existing political systems. Experimentation with new forms of government is dangerous.

Burke's concerns about the French Revolution seem sound. A reasonable person in late 1793 might conclude that replacing monarchy with some form of democratic republic is a bad idea. Former British colonists living in the new United States were not in any obvious way better off than they had been under British rule, and the French republic was a nightmare. That said, in the more than two hundred years since, we've replaced most monarchies with democracies, and overall it's been for the better. A similar point might apply to epistocracy. Or it might not.

Burke was worried about remaking society from the ground up, all at once. He was not against attempting small improvements here and there. He would tend to favor small-scale experiments.

Since we are unsure of the consequences, but have reason to expect them to be positive, we might *experiment* with voter examination systems on a relatively small scale at first. For instance, perhaps it would be best if one state in the United States tried the system first. We would want to start with a relatively noncorrupt state, such as New Hampshire, versus a corrupt state, such as Louisiana. If the experiment succeeds, then the rules could be scaled up.

Similarly, remember that few hundred years ago, we had little experience with democracy. Some advocated democracy in part because they believed it would tend to produce better and more just outcomes than monarchy. Others worried that democracies would be even more corrupt or would collapse into chaos. In light of their lack of experience, a democrat might reasonably have argued in favor of experimenting with democracy on a relatively small scale, and then scaling up only if the experiment succeeded.

Democracy, as we practice it, is unjust. We expose innocent people to high degrees of risk because we put their fate in the hands of ignorant, misinformed, irrational, biased, and sometimes immoral decision makers. Epistocracy might be able to fix this problem. If epistocracy works better, we should go with epistocracy instead.

But epistocracy might not work better. Or it might be that trying to transition to epistocracy is too costly or dangerous—we can't get there from here. In the end, then, the best argument for democracy is Burkean conservativism. Democracy is not a *fully just* social system, but it's too risky and dangerous to attempt to replace it with something else.[29]

Burkean conservativism tells us to be careful, but we also have to be careful with Burkean conservativism. Burkean conservativism warns us that attempts to make things better might make things worse. It's true that the world is complicated and our experiments may blow up in our faces. But we can repeat this line of reasoning for *any* proposed change.

CHAPTER 9

CIVIC ENEMIES

Most of my fellow citizens and most people across the world are mere strangers. I might not care much about them as individuals. But when I reflect on the role they play in civil society or the market economy, I realize that I am made better off because of them. The typical person worldwide, in their role in civil society or the market, has a small effect on my life, but that effect is positive. I am better off with that person than without them.

Unfortunately, politics tends to change that. Politics threatens an ideal of mutual respect and regard.

POLITICS MAKES US VIEW EACH OTHER AS ENEMIES

Political philosophers sometimes describe politics as a sphere of co-operative friendship.[1] Philosophers sometimes imagine political discourse to be like an idealized philosophy debate: "Come, let us calculate together what justice requires! . . . Ah yes, I concede that you have the better argument. Thank you for curing me of error. Let us do things your way!" Real-world politics is hardly ever like that. (Neither are philosophy debates.) Politics tends to make us hate each other, even when it shouldn't. We tend to divide the world into good and bad guys. We tend to view political debate not as reasonable disputes about how to best achieve our shared aims but rather as a battle between the forces of light and darkness.

It's especially bizarre that mainstream political discussion is so heated and apocalyptic, given how *little* is at stake. Republicans and Democrats disagree about many things, but in the logical space of possible political views they're not merely in the same solar system but also on the same planet. They're not debating deep existential questions about justice but instead surface disputes about the exact shape of the society they mutually accept. They've both agreed to buy the Camry; they're now just debating whether to get the sport package or hybrid.

Their disputes are tiny. Should we raise the top marginal income tax by 3 percentage points? Should we keep the minimum wage where it is or raise it by three dollars per hour? Should we pay $1 trillion a year for education or $1.2 trillion? Should employers be required to pay for birth control, or should women who work for closely held family corporations with fundamentalist owners have to pay ten to fifty dollars a month from their own pockets?

Our political tribalism spills over and corrupts our behavior outside politics. Consider research to that end by political scientists Shanto Iyengar and Sean Westwood. Iyengar and Westwood wanted to determine how much, if at all, political bias affects how people evaluate *job* candidates. They conducted an experiment in which they asked over a thousand subjects to evaluate what the subjects were told were the résumés of graduating high school students. Iyengar and Westwood carefully crafted two basic résumés, one of which was clearly more impressive than the other. They randomly labeled the job candidates as Republican or Democrat, and randomly made the candidates stronger or weaker. At the same time, they determined whether the subjects— the people evaluating the candidates—were strong or weak Republicans, independents, or strong or weak Democrats.

With this experiment, Iyengar and Westwood could answer questions such as: How much more strongly, if at all, would a Republican evaluator favor a Republican job candidate over an equally qualified Democratic job candidate? Or if a Democratic evaluator had to choose between a less qualified Democrat and a more qualified Republican, which would they prefer? Remember, subjects are not picking *political* candidates. They aren't voting. They are just being asked which candidate would be better for a private sector job.

The results are depressing: 80.4 percent of Democratic subjects picked the Democratic job candidate, while 69.2 percent of Republican subjects picked the Republican job candidate. Even when the Republican job candidate was clearly stronger, Democrats still chose the Democratic candidate 70 percent of the time. In contrast, they found that "candidate qualification had no significant effect on winner section."[2] In other words, the evaluators didn't care about how qualified the candidates were; they only cared about what the job candidates' politics were.

This is irresponsible, corrupt behavior. But it's just the kind of behavior one would expect of hooligans. Politics makes us worse.

Why are evaluators so blatantly prejudiced? Perhaps it has to do with trust. Experimental economists use what's called the trust game to test what factors influence people's willingness to trust and reciprocate with others. In the beginning of the game, the experimenter gives the first player, called the giver, ten dollars. The giver has the option of keeping all the money for themselves or they may give as much as they please to a second player, the receiver. Whatever amount the giver gives is multiplied by three, so that if the giver gives five dollars, the receiver receives fifteen dollars. The receiver may keep all this money for themselves or they may return as much of the money as they like to the giver. If two perfectly trusting and trustworthy players were playing together, the giver would give all ten dollars to the receiver, and the receiver would return half (fifteen dollars) to the giver.

Iyengar and Westwood found that differences in political affiliation reduce mutual trust in the trust game. In one experiment, they found that Democratic givers give Republican receivers about 13 percent less than they give Democratic receivers. Republican givers give Democratic receivers about 5 percent less than they give Republican receivers. These might seem like small amounts, but in the same experiment Iyengar and Westwood saw *no* effect of racial differences on trust: whites and blacks were no less trusting of people from the other race than of people from their own race.[3] So you can read their experiment as evidence that politics is *more* divisive than race, and that we are less willing or able to suppress the mutual disdain that results from political disagreements than we are willing or able to suppress our racial biases.

If these effect sizes seem small, remember that these games are designed to *punish* players for their prejudices. Players actually have something at stake here. If the giver underestimates the receiver's trustworthiness, they make less money for themselves. Thus, we should expect people in such games to be *less* prejudiced than they are in real life.

In contrast, the voting booth and democratic forum fail to punish voters for indulging such biases. Since individual votes don't matter and *hating other people is fun*, voters have every incentive to vote in ways that express their tribal biases.[4] In the trust game, if I underestimate the trustworthiness of Republicans, I lose money. In the voting booth, I can indulge the bigoted fantasy that, say, the Republicans oppose legalized abortion because they hate women, or that Democrats want to allow flag burning because they hate the United States.

In a recent commentary on this research, legal theorist Cass Sunstein notes that in 1960, only about 4 to 5 percent of Republicans and Democrats said they would be "displeased" if their children married members of the opposite party. Now, about 49 percent of Republicans and 33 percent of Democrats admit they would be displeased.[5] Sunstein says that explicit "partyism"—prejudice against people from a different political party—is now more common than explicit racism. In fact, it appears that "implicit" partyism is stronger than implicit racism, too.[6] (Part of this, presumably, results from the parties being more polarized now than in the past.)

Findings like these are upsetting. At least some people have honest, good faith disputes about how to realize shared moral values, or just what morality and justice require. We should be able to maintain such disputes without seeing each other as enemies. Sure, some moral disagreements are beyond the pale. If someone advocates the genocidal slaughter of Jews, fine, they're not a good person. But disagreements on whether the minimum wage does more harm than good are not grounds for mutual mistrust.

We are biased to see political disputants as stupid and evil rather than simply having a reasonable disagreement. All things considered, that counts in favor of disengaging with politics. If we want people to see our fellow citizens as friends, as engaged in a cooperative venture for mutual gain, as opposed to enemies, we want them to avoid politics as much as possible.

TWO WAYS POLITICS MAKES US GENUINE ENEMIES

The problem with politics is even deeper than that. It's not merely that politics makes us see each other as enemies when it shouldn't. Rather, politics tends to put us in genuinely adversarial relationships. It makes us genuine enemies with one another. The structure of democratic politics actually gives me reason to despise most of my politically active fellow citizens—even, I'll argue, most of the citizens who *share* my political beliefs. On Election Day, as my neighbors vote, they become my enemies, and I become theirs.

On one common definition, an enemy is a person who hates me, who consciously wishes me ill and consciously works toward my harm. Only a minority of people who participate in politics qualify as my enemy in this sense. As we saw in chapter 2, most voters vote for what they perceive to be the national interest. They genuinely want to help, and sincerely believe they're voting in ways that make things better, not worse, for their fellow citizens. Voters' motives seem pure and good. A few of my fellow citizens want to use the political process to harm me or people like me. But most don't think that way. They might dislike me for having views contrary to theirs, but they don't vote in ways that they believe will hurt me.

Yet there are two other senses in which politics makes us enemies. First, politics tends to make us what I will call *situational enemies*. Politics is a zero-sum game with winners and losers. It creates adversarial relationships in which we have grounds to oppose one another and undermine each other's interests, though we have no intrinsic reason to dislike one another. Second, there's a sense in which most of my fellow citizens do want to hurt me, even if they wouldn't describe themselves as having that desire. They want to do things that will in fact harm my children and me, even though they want to help. Political decisions are high stakes, but in the real world, most people involved in politics fail to make these decisions with a proper degree of care and competence. They expose me to undue risk of harm. Just as I have grounds for hating a negligent drunk driver who puts my children and me in harm's way, I have grounds for hating most of my fellow citizens whenever they engage in politics. Or so I will argue.

SITUATIONAL ENEMIES

There are scenarios in which we become each other's enemies, even though we have no intrinsic reason to dislike one another.

Consider philosopher Thomas Hobbes's "state of nature," as described in *Leviathan*. The state of nature is a hypothetical scenario in which human beings live outside society and civilization. Hobbes argues that because people in the state of nature lack any mechanisms to enforce contracts or keep predators in check, they would not trust each other. He holds that without even a basic level of mutual trust, the state of nature would become a war of all against all. Life under these conditions, he concludes, would be "solitary, poor, nasty, brutish, and short."[7] In the state of nature, Hobbes thinks, we become each other's enemies, although in better situations we would be at peace or even be friends.

Or imagine you and I are both condemned criminals in ancient Rome. Neither one of us has done anything morally wrong. Instead, imagine we've been condemned for things that shouldn't be crimes: you refused to worship Jupiter, while I helped slaves escape their masters. The barbaric Romans, ever thirsty for blood, make us fight to the death in a gladiatorial arena.

As we pick up our cudgels, we become enemies. I have nothing inherently against you. Outside the arena, I might even like you, or be your friend or partner. But inside the arena, we're forced into conflict. It's you or me. We want each other dead. You become (what we might call) my situational enemy: someone I have reason to oppose and attack not because of who you are or what you've done but simply because our situation pits us against each other.

The problem in each of these scenarios is that we're trapped in an involuntary, high-stakes, zero-sum game. In economics, a zero-sum game is a situation or interaction in which a person can win only if other people lose, and a person can win only to the degree that others lose.

Poker, for example, is a common zero-sum game. I can make only as much money as the other players at the table lose. But poker is a far nicer zero-sum game than politics. Whenever I've played poker, I've played as a volunteer, not a conscript. I don't resent the other players, even when I lose money, because I *chose* to gamble.

With political decisions, I'm a conscript, not a volunteer. While I can choose not to play poker, I can't, say, choose not to fund the National Security Agency, the invasion of Iraq, the bombing of Syria, or the criminalization of pot. I don't want whoever the current president is when you read this to be my boss, but I can't just choose not to have them as my boss, at least not without uprooting my family and fleeing the country at great personal expense.

In the next few sections, I argue that the following features of the democratic political decision-making process tend to make us situational enemies:

- Political decisions involve a *constrained set of options*. In politics, there are usually only a handful of viable choices.
- Political decisions are *monopolistic*: everyone has to accept the same decision.
- Political decisions are imposed *involuntarily* through violence.

Because political decisions are constrained, monopolistic, and imposed through violence, the political decision-making process tends to be a system of conflict.

POLITICAL OPTIONS ARE CONSTRAINED AND MONOPOLISTIC

Suppose you're in the market for a new sedan. In the United States, you have more than three hundred new models to choose from, with prices ranging from under twelve thousand dollars to well over four hundred thousand. People who want a sedan don't all want the same thing. Power and handling are important to me, but not to my twin brother. He just wants the cheapest way to get from A to B.

So what's the best sedan? There's no real answer; there are only better and worse sedans for different people. For one person, a BMW 3-series will be best. For another, the Mazda 3 might be best. Even the miserable Nissan Versa might be best for some people. While for any one of us there might be a uniquely best sedan, there's no best sedan for *all* of us.

What if instead of asking what the best sedan is, we ask what the best society is, what the best institutions and laws are, and who the best leaders would be? Is there some reason to think that there is a uniquely best answer for all people to these questions?

When you cast a ballot, you don't get three hundred choices the way you get three hundred choices for a family sedan. In most democracies, you get a handful. In the United States, you get two. (This is not an accidental feature of US politics. Rather, our type of voting system renders third parties unviable.)[8]

The problem isn't just that the choices are constrained; they aren't good. As I discussed over the previous chapters, not everything or even most of what democratic governments do is a straightforward result of the electorate's collective preferences. The electorate nevertheless does get to choose winners in an election. Furthermore, the quality of the candidates on the ballot depends in significant part on the quality of the electorate, and since, as we saw especially in previous chapters, the electorate is of low quality, we should expect democracies to deliver us poor-quality candidates.[9] There's little reason to think that in any major election, democratic communities somehow determine, before the election takes place, who the two or three best candidates are, and then pick the best from this elite set. Instead, as we saw in previous chapters, if the electorate were better informed, it would have different policy preferences and so would likely prefer different candidates.

On the day I wrote the first draft of this sentence, the best-selling album in the United States was Sia's *1000 Forms of Fear*. I find Sia's music simplistic and irritating. I much prefer the progressive metal band Opeth. But Sia's popularity doesn't make my life any better or worse. I can simply decide not to listen to her music. In fact, I'd never heard of Sia and hadn't heard any of her music until I wrote this paragraph. I had to look up the best seller on Billboard 200 and then listen to her on iTunes to form an opinion.

Or consider this: Pizza Hut is the most popular pizza chain in the United States. I think their pizza is yucky. I'm not a food snob, but I much prefer the wood-fired Neapolitan pizzas at Pizzeria Orso. Yet it makes little difference to me that Pizza Hut is popular.[10] I never have to eat there again.

Imagine instead that we put decisions to a democratic vote about what to eat or listen to. Suppose we had to choose one pizza maker or one music performer for everyone. It will be Domino's versus Pizza Hut—Pizzeria Orso is out. It will be Justin Bieber versus Sia—Opeth is out. If we turned these market decisions into political decisions, we would probably decide that everyone must eat Pizza Hut and listen to Sia.

Political commentators Aaron Ross Powell and Trevor Burrus explain why all this produces conflict:

> Politics takes a continuum of possibilities and turns it into a small group of discrete outcomes, often just two. Either this guy gets elected, or that guy does. Either a given policy becomes law or it doesn't. As a result, political choices matter greatly to those most affected. An electoral loss is the loss of a possibility. These black and white choices mean politics will often manufacture problems that previously didn't exist, such as the "problem" of whether we—as a community, as a nation—will teach children creation or evolution.[11]

On this point, philosophers David Schmidtz and Christopher Freiman add:

> The fewer issues subject to political oversight, the less urgent the need for consensus on contentious questions. For example, selecting a "one-size-fits-all" car model is not currently a source of political conflict. Individuals browse a wide variety of cars and buy whatever best suits their needs and budget. No particular car needs to suit every member of the community. Polities do not put the question of the right car or the right shoe size to a popular vote and enforce the majority decision. In conditions of pluralism, we similarly eschew one-size-fits-all solutions to divisive political problems concerning religion, education, medicine, and so on. . . . By contrast, when issues fall within the purview of

politics—even democratic politics—minorities risk finding themselves marginalized.[12]

Political choices are constrained. While there are many possible options, in any decision only a few options are on the table. Political decisions are also monopolistic. After the decision, there will be only one option left, which everyone must accept.

Outside politics, it usually makes little difference that you have different tastes than I do. I can tolerate your different preferences or even in some cases celebrate them, because your preferences impose little cost on me. But once we make decisions political, your different preferences become a source of genuine conflict. For you to get your way is for you to stop me from getting mine.

POLITICAL DECISIONS ARE IMPOSED INVOLUNTARILY, THROUGH VIOLENCE

The problem with political decisions isn't merely that most of us don't get our own way. It's also that these decisions are usually imposed on us, against our will, by threats of violence.

Governments do not merely advise us to follow their rules, hoping that we'll comply out of the goodness of our hearts. They enforce their laws and rules with violence, or threats of violence.

I'll illustrate this point by modifying an example from Huemer. Imagine you get a hundred-dollar ticket for failing to wear a helmet while riding your motorcycle.[13] When the government issues you a ticket, it commands you to pay it a hundred dollars. If you don't immediately pay the ticket, it responds by issuing even more commands. It will send you an angry letter and command you to pay it even more money. If you still ignore its command, it will revoke your license, which means that it commands you not to drive. But now suppose you ignore these commands and continue to drive. Eventually, the government will arrest and imprison you. When it tries to arrest you, if you do not heed its command to submit, its agents will physically assault, beat, and kill you, if necessary.

For someone to say, "There ought to be law requiring X" is, in effect, to say, "I want to threaten people with violence unless they do X." A political battle is a battle over who will acquire the power to force the other side to bend to its will. To say, "Employers should have to pay for their employees' contraception" is to say, "I advocate using violence against employers who don't pay for their employee's contraception." To say, "Cocaine should be illegal" is to say, "I advocate using violence against people who snort cocaine." To say, "Restaurateurs should be required by law to post nutrition facts on their menus" is to say, "I advocate using violence against restaurateurs who fail to post nutrition facts on their menus." To say, "Flag burning should be illegal" is to say, "I advocate using violence against people who burn flags." Perhaps some of this violence is justified—I haven't argued that it's not. My point here is that just that political decisions are enforced through institutionalized violence.[14]

ALL AGAINST ALL

In reviewing the findings of political psychology, we see that people tend to dislike each other over mere political disagreements. Even in the context of a philosophy seminar, if half the students start arguing for classical liberalism while the other half advocate communitarianism, there's a good chance that ten years later, the classical liberals will be closer friends with each other than with the communitarians, and vice versa.

There's a world of difference between merely having different political opinions and acting on them. Once groups of people leave their homes and schools, and instead start donating, campaigning, picketing, or voting, their collective political attitudes and behaviors begin to make a real difference. They aren't just *advocating* different views; they're working to *impose* their views on others who disagree.

Political decisions lead to real conflict. When we make collective political decisions, we tend to have only a few options to decide among. After the decision, we are stuck with one option, and that option is enforced with violence. Politics puts us in something uncomfortably like a gladiatorial situation. If you're on the other team, you're quite literally trying to force me to bend to your will. For that reason, I have grounds to dislike you. Perhaps it's not your fault that we're in this conflict, but we are nevertheless in conflict. As soon as you pick up the cudgel, I'm reaching for mine.

Those who favor expansive politics will respond, "Sure, political decisions have these features. But instead of saying this makes us genuine situational enemies, why not say it creates situations in which we need to compromise?"

There may be a core set of problems about which people have to make collective decisions. I won't try to articulate a theory here of just what goes in that set. Instead, I simply respond by saying that this set almost surely is smaller than the things we actually submit to collective control. My friends on both the Left and Right agree, for I frequently see them complain that people on the other side are treating as a political matter something that shouldn't be the purview of politics at all. We all seem to agree the scope of actual politics is often larger than the sphere of necessary politics.

A TOAST TO THE DEATH OF THE INCOMPETENT KING

There's yet another way democracy makes us enemies. In previous chapters, I examined at great length much of the empirical research on the political brain. I showed that most democratic citizens are hobbits and hooligans. Most hobbits are potential hooligans. Most voters are not merely ignorant but also are misinformed and irrational. Ignorance and irrationality are resilient. People resist attempts to reach consensus or learn more. They dig in their heels. Attempts to eradicate ignorance and irrational frequently make these problems even worse. Political participation, including democratic deliberation, is more likely to corrupt and stultify than to ennoble and enlighten us.

These hobbits and hooligans wield political power over me. It turns out they have altruistic intentions when they wield this power. At the same time, they wield that power in a highly incompetent way. This, I argue, gives me some reason to hate them, to regard them as my enemies and I as theirs.

To see why, recall the story of King Carl the Incompetent from chapter 6. Carl wants to make his subjects' lives go better. But he doesn't take proper care to know what he's doing. He doesn't have the information he needs, and doesn't reason in a reliable way about what little information he has.

Carl means well, but he's dangerous. The following hold true of him:

- While he doesn't desire to hurt his subjects *under that description*, he often desires to do things that will in fact hurt them.
- While he doesn't desire to impose undue risk on his subjects *under that description*, he frequently desires to act in ways that in fact impose undue risk.
- Carl has ample evidence that he is incompetent, but he doesn't pay much attention to that evidence, nor does he process the evidence that he is incompetent in a rational way. Accordingly, he doesn't take any steps to reduce his incompetence or protect his subjects from it.

In light of the above, Carl's subjects have good reason to despise him. Almost every time Carl makes a decision, he imposes serious risk of harm on his subjects. If the subjects are lucky, Carl will pick a decent or good policy. But even then, Carl doesn't know what he's doing. When he makes a good decision, it's by accident. If the subjects are unlucky, Carl causes serious harm. He wields an incredible amount of power in an irresponsible way.

I wouldn't be surprised to hear Carl's subjects raise a glass at the pub and wish for the king's early death. They might feel a bit bad about that. After all, Carl genuinely means well. Still, the subjects are right to see him as a threat to their and their children's well-being.

In modern democracies, rather than having a one-headed incompetent king, we have a many-headed incompetent king. In a democracy, the incompetent, irresponsible ruler isn't some bearded fellow in a castle but rather almost everyone else I see. If Carl's irresponsible behavior gives his subjects grounds to hate him, I some have reason to hate my fellow citizens as well.

Few voters consciously think, "I really hope this politician will hurt others." There's an important sense, however, in which most politically active citizens do desire to harm or impose unjustified risk of harm on their fellow citizens.

To illustrate this, consider the character Betty Benevolence, whom I first introduced in *The Ethics of Voting*. Betty Benevolence has an overwhelming desire to help other people. Yet she has mistaken beliefs about what actually helps other people. She always tries to help them by doing something that in fact harms them. So, for instance, if she sees a drowning child, she'll throw water at its face. If she sees a sick man, she injects him with smallpox. If she sees someone in pain, she kicks their shins.[15] She sees herself as desiring to help people, but at the same time, desires to do things that will in actuality hurt them. There's a sense in which Betty wants to hurt people, although she wouldn't describe herself as having that desire.[16]

Or suppose Sammy the Surgeon genuinely wishes to help his patients. But suppose Sammy has an unreliable method for deciding how to help. Whenever a patient complains of an ailment, Sammy throws a dart at an anatomy chart. He then recommends to his patients that they let him remove whatever body organ or part he struck with the dart. Sammy sincerely believes that his dart-throwing method of medicine reliably selects the best treatment for his patients' ailments. Here, Sammy desires to help people, yet at the same time, he desires to do things that will in fact expose them to undue risk of harm. There's a sense in which Sammy wants to expose his patients to undue risk, although he wouldn't describe himself as having that desire.[17]

The voting public is composed mostly of hooligans, people who act like Carl, Betty, or Sammy. These three don't consider themselves my enemies, but they desire to do things that will in actuality harm me or put me at great risk of harm. Their behavior gives me some reason to hate them or wish them ill, although there is nothing but love in their hearts.

I don't want to overstate this. Suppose Carl is incompetent, but has many competent ministers, who get away with making relatively smart decisions behind Carl's back. In that case, Carl's subjects would have grounds to hate him a little less. Similarly, as discussed in chapter 7, government agents in modern democracies often act better than we might expect, as they get away with doing things the incompetent electorate would not support. In that case, I have weaker grounds for despising my fellow voters than I otherwise would.

In civil society, most of my fellow citizens are my civic friends, part of a great cooperative scheme. One of the repugnant features of democracy is that it transforms these people into threats to my well-being. My fellow citizens exercise power over me in risky and incompetent ways. This makes them my civic enemies.

NOTES

CHAPTER 1

Hobbits and Hooligans

1. Letter from John Adams to Abigail Adams, May 12, 1780, https://www.masshist.org/digitaladams/archive/doc?id=L17800512jasecond (accessed January 20, 2016). Spelling modified to contemporary English.

2. Schumpeter 1996, 262.

3. For an argument that if people were perfectly just, they would dispense with politics and instead live under a form of cooperative anarchism, see Brennan 2014.

4. For an excellent defense of this view, see Conly 2012.

5. Of course, sometimes our rights of speech do give us a kind of power over others, which is why some philosophers question whether there might be limits on free speech, such as hate speech. I take no stance on this question here.

6. Christiano 1996, 2008.

7. Estlund 2007.

8. González-Ricoy 2012, 50.

9. For a more comprehensive summary and critique of the different kinds of pure proceduralist theories, however, see Estlund 2007, chapters 2–5. Estlund notes that the most plausible form of pure proceduralism contends that democracy is inherently just simply because it is fair. Yet he argues that flipping a coin and rolling dice are equally fair, and so the pure proceduralist has no particularly good grounds for advocating democracy.

10. This is a summary of Estlund 2007.

11. The contrast here is not the same thing as that between consequentialism and deontology. Consequentialist moral theories maintain that what makes actions right and wrong is entirely a matter of the consequences of those actions. Deontological moral theories hold that what makes actions right or wrong is not entirely

determined by those actions; some actions might be intrinsically right or wrong. An instrumentalist about democracy could accept either a consequentialist or deontological theory of justice. The instrumentalist is only committed to the claim that democracy is not intrinsically just.

12. Estlund (2003) coined this term.

13. For a lengthy defense of this, see López-Guerra 2014.

14. Estlund 2007, 30.

15. Strictly speaking, it might be that excluding people for the wrong reasons was not the injustice but rather that *including* people for the wrong reasons was the problem. Perhaps the problem wasn't that the belief that being black disqualified you from voting but that being white qualified you.

16. Somin 2013.

CHAPTER 2

Ignorant, Irrational, Misinformed Nationalists

1. Of course, part of the reason they're less than perfect is because they have insurance. As economist Gordon Tullock joked, the optimal safety device for cars—the device that might do the best to reduce accidents—would be to put a six-inch spike on the steering wheel of every vehicle.

2. Converse 1990, 372.

3. Somin 2013, 17.

4. Ibid., 17–37 (emphasis added).

5. Bartels 1996, 194.

6. Friedman 2006, v.

7. Cited in Converse 1990, 3.

8. Hardin 2009, 60.

9. Somin 2013, 17–21.

10. Somin 2004, 3–4.

11. Somin 2013, 22.

12. "Americans Stumble on Math of Big Issues," *Wall Street Journal*, January 7, 2012.

13. Page and Shapiro 1992, 10.

14. *PR Newswire*, "Newsweek Polls Americans on Their Knowledge of Being American; 38 Percent Failed," http://www.prnewswire.com/news-releases/newsweek-polls-americans-on-their-knowledge-of-being-american-38-percent-failed-118366914.html (accessed December 31, 2015).

15. Somin 2013, 29.

16. *Newsweek* staff, "Take the Quiz: What We Don't Know," http://www.newsweek.com/take-quiz-what-we-dont-know-66047 (accessed December 31, 2015).

17. Somin 2013, 31.

18. Ibid., 32.

19. See, for example, Althaus 2003, 11.

20. Pew Research Center, "What Voters Know about Campaign 2012," http://www
.people-press.org/2012/08/10/what-voters-know-about-campaign-2012/#knowledge
-differences-between-voters-and-non-voters (accessed December 31, 2015).

21. Somin 2013, 42.

22. Ibid., 92.

23. Caplan 2007, 5.

24. Juan DeJesus, "1 in 4 Americans Don't Know Who We Fought for Independence," http://www.nbcnewyork.com/news/local/Mari-97694414.html (accessed
January 1, 2016).

25. Caplan 2007.

26. Zogby Analytics, poll, July 21–27, 2006.

27. Somin 2013, 102.

28. Ibid., 19.

29. Caplan et al. 2013.

30. Ibid.; Healy and Malholtra 2010.

31. Somin 2013, 18–21.

32. Ibid., 20.

33. "Ask a Librarian," http://asklib.hcl.harvard.edu/a.php?qid=137327 (accessed January 1, 2016).

34. Some might object that a vote can influence a politician's mandate, but political scientists are skeptical such mandates exist. See Mackie 2009. Alexander Guerrero (2010) argues that an individual vote has the possibility of changing the *kind* of normative authority a representative has. Without getting too much into Guerrero's theory, the problem is that Guerrero still never shows us individual votes matter. If he thinks there is some threshold number or percentage of votes at which a representative's normative authority changes, then, as with breaking a tie, the probability that an individual vote will decisively pass that threshold is vanishingly small, and so even on Guerrero's account, an individual vote should be considered of vanishingly small value. On the other hand, if Guerrero believes that normative authority changes marginally, a little bit with each vote, he needs to show us that the marginal benefits exceed the marginal costs. He does not. Accordingly, Guerrero's defense of the rationality of voting fails.

35. See Brennan and Lomasky 2003, 56–57, 119.

36. Ibid.; Landsburg 2004.

37. See Gelman, Silver, and Edlin 2012.

38. Althaus 2003, 11–12.

39. Ibid., 11.

40. Ibid.

41. Ibid., 16; Delli Carpini and Keeter 1996, 135–77. For example, less than 40 percent of all blacks can identify which political party was more conservative, but the majority of whites can (Delli Carpini and Keeter 1996, 166). On the 1988 survey,

high-income older men get average scores that are nearly three times as high as the average score of low-income black women (ibid., 162). See also Delli Carpini and Keeter 1991; Neuman 1986; Palfrey and Poole 1987; Althaus 1998.

42. Gilens 2012, 106–11.

43. Althaus 2003, 129; Caplan 2007. Both Althaus and Caplan correct for the influence of demographic factors.

44. Mackie 2009, 8.

45. Murray 2012.

46. Somin 2013, 83.

47. Lodge and Taber 2013, 169.

48. Huddy, Sears, and Levy 2013, 11.

49. Jonathan Haidt, "The New Science of Morality." *Edge*, http://www.edge.org /3rd_culture/morality10/morality.haidt.html (accessed January 2, 2016). Haidt is summarizing research (which he endorses) by Mercier and Sperber.

50. Westen et al. 2006; Westen 2008.

51. Haidt 2012; Westen et al. 2006; Westen 2008.

52. Tajfel 1981, 1982; Tajfel and Turner 1979.

53. Chong 2013, 111–12, citing Cohen 2003.

54. See, for example, Taber and Young 2013, 530; Lodge and Taber 2013, 149–69.

55. Somin 2013, 78–79.

56. Ibid., 79.

57. Noel 2010, 12–13.

58. See Mutz 2006, 128.

59. Ibid., 120.

60. Ibid., 92, 110, 112–13.

61. Ibid., 30. The more people join voluntary associations, the less they engage in cross-cutting discussions. What demographic factors best predict that one will engage in cross-cutting political dialogue? Apparently, being nonwhite, poor, and uneducated. The reason for this is that white, rich, educated people have more control over the kinds of interactions they have with others. People generally do not enjoy having cross-cutting political discussions. They enjoy agreement. So those with the most control over their lives choose not to engage in cross-cutting conversations. See ibid., 27, 31, 46–47.

62. Althaus 2003, 9–14.

63. Lord, Ross, and Lepper 1979; Taber and Lodge 2006.

64. Nyhan and Reifler 2010; Bullock 2006; Amanda Marcotte, "According to a New Study, Nothing Can Change an Anti-Vaxxer's Mind, http://www.slate.com /blogs/xx_factor/2014/03/03/effective_messages_in_vaccine_promotion_when_it _comes_to_anti_vaxxers_there.html (accessed January 2, 2016).

65. Kahan et al. 2013.

66. Train, "Calling All Angels," *My Private Nation*, Columbia Records, 2003.

67. Tversky and Kahneman 1973.

68. Costs of War Project, Watson Institute for International and Public Affairs, http://watson.brown.edu/research/projects/costs_of_war (accessed January 2, 2016).

69. Mueller and Stewart 2011.

70. Krause 2013.

71. Erisen, Lodge, and Taber 2014; Taber and Lodge 2006.

72. Taken from Kahneman 2003, 1458.

73. For a thorough overview of the literature and discussion of the impact this has on democracy, see Kelly 2012.

74. Asch 1952, 457–58; Asch 1955, 37.

75. Berns et al. 2005.

76. Subjects (in ibid.) were given a mental rotation task: determining whether two objects on a computer screen were different, or merely the same object rotated in space. The baseline error rate was a mean 13.8 percent. The error rates in the presence of wrong information given by a group of confederates and by a computer were 41 and 32 percent, respectively (ibid., 248). When asked why they went along with the group, 82.8 percent said that on some trials they were sure they were right, and serendipitously, so was the group; 58.6 percent said that on some trials they were not sure but decided to go with the group; and 3.4 percent said they were sure they were right but nonetheless decided to go with the group. The presence of external information was shown to decrease activity in the occipital and parietal parts of the brain, known to govern perceptual tasks. The authors say, "It was striking that the effects of social conformity were detected only in the most posterior aspects—the occipital and parietal lobes" (ibid., 251). "The lack of concomitant activity changes in more frontal areas was highly suggestive of a process based, at least partially, in perception. Of course, changes in frontal activity could have occurred below our detection threshold, but with 32 participants, we think this unlikely" (ibid.).

77. Presumably there is a major evolutionary advantage to being able to track the truth, without distortion. But presumably there is also a major evolutionary advantage to being able to "go along to get along."

78. Caplan 2007.

79. Chong 2013, 101; Funk 2000; Funk and Garcia-Monet 1997; Miller 1999; Mutz and Mondak 1997; Feddersen, Gailmard, and Sandroni 2009; Brennan and Lomasky 2003, 108–14; Green and Shapiro 1994; Markus 1988; Conover, Feldman, and Knight 1987; Kinder and Kiewiet 1979; Huddy, Jones, and Chard 2001; Rhodebeck 1993; Ponza et al. 1988; Sears and Funk 1990; Caplan 1997; Holbrook and Garand 1996; Mutz 1992; Mutz 1993; Mansbridge 1993; Citrin and Green 1990; Sears et al. 1980; Sears and Lau 1983; Sears, Hensler, and Speer 1979.

80. Cited in Kinder 2006, 199.

81. Jennings 1992; Converse and Pierce 1996; Zaller 1992.

82. Jeffrey M. Jones, "In U.S., New Record 43% Are Political Independents," Gallup, January 7, http://www.gallup.com/poll/180440/new-record-political-independents .aspx (accessed January 21, 2016).

83. Noel 2010, 12–13; Keith et al. 1992.
84. Somin 2013, 112.

CHAPTER 3

Political Participation Corrupts

1. For a moral defense of hobbits, see Brennan 2011a, chapters 1–2.
2. Mill 1975, 196–97.
3. See Tocqueville 1969, 243–44.
4. Dagger 1997, 102–4.
5. Delli Carpini and Keeter 1996, 135–77; Caplan 1997, 255–56; Birch 2009, 62; Mackerras and McAllister 1999; McAllister 1986; Selb and Lachat 2007.
6. "Philosophy Students Excel on Standardized Tests, http://www.pages.drexel.edu/~pa34/philexcel.htm (accessed January 4, 2016).
7. "IQ Estimates by College Major," Statistic Brain Research Institute, http://www.statisticbrain.com/iq-estimates-by-intended-college-major/ (accessed January 4, 2016).
8. Birch 2009, 49–51, 57–67, 140.
9. Lever 2010, 906. See also Lever 2008; Loewen, Milner, and Hicks 2008; Milner, Loewen, and Hicks 2007.
10. Landemore 2012, 97.
11. Manin, Stein, and Mansbridge 1987, 354, 363.
12. Cohen 2006, 163, 174.
13. Elster 1998, 12.
14. Gutmann and Thompson, 1996, 9.
15. Habermas 2001, 65.
16. J. Cohen 2009, 91–92. I ignore Cohen's proceduralism here, since pure proceduralism is controversial and may be seen as incompatible with the education argument.
17. Huemer 2013, 62.
18. Berggren, Jordahl, and Poutvaara 2010.
19. Mendelberg 2002, 154.
20. Ibid., 156.
21. Ibid., 158.
22. Ibid.
23. Ibid., 159.
24. Ibid., 163–64.
25. Ibid., 165–67.
26. Ibid., 170–72.
27. Ibid., 173.
28. Ibid., 176, citing Kerr, MacCoun, and Kramer 1996.
29. Mendelberg 2002, 181.

30. Ibid., 174.

31. Ibid., 168.

32. Ibid., 169.

33. Ibid., 180.

34. See, for example, Landemore 2012, 118–19; Pincock 2012.

35. Sunstein 2002.

36. Downs 1989.

37. Ellsworth 1989, 213; Cohen 1982, 210–11; Marsden 1987, 63–64.

38. Ryfe 2005, 54.

39. Ibid.

40. See Mutz 2006.

41. See Stokes 1998.

42. Hibbing and Theiss-Morse 2002.

43. See ibid., 2002.

44. Mutz 2006, 89.

45. Somin 2013, 53.

46. Feldman 2006; Elga 2007.

47. Mutz 2006, 5.

48. See, for example, Goodin 2006.

49. Mendelberg 2002, 154.

50. Mutz (2008) also complains about this.

51. Landemore 2012, 143.

52. Mendelberg 2002, 181.

53. "Fraternity Mission," Sigma Alpha Epsilon, http://www.sae.net/page.aspx?pid=753 (accessed January 4, 2016).

54. "The Creed of Sigma Nu Fraternity," Sigma Nu Fraternity, http://www.sigmanu.org/about/the_creed.php (accessed January 4, 2016).

55. "Become a Beta," Beta Theta Pi, http://beta.org/about/become-a-beta/ (accessed January 21, 2016).

56. "Our Mission," Phi Delta Theta, http://www.phideltatheta.org/about/ (accessed January 4, 2016).

57. Russell Westerholm, "Wesleyan University, 'Rape Factory' Frat House and Victim Reach Settlement in Lawsuit, *University Herald*, September 12, 2013, http://www.universityherald.com/articles/4521/20130912/wesleyan-university-rape-factory-frat-house-victim-reach-settlement-lawsuit.htm (accessed January 4, 2016); Frintner and Rubinson 1993; Koss and Gaines 1993; Humphrey and Kahn 2000.

58. Kremer and Levy 2008.

59. McCabe and Trevino 1997.

60. Alan Reifman, "How Fraternities and Sororities Impact Studies (or Do They?)," *Psychology Today*, September 1, 2011, http://www.psychologytoday.com/blog/the-campus/201109/how-fraternities-and-sororities-impact-students-or-do-they (accessed January 4, 2016).

CHAPTER 4

Politics Doesn't Empower You or Me

1. Stanton 1894, 482–83.

2. Cholbi 2002, 549.

3. Cited in Harper 1898, 801.

4. Brennan 2016.

5. For a further refutation of consent theories of political legitimacy, see Huemer 2013, 20–58; Wellman and Simmons 2005, 116–18.

6. Huemer 2013, 32–33. Huemer cites three separate recent cases in which the Supreme Court held that the government has no duties to individual citizens but only to the public at large.

7. Wellman 2005, 9.

8. Australian Electoral Commission, "Voting within Australia: Frequently Asked Questions," 2013, http://www.aec.gov.au/faqs/voting_australia.htm#not-vote (accessed January 5, 2016).

9. Birch 2009, 9.

10. Matt Zwolinski, "Medical vs. Democratic Consent," Bleeding Heart Libertarians, June 1, 2011, http://bleedingheartlibertarians.com/2011/06/medical-vs-democratic-consent/ (accessed January 5, 2016).

11. Faden and Beauchamp 1986, 235–373.

12. See, for example, Mackie 2009.

13. See, for example, Dahl 1990; Noel 2010. See also Grossback, Peterson, and Stimson 2006; Grossback, Peterson, and Stimson 2007. In fact, the US Advanced Placement Government exam sometimes asks students to answer the question, "Why are political scientists skeptical of the mandate theory of elections?"

14. Catherine Rampell, "Your Senator Is (Probably) a Millionaire," *New York Times*, November 25, 2009, http://economix.blogs.nytimes.com/2009/11/25/your-senator-is-probably-a-millionaire/?_php=true&_type=blogs&_r=0 (accessed January 5, 2016). The *Economist* claims that the average net worth of a congressperson is only $440,000; see "Politics and the Purse," *Economist*, September 19, 2013, http://www.economist.com/blogs/graphicdetail/2013/09/daily-chart-14 (accessed January 5, 2016).

15. Alfred Gottschalck, Marina Vornovytskyy, and Adam Smith, "Household Wealth in the U.S.: 2000 to 2011," https://www.census.gov/people/wealth/files/Wealth%20Highlights%202011.pdf (accessed January 5, 2016).

16. "Fredrik Reinfeldt Net Worth," Celebrity Net Worth, http://www.celebritynetworth.com/richest-politicians/presidents/fredrik-reinfeldt-net-worth/ (accessed January 5, 2016).

17. For versions of this argument, see Rousseau 1997; Gould 1988, 45–85. Carol Gould argues that democracy is necessary for the good of autonomous self-government and goes on to assert that citizens are entitled to democracy.

18. Christiano 2009, 238.

19. Christiano 2008, 65.

20. See ibid., 61–63, 101, 115, 154, passim.

21. Christiano's argument is more complicated. In a nutshell, he holds that justice requires that everyone be treated as equals and have their interests advanced equally by society. Everyone has three fundamental interests, including an interest in being at home in the world. In order for people to be sure that their interests are being advanced equally, justice must not merely be done; it must be seen as being done. And in light of the various cognitive biases, self-serving biases, and cognitive weaknesses we all have, the only way for justice to be seen as being done is if everyone is given equal political power. This is an argument for why democracy is justified, but it also contains subarguments that purport to show that political liberties are valuable to each individual. My discussion here of the social construction and status arguments makes trouble for Christiano.

22. For a sophisticated argument on behalf of this claim, see Tuck 2008, 30–98.

23. For a defense of the claim that all participants and even eligible nonparticipants are causally responsible for electoral outcomes, see Goldman 1999.

24. Christiano 2008, 61, citing Walzer 1988, 14.

25. Someone might object to this metaphor by saying that in a democracy, we the people are the ocean. Each of us is an equally efficacious water molecule. Perhaps. But waves go through this ocean, and each molecule is powerless against the waves.

26. Berlin 1998.

27. Pettit 1996, 578, 581.

28. Lovett 2014.

29. Ibid.

30. Pettit 2012.

31. One might attempt to argue that having the right to vote is, by the very definition of domination, a necessary condition for being nondominated. This seems to render domination so defined of no obvious value, however.

32. One might try to assert that a citizen is dominated if and only if they lack the vote. On this view, for a person to have a right to vote automatically means they are not dominated, regardless of what their country does to them. This seems too implausible to merit further discussion.

33. See, for example, Pettit 2012, 181. Pettit goes so far as to maintain that republican democracy is preferable to utopian anarchy, that even a society of angels who always and infallibly did the right thing would be improved if they created a republican government. I find this utterly bizarre.

34. Rawls 1996, 5–6.

35. For example, imagine that an influential economist has a mistaken view of fiscal policy. If this view were widely believed, people would vote accordingly, and this would retard economic growth. If the government were to censor the economist, this would in turn stop voters from voting for politicians who follow that economist's bad advice.

36. Freeman 2007, 470.

37. Ibid.

38. The dominant position in political science is that campaign expenditures are a consumption good, not a production good. Money tends to chase winners, not to make them. While lobbying and corruption exist, campaign finance isn't the problem; there's little evidence that campaign finance changes either who wins or what policies the winners implement. See, for example, Ansolabehere, de Figueiredo, and Snyder 2003; Stratmann 2005; Hall and Deardroff 2006; Baumgartner et al. 2009.

39. Freeman 2007, 54.

40. Ibid., 55.

41. Samuel Freeman, "Can Economic Liberties Be Basic Liberties," Bleeding Heart Libertarians, June 13, 2012, http://bleedingheartlibertarians.com/2012/06/can -economic-liberties-be-basic-liberties/ (accessed January 7, 2016).

42. Ibid.

43. Tomasi 2012.

44. See, for example, Brennan 2012b; Westen 2008; Haidt 2012.

45. Rawls 1996, 293.

46. See ibid., 315–29; Rawls 2001, 18–26.

47. I'm pretty sure I got this example from Ben Saunders.

48. For a good example of this, see Pettit 2012, 155–63. Pettit argues over many pages that even a person constrained by others might not be subjugated, provided that the constrained person controls the constraints. In the *Odyssey*, for instance, Ulysses decides he wants to hear the sirens' song. He tells his crew to bind him to the mast, put wax in their ears, and ignore any orders he gives to sail to the sirens. Though the crew ties him up and ignores his commands, Ulysses remains in control in some sense. He's not being subjugated, dominated, or controlled by his crew. Pettit contends that a democratic body can collectively exert the same kind of control over the laws. But it remains unclear how an individual who is a member of this collective can in any way be said to have control or influence. The collective controls the government that constrains the individuals, but it doesn't follow that the individuals who form the collective therefore control the government that constrains them.

49. Thanks to Rob Tempio for bringing this to my attention.

50. Phil Gregory, "Jaded View of U.S. Government Deters Many from Political Involvement, Survey Finds," *NewsWorks*, July 13, 2105, http://www.newsworks.org /index.php/local/new-jersey/83999-jaded-view-of-us-government-deters-many-from -political-involvement-survey-finds (accessed January 7, 2016).

CHAPTER 5

Politics Is Not a Poem

1. Schmidtz and Brennan 2010, 189.

2. Anderson 2009, 215.

3. Gilbert 2012, 13.

4. Griffin 2003, 120.

5. Estlund 2007, 37.

6. Nozick 1990, 286.

7. Mill 1975; Caplan 2007; Brennan 2011a.

8. See, for example, Huemer 2013, 51–80.

9. Christiano 2008, 98.

10. Ibid., 99.

11. Ibid.

12. Christiano 2004, 287.

13. Fedderson, Gailmard, and Sandroni 2009.

14. By *political judgment*, I mean here to include everything I think Christiano would include, meaning both the ability to determine what the appropriate final ends of government ought to be as well as the ability to determine what the most effective means of achieving those ends is.

15. One might hold the following view of university teaching: we professors don't really have better political judgment than our students but rather are good at making them have better judgment. Yet we professors have also taken a great number of courses from other professors who are supposedly (according to this perspective) good at making students have better judgment. Did our professors make all the other students develop better judgment, but fail to help us—the ones who became professors—have better judgment? So I don't see a way out of the view that if you're a professor of X, you should believe you have better judgment with regard to X than the average person.

16. For a theory of good representatives, see, for example, Dovi 2007.

17. Christiano 2008, 47.

18. Christiano 2001, 208; Christiano 2008.

19. See Rawls 1971, 234; Rawls 1996, 318–19; Rawls 2001, 131; Freeman 2007, 76.

20. Wall 2006, 257–58.

21. Freeman 2007, 76.

22. If it turned out these attitudes toward scarves resulted not from an arbitrary social practice but rather deep features in our evolved psychology, this argument would still stand. Our psychological tendencies would be lamentable, and scarves would be valuable only in light of these lamentable tendencies.

23. On this point, blogger Will Wilkinson has an excellent post from shortly after the 2008 US presidential election. Wilkinson says that given that we tend to think of the presidency as "the highest peak, the top of the human heap," and given our history of oppressing blacks, the fact that a black man won the presidency is momentous. At the same time, it would be better if we stopped thinking of the presidency as a majestic office and instead as the "chief executive of the national public goods administrative agency." Wilkinson continues, "I hope never to see again streets thronging with people chanting the glorious leader's name." See Will Wilkinson, "One Night of Romance," Fly Bottle, November 5, 2008, http://www.willwilkinson .net/flybottle/2008/11/05/one-night-of-romance/ (accessed January 7, 2016).

24. For further discussion of this example, see Brennan and Jaworski 2015.

25. Rawls 1971, 144.

26. Delli Carpini and Keeter 1996, 162.

27. Caplan 2007; Althaus 2003; Somin 2013; Brennan and Hill 2014.

28. Boukus, Cassil, and Ann S. O'Malley 2009.

29. Brennan and Hill 2014, 123.

30. I am not challenging the expressive theory of voting here. The expressive theory of voting is a *descriptive* theory, which claims that many citizens vote in order to express attitudes. The expressive theory holds (roughly) that citizens know that their votes won't change the outcome of an election, and so they vote to express solidarity with certain causes. One person votes Democrat to express solidarity with the poor, while another votes Republican to express concern for personal responsibility. See Brennan and Buchanan 1984; Brennan and Lomasky 2003; Brennan and Hamlin 2000.

31. Saunders 2010, 72.

CHAPTER 6

The Right to Competent Government

1. For an argument to the effect that anyone committed to universal adult suffrage must also accept youth voting, see López-Guerra 2014.

2. The right to rule thus encompasses both a permission and claim right.

3. Cf. Estlund 2007, 2.

4. Ibid., 2. In earlier political philosophy, the terms were used in sloppy or nonuniform ways. In the last ten years or so, however, it has become the convention to use the terms exactly as I define them here.

5. For examples of successful appeals, reversals, and remanding of cases, see Sullivan v. Fogg (613 F.2d 465, 2nd Cir. 1980), in which a juror was delusional; State v. Majid (2009 WL 1816946), in which a juror was sleeping; Spencer v. Georgia, in which there was a racist juror; Jackson v. United States (1968), in which a conviction was reversed and remanded because it came to light that one of the jurors had been involved in a love triangle similar to that of the defendant.

6. The relationship between a jury and defendant provides grounds for holding that jurors have something like fiduciary duties toward defendants. The analogy to fiduciary duties appears to understate jurists' obligations, though. When fiduciaries breach their principals' trust, this is normally considered an intentional tort. Principals can sue their fiduciaries for damages. Yet most fiduciary-principal relationships are contractual and voluntary.

7. As Christopher Heath Wellman and A. John Simmons (2005, 118) observe, "For many citizens there are few acceptable options to remaining in their states and obeying (most) law, and for most persons active resistance to the state is in effect impossible. And for none of us is there any option to living in some state or other,

all of which make (at least) the same core demands on us. These facts raise serious doubts about the voluntariness of any widely performed acts that might be alleged to be binding acts of political consent."

8. One might object that the right to competent government is largely unenforceable. One might claim that because the right isn't enforceable, it doesn't exist. I'm not sure that this assertion—that the right is unenforceable—is true. In chapter 8, I'll examine a few possible ways of trying to enforce this right. Even if the right were unenforceable, however, that doesn't tell us whether or not it exists. A person can possess a right to something even when they cannot effectively enforce that right. For instance, Joseph Stalin murdered millions of people with impunity. We would still say that these people had rights to life, even though they lacked effective enforcement of their rights. In a world in which, due to bad luck, no one knew how to enforce the right to life, that would not mean that people had no right to life or that it would be legitimate to kill whomever you'd like.

9. See, for example, Glennon 2014.

10. Craigie 2011.

11. Alesina, Spolaore, and Wacziarg 2005, 1504.

12. Nathanson 2000.

13. Alston, Kearl, and Vaughan 1992; Rockoff 1984; Hayek 1945.

14. Weiner 2012.

CHAPTER 7

Is Democracy Competent?

1. Brennan 2012a, 125–26; Read 1958.

2. Converse 1990, 381–82.

3. Condorcet 1976, 48–49.

4. Page and Hong 2001.

5. That being said, not all contemporary defenses of democracy are a priori. For some consequentialist defenses, see Shapiro 2003; Knight and Johnson 2011; Oppenheimer and Edwards 2012.

6. Landemore 2012, 9.

7. Ibid., 195.

8. Althaus 2003, 129; Caplan 2007. Both Althaus and Caplan correct for the influence of demographic factors.

9. Ibid.

10. David Dunning and Justin Kruger have famously shown that incompetent people are unable to identify who the most competent people are. Instead, incompetent people view themselves as competent, and when asked to select more competent people, they tend to select those who are just slightly more competent than themselves. See Ehrlinger et al. 2008; Dunning et al. 2003; Kruger and Dunning 1999, 2002.

11. Somin 1998, 431. For empirical confirmation of these claim, see Bartels 1996; Alvarez 1997.

12. Jakee and Sun 2006.

13. Althaus 2003, 40.

14. See, for example, Grofman and Feld 1988; Barry 1965; Dagger 1997, 96–97; List and Goodin 2001; Goodin 2003.

15. Estlund 1994, 131.

16. Importantly, for the jury theorem to hold, individual voters' probabilities must be statistically independent, voters must vote sincerely, and voters must vote for what they think is best. Much of the debate over whether the jury theorem applies to real democracies concerns whether these conditions actually hold.

17. So, for example, Estlund (2007, 136–58) doesn't dispute the mathematics of Condorcet's jury theorem but just denies that it tells us anything about real-life democracies. Similarly, even though it would be ideologically convenient for me if the jury theorem applied to actual democracies (because I think democracies are largely incompetent, and because I think I can prove that the average and median levels of competence among voters is < 0.5), I also think it is just a mathematical curiosity.

18. Somin 2013, 114.

19. Ibid., 114; Hong and Page 2004, 163–86.

20. Thompson 2014, 1024.

21. Landemore 2012, 3.

22. Page 2007, 7.

23. One problem with Page's work is that he tends to treat experts as nondiverse, as if they all have the same models of the world. But perhaps Page's work makes a better argument for having many diverse experts make decisions rather than for having many diverse nonexperts make decisions.

24. Page's models work best for cases where issues are easily quantified or where qualitative answers to questions can be easily separated into distinct categories. It's not as clear how they apply other kinds of issues. Note also that Page does not mean, for example, that including more people from different vocations or different races tends to lead to group wisdom. Rather, what he means is that having many people with diverse, sophisticated models of the world tends to lead to group wisdom. In addition, insofar as uneducated people tend to have simplistic, unsophisticated models of the world, their input into collective decision making tends to lead to less accuracy. Page seems to recognize this at times, but then often appears to overreach in how well his models of diversity apply to actual democratic decision making. For a quick but sharp criticism of Page on this point, see Tetlock 2007.

25. Page 2007, 212–14, 391–91; Page and Lamberson 2009.

26. Page 2007, 346–47. Page (ibid., 147) observes, "The best problem solvers tend to be similar; therefore, a collection of the best problem solvers performs little better than any one of them individually. A collection of random, but intelligent, problem

solvers tends to be diverse. This diversity allows them to be collectively better. Or to put it more provocatively, *diversity trumps ability*."

27. Page 2012.

28. Page 2007, 345.

29. Emily Alpert, "Related Story: Gun Crime Has Plunged, But Americans Think It's Up, Says Study," *Los Angeles Times*, May 7, 2013, http://articles.latimes.com/2013/may/07/nation/la-na-nn-gun-crimes-pew-report-20130507 (accessed January 11, 2016).

30. Landemore 2012, 196. This was also her response at the August 30, 2014, American Political Science Association meeting in which I pressed these complaints.

31. Ezra Klein, "The Budget Myth That Just Won't Die: Americans Still Think 28 Percent of the Budget Goes to Foreign Aid," *Washington Post*, November 7, 2013, http://www.washingtonpost.com/blogs/wonkblog/wp/2013/11/07/the-budget-myth-that-just-wont-die-americans-still-think-28-percent-of-the-budget-goes-to-foreign-aid/ (accessed January 11, 2016).

32. Jamelle Bouie, "The Gulf That Divides Us: The *Whiteness Project* Underscores Why There Is So Little Empathy between Whites and Blacks," *Slate*, October 17, 2004, http://www.slate.com/articles/news_and_politics/politics/2014/10/the_whiteness_project_whites_and_blacks_are_still_living_in_separate_worlds.html (accessed January 11, 2016).

33. Landemore 2012, 200.

34. Ibid., 203.

35. Caplan 2007, x.

36. Ibid., 85.

37. Ibid.

38. Clemens 2011.

39. For a summary of the studies on this issue, see Brennan 2012a, 150–54.

40. Tetlock 2005.

41. Landemore 2012, 205.

42. See Bryan Caplan, "Tackling Tetlock," Library of Economics and Liberty, December 26, 2005, http://econlog.econlib.org/archives/2005/12/tackling_tetloc_1.html (accessed January 11, 2016). Caplan cites Tetlock 2005. See also Caplan 2007.

43. Caplan 2007, 83.

44. Sen 1999, 178.

45. See, for example, Rosato 2003.

46. See Brennan 2015.

47. Somin 2013, 96.

48. Brennan and Hill 2014, 100.

49. Gilens 2012, 80, passim.

50. Ibid., 106–11.

51. Ibid., 241.

52. See, for example, Ansolabehere, Figueiredo, and Snyder 2003; Stratman 2005.

53. See, for example, Oppenheimer and Edwards 2012, 119–222.

CHAPTER 8

The Rule of the Knowers

1. See Kavka 1995.

2. Epistocrats might favor most of the improvements Robert Goodin (2008) suggests.

3. Christiano 2006.

4. A more radical proposal, one that I think has a better chance of working, would be to govern using information markets. See Hanson 2013.

5. Christiano 2008, 104 (emphasis added).

6. Cohen 2009; Levy 2013; Schmidtz, forthcoming; Estlund, forthcoming.

7. Brennan 2011b.

8. See ibid., 87.

9. Saunders 2010, 72.

10. López-Guerra 2014, 4.

11. Ibid., 26.

12. Ibid., 41.

13. Ibid., 41–42.

14. Wiener 2012.

15. Lopéz-Guerra 2011.

16. See, for example, Gaus 1996, 279–88; Rawls 1996, 165, 216, 233, 240, 339; Michelman 2002; Brettschneider 2007; Christiano 2008, 257–58, 278–86.

17. See, for example, Waldron 2006, 1346.

18. Estlund 2007, 262.

19. Note also that democrats tend to favor universal public education in part because they think such education is needed to make citizens prepared to participate in politics. They typically favor having citizens make decisions after reasoned public discourse and deliberation, too, rather than on spur-of-the-moment emotions. Most democrats are thus already committed to the view that some citizens have better moral and political knowledge than others. After all, some of us have received and internalized good political education, while others have not. Some of us have engaged in reasoned public discourse and deliberation, while others have not. Given their commitments to deliberation and education, democratic theorists would be hard put to argue that *all* adult citizens are already politically competent.

20. Ibid., 262, 36.

21. Ibid., 215.

22. See Ehrlinger et al. 2008; Dunning et al. 2003; Kruger and Dunning 1999, 2002.

23. Caplan (2007) claims that voters tend to vote for candidates whom they believe will promote the national common good and increase national prosperity. But voters are irrational in how they evaluate candidates by this standard. Voters have the right standards for selecting candidates, but are terrible at applying these standards.

24. Healy and Malhotra 2010.

25. Leigh 2009.

26. Todorov et al. 2005; Ballew and Todorov 2007; Lenz and Lawson 2008.

27. The process begins by randomly selecting five hundred citizens from all adult citizens. A second lottery further cuts this five hundred down to one hundred. These one hundred randomly chosen citizens would then produce a list of one hundred other citizens from the original five hundred, whom they wish to serve as potential electors. To make it onto the list of potential electors, each elector must receive sixty-six approving votes from the hundred previously selected citizens. The list of fifty potential electors would then be cut by lottery down to twenty-five electors. The twenty-five electors would then produce a list of a hundred citizens from the original five hundred, whom they wish to serve on a council that will be charged with determining a legal doctrine of political competence. Each of these hundred citizens would need to receive, say, eighteen out of twenty-five votes. Finally, the hundred selected potential council members would be randomly cut to twenty-one actual council members.

28. Feddersen, Gailmard, and Sandroni 2009.

29. For a good example of this kind of argument, see Knight and Johnson 2011. Jack Knight and James Johnson call their argument "pragmatic," and it is indeed that, but it ultimately rests on Burkean conservative ideas.

CHAPTER 9

Civic Enemies

1. For accounts of various senses in which fellow citizens could be seen as friends, see Schwarzenbach 1996; Cooper 2005.

2. Iyengar and Westwood 2015, 699.

3. Ibid., 714.

4. For experimental evidence confirming this explanation, see Waytz, Young, and Ginges 2014.

5. Sunstein 2014, citing Iyengar, Sood, and Lelkes 2012.

6. Iyengar and Westwood (2014) also test implicit associations, and find stronger negative associations with rival political parties than with different races. Of course, part of the story here is that Republicans and Democrats are more ideologically dissimilar now than they were in the 1950s. In the 1950s, Republicans and Democrats in the House and Senate had significant ideological overlap. Some Democrats were to the right of some Republicans. Now, all Republicans in Congress are to the right of all Democrats in Congress.

7. Hobbes 1994, I.xiii.8.

8. Riker 1982.

9. See, for example, Nagel 2010; Ehrlinger et al. 2008; Dunning et al. 2003; Kruger and Dunning 1999, 2002.

10. I admit it makes some difference. If Sia's music is popular, there's an increased chance I'll hear a Muzak version of it next time I shop at Target. If Pizzeria Orso were as popular as Pizza Hut, I could get good pizza almost everywhere.

11. Aaron Ross Powell and Trevor Burrus, "Politics Makes Us Worse," Libertarianism.org, September 13, 2012, http://www.libertarianism.org/publications /essays/politics-makes-us-worse (accessed January 14, 2016).

12. Schmidtz and Freiman 212, 425.

13. This modifies Huemer 2013, 9–10.

14. On this point, a colleague once remarked, "Aren't many nonpolitical institutions enforced through violence? Property rights, for instance, are ultimately enforceable through violence." That's right, but I think this also shows how certain levels of abstraction can be misleading. There's a difference of degree.

15. Brennan 2011a, 162.

16. In technical terms, she has a *de re* desire to harm others, but a *de dicto* desire to help.

17. He has a *de re* desire to impose undue risk on his patients, but a *de dicto* desire not to expose them to undue risk.

BIBLIOGRAPHY

Alesina, Albert, Enrico Spolaore, and Romain Wacziarg. 2005. "Trade, Growth, and the Size of Countries." In *The Handbook of Economic Growth, Volume 1B*, edited by Philippe Aghion and Steven Durlauf, 1499–542. Amsterdam: Elsevier.

Alston, Richard M., J. R. Kearl, and Michael B. Vaughan. 1992. "Is There a Consensus among Economists in the 1990s?" *American Economic Review* 82:203–9.

Althaus, Scott. 1998. "Information Effects in Collective Preferences." *American Political Science Review* 92:545–58.

———. 2003. *Collective Preferences in Democratic Politics*. New York: Cambridge University Press.

Alvarez, Michael. 1997. *Information and Elections*. Ann Arbor: University of Michigan Press.

Anderson, Elizabeth. 2009. "Democracy: Instrumental vs. Non-Instrumental Value." In *Contemporary Debates in Political Philosophy*, ed. Thomas Christiano and John Christman, 213–28. Malden, MA: Blackwell.

Ansolabehere, Stephen, John M. de Figueiredo, and James M. Snyder Jr. 2003. "Why Is There So Little Money in U.S. Politics?" *Journal of Economic Perspectives* 17 (1): 105–30.

Asch, Solomon E. 1952. *Social Psychology*. New York: Prentice Hall.

———. 1955. "Opinions and Social Pressure." *Scientific American* 193 (5): 31–35.

Ballew, Charles C., II, and Alexander Todorov. 2007. "Predicting Political Elections from Rapid and Unreflective Face Judgments." *Proceedings of the National Academy of Sciences* 104:17948–53.

Barry, Brian. 1965. "The Public Interest." In *Political Philosophy*, edited by A. M. Quinton, 45–65. New York: Oxford University Press.

Bartels, Larry. 1996. "Uninformed Votes: Information Effects in Presidential Elections." *American Political Science Review* 40:194–230.

Baumgartner, Barry, Jeffrey M. Berry, Marie Hojnacki, David C. Kimball, and Beth L. Leech. 2009. *Lobby and Policy Change: Who Loses, Who Wins, and Why*. Chicago: University of Chicago Press.

Berggren, Niclas, Henrik Jordahl, and Panu Poutvaara. 2010. "The Right Look: Conservative Politicians Look Better and Their Voters Reward It." Working Paper Series 855, Social Research Institute of Industrial Economics.

Berlin, Isaiah. 1998. "Two Concepts of Liberty." In *The Proper Study of Mankind: An Anthology of Essays*. New York: Farrar, Straus and Giroux.

Berns, Gregory S., Jonathan Chappelow, Caroline F. Zink, Guiseppe Pagnoni, Megan E. Martin-Skurski, and Jim Richards. 2005. "Neurobiological Correlates of Social Conformity and Independence during Mental Rotation." *Biological Psychiatry* 58:245–53.

Birch, Sarah. 2009. *Full Participation: A Comparative Study of Compulsory Voting*. Manchester, UK: Manchester University Press.

Boukus, Ellyn R., Alwyn Cassil, and Ann S. O'Malley. 2009. "A Snapshot of the U.S. Physicians: Key Findings from the 2008 Health Tracking Physician Survey." *Data Bulletin* 35. http://www.hschange.com/CONTENT/1078/ (accessed January 8, 2016).

Brennan, Geoffrey, and James Buchanan. 1984. "Voter Choice." *American Behavioral Scientist* 28:185–201.

Brennan, Geoffrey, and Alan Hamlin. 2000. *Democratic Devices and Desires*. New York: Cambridge University Press.

Brennan, Geoffrey, and Loren Lomasky. 2003. *Democracy and Decision: The Pure Theory of Electoral Preference*. New York: Cambridge University Press.

Brennan, Jason. 2011a. *The Ethics of Voting*. Princeton, NJ: Princeton University Press.

———. 2011b. "The Right to a Competent Electorate." *Philosophical Quarterly* 61:700–724.

———. 2012a. *Libertarianism: What Everyone Needs to Know*. New York: Oxford University Press.

———. 2012b. "Political Liberty: Who Needs It?" *Social Philosophy and Policy* 29:1–27.

———. 2013. "Epistocracy and Public Reason." In *Philosophical Perspectives on Democracy in the Twenty-First Century*, edited by Ann Cudd and Sally Scholz, 191–204. Berlin: Springer.

———. 2014. *Why Not Capitalism?* New York: Routledge Press.

———. 2016. "Democracy and Freedom." In *The Oxford Handbook of Freedom*, edited by David Schmidtz. New York: Oxford University Press.

Brennan, Jason, and Lisa Hill. 2014. *Compulsory Voting: For and Against*. New York: Cambridge University Press.

Brennan, Jason, and Peter Jaworski. 2015. "Markets without Symbolic Limits." *Ethics* 125:1053–77.

Brettschneider, Corey. 2007. *Democratic Rights: The Substance of Self-Government*. Princeton, NJ: Princeton University Press.

Bullock, John. 2006. "The Enduring Importance of False Political Beliefs." Paper presented at the annual meeting of the Western Political Science Association, March 17.

Caplan, Bryan. 2007. *The Myth of the Rational Voter: Why Democracies Choose Bad Policies*. Princeton, NJ: Princeton University Press.

Caplan, Bryan, Eric Crampton, Wayne A. Grove, and Ilya Somin. 2013. "Systematically Biased Beliefs about Political Influence: Evidence from the Perceptions of Political Influence on Policy Outcomes Survey." *PS: Political Science and Politics* 46:760–67.

Cholbi, Michael. 2002. "A Felon's Right to Vote." *Law and Philosophy* 21:543–65.

Chong, Dennis. 2013. "Degrees of Rationality in Politics." In *The Oxford Handbook of Political Psychology*, edited by David O. Sears and Jack S. Levy, 96–129. New York: Oxford University Press.

Christiano, Thomas. 1996. *The Rule of the Many: Fundamental Issues in Democratic Theory*. Boulder, CO: Westview Press.

———. 2001. "Knowledge and Power in the Justification of Democracy." *Australasian Journal of Philosophy* 79 (2): 197–215.

———. 2004. "The Authority of Democracy." *Journal of Political Philosophy* 12 (3): 266–90.

———. 2006. "Democracy." In *Stanford Encyclopedia of Philosophy*, edited by Edward N. Zalta. http://plato.stanford.edu/entries/democracy/ (accessed January 12, 2016).

———. 2008. *The Constitution of Equality: Democratic Authority and Its Limits*. New York: Oxford University Press.

———. 2009. "Debate: Estlund on Democratic Authority." *Journal of Political Philosophy* 17:228–40.

Citrin, Jack, and Donald Green. 1990. "The Self-Interest Motive in American Public Opinion." *Research in Micropolitics* 3:1–28.

Clemens, Michael. 2011. "Economics and Emigration: Trillion-Dollar Bills on the Sidewalk?" *Journal of Economic Perspectives* 23:83–106.

Cohen, E. G. 1982. "Expectation States and Interracial Interaction in School Settings." *Annual Review of Sociology* 8:209–35.Cohen, G. A. 2009. *Rescuing Justice and Equality*. New York: Oxford University Press.

Cohen, Geoffrey. 2003. "Party over Policy: The Dominating Impact of Group Influence on Political Beliefs." *Journal of Personality and Social Psychology* 85:808–22.

Cohen, Joshua. 2006. "Deliberation and Democratic Legitimacy." In *Contemporary Political Philosophy*, edited by Robert Goodin and Philip Pettit, 159–70. Boston: Wiley-Blackwell.

———. 2009. "Deliberation and Democratic Legitimacy." In *Democracy*, edited by David Estlund, 87–106. Malden, MA: Blackwell.

Condorcet, Marquis de. 1976. "Essay on the Application of Mathematics to the Theory of Decision-Making." In *Condorcet: Selected Writings*, edited by Keith M. Baker, 48–49. New York: Macmillan Press.

Conly, Sarah. 2012. *Against Autonomy: Justifying Coercive Paternalism*. Cambridge: Cambridge University Press.

Conover, Pamela, Stanley Feldman, and Kathleen Knight. 1987. "The Personal and Political Underpinnings of Economic Forecasts." *American Journal of Political Science* 31:559–83.

Converse, Philip E. 1964. "The Nature of Belief Systems in Mass Publics." In *Ideology and Discontent*, ed. D. E. Apter. London: Free Press of Glencoe, 1964.

———. 1990. "Popular Representation and the Distribution of Information." In *Information and Democratic Processes*, edited by John A. Ferejohn and James H. Kuklinski, 369–88. Urbana: University of Illinois Press.

Converse, Philip E., and Richard Pierce. 1986. *Political Representation in France*. Cambridge MA: Harvard University Press.

Cooper, John. 2005. "Political Animals and Civic Friendship." In *Aristotle's Politics: Critical Essays*, edited by Richard Kraut and Steven Skultety, 65–91. Boulder, CO: Rowman and Littlefield.

Craigie, Jillian. 2011. "Competence, Practical Rationality, and What a Patient Values." *Bioethics* 26:326–33.

Dahl, Birger. 1994. *Venezia, et Kulterhistorisk Eventyr*. Oslo: Tell Forlag.

Dahl, Robert A. 1989. *Democracy and Its Critics*. New Haven: Yale University Press.

———. 1990. "The Myth of the Presidential Mandate." *Political Science Quarterly* 105:355–72.

Dagger, Richard. 1997. *Civic Virtue: Rights, Citizenship, and Republican Liberalism*. New York: Oxford University Press.

Delli Carpini, Michael X., and Scott Keeter. 1991. "Stability and Change in the U.S. Public's Knowledge of Politics." *Public Opinion Quarterly* 55:583–612.

———. 1996. *What Americans Know about Politics and Why It Matters*. New Haven, CT: Yale University Press.

Dovi, Suzanne. 2007. *The Good Representative*. Malden, MA: Blackwell.

Downs, Donald Alexander. 1989. *The New Politics of Pornography*. Chicago: University of Chicago Press.

Dunning, David, Kerri Johnson, Joyce Ehrlinger, and Justin Kruger. 2003. "Why People Fail to Recognize Their Own Incompetence." *Current Directions in Psychological Science* 12:83–86.

Ehrlinger, Joyce, Kerri Johnson, Matthew Banner, David Dunning, and Justin Kruger. 2008. "Why the Unskilled Are Unaware: Further Explorations of (Absent) Self-Insight among the Incompetent." *Organizational Behavior and Human Decision Processes* 105:98–121.

Elga, Adam. 2007. "Reflection and Disagreement." *Noûs* 41:478–502.

Ellsworth, Phoebe C. 1989. "Are Twelve Heads Better Than One." *Law and Contemporary Problems* 52:205–24.

Elster, Jon. 1998. "The Market and the Forum: Three Varieties of Political Theory." In *Deliberative Democracy: Essays on Reason and Politics*, edited by James Bohman and William Rehg, 3–34. Cambridge, MA: MIT Press.

Erisen, Cengiz, Milton R. Lodge, and Charles S. Taber. 2014. "Affective Contagion in Effortful Political Thinking." *Political Psychology* 35:187–206.

Estlund, David. 1994. "Opinion Leaders, Independence, and Condorcet's Jury Theorem." *Theory and Decision* 36:131–62.

————. 2003. "Why Not Epistocracy." *Desire, Identity, and Existence: Essays in Honor of T. M. Penner*, edited by Naomi Reshotko, 53–69. New York: Academic Printing and Publishing.

————. 2007. *Democratic Authority: A Philosophical Framework*. Princeton, NJ: Princeton University Press.

————. Forthcoming. *Utopophobia*. Princeton, NJ: Princeton University Press.

Faden, Ruth, and Tom L. Beauchamp. 1986. *A History and Theory of Informed Consent*. New York: Oxford University Press.

Feddersen, Timothy, Sean Gailmard, and Alvaro Sandroni. 2009. "A Bias toward Unselfishness in Large Elections: Theory and Experimental Evidence." *American Political Science Review* 103:175–92.

Feldman, Richard. 2006. "Epistemological Puzzles about Disagreement." In *Epistemology Futures*, edited by Stephen Hetherington, 216–36. Oxford: Oxford University Press.

Freeman, Samuel. 2007. *Rawls*. New York: Routledge Press.

Friedman, Jeffrey. 2006. "Democratic Competence in Normative and Positive Theory: Neglected Implications of 'The Nature of Belief Systems in Mass Publics.'" *Critical Review* 18:i–xliii.

Frintner, Mary Pat, and Laura Rubinson. 1993. "Acquaintance Rape: The Influence of Alcohol, Fraternity Membership, and Sports Team Membership." *Journal of Sex Education and Therapy* 19:272–84.

Funk, Carolyn L. 2000. "The Dual Influence of Self-Interest and Societal Interest in Public Opinion." *Political Research Quarterly* 53:37–62.

Funk, Carolyn L., and Patricia Garcia-Monet. 1997. "The Relationship between Personal and National Concerns in Public Perceptions of the Economy." *Political Research Quarterly* 50:317–42.

Gaus, Gerald. 1996. *Justificatory Liberalism: An Essay on Epistemology and Political Theory*. New York: Oxford University Press.

Gelman, Andrew, Nate Silver, and Aaron Edlin. 2012. "What Is the Probability That Your Vote Will Make a Difference?" *Economic Inquiry* 50:321–26.

Gilbert, Pablo. 2012. Is There a Human Right to Democracy? A Response to Cohen. *Revista Latinoamericana de Filosofía Política* 1:1–37.

Gilens, Martin. 2012. *Affluence and Influence: Economic Inequality and Political Power in America*. Princeton, NJ: Princeton University Press.

Glennon, Michael. 2014. *National Security and Double Government*. New York: Oxford University Press.

Goldman, Alvin. 1999. "Why Citizens Should Vote: A Causal Responsibility Approach." *Social Philosophy and Policy* 16:201–17.

González-Ricoy, Iñigo. 2012. "Depoliticising the Polls: Voting Abstention and Moral Disagreement." *Politics* 32:46–51.

Goodin, Robert E. 2003. *Reflective Democracy*. New York: Oxford University Press.

Goodin, Robert E. 2006. "Talking Politics: Perils and Promise." *European Journal of Political Research* 45:235–61.

———. 2008. *Innovating Democracy: Democratic Theory and Practice After the Deliberative Turn*. New York: Oxford University Press.

Gould, Carol. 1988. *Rethinking Democracy: Freedom and Social Cooperation in Politics, Economics, and Society*. New York: Cambridge University Press.

Green, Donald, and Ian Shapiro. 1994. *Pathologies of Rational Choice Theory: A Critique of Applications in Political Science*. New Haven, CT: Yale University Press.

Griffin, Christopher. 2003. "Democracy as a Non-Instrumentally Just Procedure." *Journal of Political Philosophy* 11:111–21.

Grofman, Bernard, and Scott Feld. 1988. "Rousseau's General Will: A Condorcetian Perspective." *American Political Science Review* 82:567–76.

Grossback, Lawrence J., David A. M. Peterson, and James A. Stimson. 2006. *Mandate Politics*. New York: Cambridge University Press.

———. 2007. "Electoral Mandates in American Politics." *British Journal of Political Science* 37:711–30.

Guerrero, Alexander R. 2010. "The Paradox of Voting and the Ethics of Political Representation." *Philosophy and Public Affairs* 38:272–306.

Gutmann, Amy, and Dennis Thompson. 1996. *Democracy and Disagreement*. Cambridge: Cambridge University Press.

Habermas, Jürgen. 2001. *Moral Consciousness and Communicative Action*. Cambridge, MA: MIT Press.

Haidt, Jonathan. 2012. *The Righteous Mind: Why Good People Are Divided by Politics and Religion*. New York: Pantheon.

Hall, Robert, and Allen Deardroff. 2006. "Lobbying as Legislature Subsidy." *American Political Science Review* 100:69–84.

Hanson, Robin. 2013. "Should We Vote on Values, But Bet on Beliefs? *Journal of Political Philosophy* 21:151–78.

Hardin, Russell. 2009. *How Do You Know? The Economics of Ordinary Knowledge*. Princeton, NJ: Princeton University Press.

Harper, Ida Husted. 1898. *The Life and Work of Susan B. Anthony*. Vol. 2. New York: Bowen-Merrill Company.

Hayek, Friedrich A. 1945. "The Use of Knowledge in Society." *American Economic Review* 35:519–30.

Healy, Andrew, and Neil Malholtra. 2010. "Random Events, Economic Losses, and Retrospective Voting: Implications for Democratic Competence." *Quarterly Journal of Political Science* 5:193–208.

Hibbing, John R., and Elizabeth Theiss-Morse. 2002. *Stealth Democracy: Americans' Beliefs about How Government Should Work*. Cambridge: Cambridge University Press.

Hobbes, Thomas. 1994. *Leviathan*. Edited by Edwin Curly. Indianapolis: Hackett.

Holbrook, Thomas, and James C. Garand. 1996. "Homo Economus? Economic Information and Economic Voting." *Political Research Quarterly* 49 (2): 351–75.

Hong, Lu, and Scott Page. 2004. "Groups of Diverse Problem Solvers Can Out-perform Groups of High-Ability Problem Solvers," *Proceedings of the National Academy of Sciences* 101 (46): 16385–89.

Huddy, Leonie, Jeffrey Jones, and Richard Chard. 2001. "Compassion vs. Self-Interest: Support for Old-Age Programs among the Non-Elderly." *Political Psychology* 22:443–72.

Huddy, Leonie, David Sears, and Jack S. Levy. 2013. Introduction to *The Oxford Handbook of Political Psychology, 2nd Edition*, edited by Leonie Huddy, David Sears, and Jack S. Levy, 1–21. New York: Oxford University Press.

Huemer, Michael. 2013. *The Problem of Political Authority: An Examination of the Right to Coerce and the Duty to Obey.* New York: Palgrave MacMillan.

Humphrey, Stephen E., and Arnold S. Kahn. 2000. "Fraternities, Athletic Teams, and Rape: Importance of Identification with a Risky Group." *Journal of Interpersonal Violence* 15:1313–22.

Iyengar, Shanto, Guarav Sood, and Yphtach Lelkes. 2012. "Affect, Not Ideology: A Social Identity Perspective on Polarization." *Public Opinion Quarterly*, doi: 10.1093/poq/nfs038.

Iyengar, Shanto, and Sean J. Westwood. 2015. "Fear and Loathing across Party Lines: New Evidence on Group Polarization." *American Journal of Political Science* 59 (3): 690–707.

Jakee, Keith, and Guang-Zhen Sun. 2006. "Is Compulsory Voting More Democratic?" *Public Choice* 129:61–75.

Jennings, M. Kent. 1992. "Ideological Thinking among Mass Publics and Political Elites. *Public Opinion Quarterly* 56 (4): 419–41.

Kahan, Dan, Ellen Peters, Erica Cantrell Dawson, and Paul Slovic. 2013. "Motivated Numeracy and Enlightened Self-Government." Unpublished manuscript, Yale Law School, Public Working Paper No. 307, http://papers.ssrn.com/sol3/papers.cfm?abstract_id=2319992 (accessed January 2, 2016).

Kahneman, Daniel. 2003. "Maps of Bounded Rationality: Psychology for Behavioral Economics." *American Economic Review* 93:1449–75.

Kavka, Gregory. 1995. "Why Even Morally Perfect People Would Need Government." *Social Philosophy and Policy* 12:1–18.

Keith, Bruce E., David B. Magleby, Candice J. Nelson, Elizabeth Orr, Mark C. Westlye, and Raymond E. Wolfinger. 1992. *The Myth of the Independent Voter.* Berkeley: University of California Press.

Kelly, James Terence. 2012. *Framing Democracy: A Behavioral Approach to Democratic Theory.* Princeton, NJ: Princeton University Press.

Kennings, M. Kent. 1992. "Ideological Thinking among Mass Publics and Political Elites," *Public Opinion Quarterly* 56: 419–51.

Kerr, Norbett, Robert MacCoun, and Geoffrey Kramer. 1996. "Bias in Judgment: Comparing Individuals and Groups." *Psychological Review* 103:687–719.

Kinder, Donald. 2006. "Belief Systems Today." *Critical Review* 18:197–216.

Kinder, Donald, and Roderick Kiewiet. 1979. "Economic Discontent and Political Behavior: The Role of Personal Grievances and Collective Economic Judgments in Congressional Voting." *American Journal of Political Science* 23:495–527.

Knight, Jack, and James Johnson. 2011. *The Priority of Democracy: Political Consequences of Pragmatism*. Princeton, NJ: Princeton University Press.

Koss, Mary P., and John A. Gaines. 1993. "The Prediction of Sexual Aggression by Alcohol Use, Athletic Participation, and Fraternity Affiliation." *Journal of Interpersonal Violence* 8:94–108.

Krause, Sharon. 2013. *Civil Passion: Moral Sentiment and Democratic Deliberation*. Princeton, NJ: Princeton University Press.

Kremer, Michael, and Dan Levy. 2008. "Peer Effects and Alcohol Use among College Students." *Journal of Economic Perspectives* 22:189–206.

Kruger, Justin, and David Dunning. 1999. "Unskilled and Unaware of It: How Difficulties in Recognizing One's Own Incompetence Lead to Inflated Self-Assessments." *Journal of Personality and Social Psychology* 77:1121–34.

———. 2002. "Unskilled and Unaware—But Why? A Reply to Krueger and Mueller." *Journal of Personality and Social Psychology* 82:189–92.

Krugman, Paul, and Wells, Robin. 2009. *Economics*. New York: Worth Publishers.

Landemore, Hélène. 2012. *Democratic Reason: Politics, Collective Intelligence, and the Rule of the Many*. Princeton, NJ: Princeton University Press.

Landsburg, Steven E. 2004. "Don't Vote: It Makes More Sense to Play the Lottery." *Slate*. http://www.slate.com/id/2107240/ (accessed January 1, 2016).

Leigh, Andrew. 2009. "Does the World Economy Swing National Elections?" *Oxford Bulletin of Economics and Statistics* 71:163–81.

Lenz, Gabriel, and Chappell Lawson. 2008. "Looking the Part: Television Leads Less Informed Citizens to Vote Based on Candidates' Appearance." Unpublished manuscript, Department of Political Science, Massachusetts Institute of Technology, Cambridge, MA.

Lever, Annabelle. 2008. "'A Liberal Defense of Compulsory Voting': Some Reasons for Skepticism." *Politics* 28:61–64.

———. 2010. "Compulsory Voting: A Critical Perspective." *British Journal of Political Science* 40:897–915.

Levy, Jacob. 2013. "There Is No Such Thing as Ideal Theory." Paper presented at the Association for Political Theory, October 13, Vanderbilt University, Nashville, TN.

List, Christian, and Robert Goodin. 2001. "Epistemic Democracy: Generalizing the Condorcet Jury Theorem." *Journal of Political Philosophy* 9:277–306.

Lodge, Milton R., and Charles S. Taber. 2013. *The Rationalizing Voter*. New York: Cambridge University Press.

Loewen, Peter John, Henry Milner, and Bruce M. Hicks. 2008. "Does Compulsory Voting Lead to More Informed and Engaged Citizens? An Experimental Test." *Canadian Journal of Political Science* 41:655–67.

Lopéz-Guerra, Claudio. 2011. "The Enfranchisement Lottery." *Politics, Philosophy, and Economics* 10:211–33.

———. 2014. *Democracy and Disenfranchisement: The Morality of Election Exclusions.* New York: Oxford University Press.

Lord, Charles, Lee Ross, and Mark R. Lepper. 1979. "Biased Assimilation and Attitude Polarization: The Effects of Prior Theories on Subsequently Considered Evidence." *Journal of Personality and Social Psychology* 37:2098–109.

Lovett, Frank. 2014. "Republicanism." *Stanford Encyclopedia of Philosophy.* Edited by Edward N. Zalta. http://plato.stanford.edu/entries/republicanism/ (accessed January 6, 2016).

Mackerras, Malcolm, and Ian McAllister. 1999. "Compulsory Voting, Party Stability, and Electoral Advantage in Australia." *Electoral Studies* 18:217–33.

Mackie, Gerry. 2009. "Why It's Rational to Vote." Unpublished manuscript, University of California at San Diego.

Manin, Bernard, Elly Stein, and Jane Mansbridge. 1987. "On Legitimacy and Political Deliberation." *Political Theory* 15:333–68.

Mansbridge, Jane. 1993. "Self-Interest and Political Transformation." In *Reconsidering the Democratic Public*, edited by George E. Marcus and Russell L. Hanson, 91–109. University Park: Pennsylvania State University Press.

Markus, Gregory. 1988. "The Impact of Personal and National Economic Conditions on the Presidential Vote: A Pooled Cross-Sectional Analysis." *American Journal of Political Science* 32:137–54.

Marsden, Nancy. 1987. "Note: Gender Dynamics and Jury Deliberations." *Yale Law Journal* 96:593–612.

McAllister, Ian. 1986. "Compulsory Voting, Turnout, and Party Advantage in Australia." *Politics* 21:89–93.

McCabe, Donald, and Linda Trevino. 1997. "Individual and Contextual Influences on Academic Dishonesty: A Multicampus Investigation." *Research in Higher Education* 38:379–96.

Mendelberg, Tali. 2002. "The Deliberative Citizen: Theory and Evidence." In *Research in Micropolitics, Volume 6: Political Decision Making, Deliberation, and Participation*, edited by Michael X. Delli Carpini, Leonie Huddy, and Robert Y. Shapiro, 151–93. Amsterdam: Elsevier.

Michelman, Frank I. 2002. "Rawls on Constitutionalism and Constitutional Law." In *The Cambridge Companion to Rawls*, edited by Samuel Freeman, 394–95. New York: Cambridge University Press.

Mill, John Stuart. 1975. *Three Essays: "On Liberty," "Representative Government," and "The Subjection of Women."* Edited by Richard Wollheim. New York: Oxford University Press.

Miller, Dale. 1999. "The Norm of Self-Interest." *American Psychologist* 54:1053–60.

Milner, Henry, Peter John Loewen, and Bruce M. Hicks. 2007. "The Paradox of Compulsory Voting: Participation Does Not Equal Political Knowledge." *IRPP Policy Matters* 8:1–48.

Mueller, John, and Mark G. Stewart. 2011. *Terror, Security, and Money: Balancing the Risks, Benefits, and Costs of Homeland Security.* New York: Oxford University Press.

Murray, Charles. 2012. *Coming Apart: The State of White America, 1960–2010*. New York: Crown Forum.

Mutz, Diana. 1992. "Mass Media and the Depoliticization of Personal Experience." *American Journal of Political Science* 36:483–508.

———. 1993. "Direct and Indirect Routes to Politicizing Personal Experience: Does Knowledge Make a Difference?" *Public Opinion Quarterly* 57:483–502.

———. 2006. *Hearing the Other Side: Deliberative versus Participatory Democracy*. Cambridge: Cambridge University Press.

———. 2008. "Is Deliberative Democracy a Falsifiable Theory?" *Annual Review of Political Science* 11:521–38.

Mutz, Diana, and Jeffrey Mondak. 1997. "Dimensions of Sociotropic Behavior: Group-Based Judgments of Fairness and Well-Being." *American Journal of Political Science* 41:284–308.

Nagel, Mato. 2010. "A Mathematical Model of Democratic Elections." *Current Research Journal of Social Sciences* 2 (4): 255–61.

Nathanson, Stephen. 2000. "Should We Execute Those Who Deserve to Die?" In *Philosophy of Law, Sixth Edition*, edited by Joel Feinberg and Jules L. Coleman, 841–50. Belmont, CA: Wadsworth.

Neuman, W. Russell. 1986. *The Paradox of Mass Politics: Knowledge and Opinion in the American Electorate*. Cambridge, MA: Harvard University Press.

Noel, Hans. 2010. "Ten Things Political Scientists Know That You Don't." *Forum* 8:1–19.

Nozick, Robert. 1990. *The Examined Life: Philosophical Meditations*. New York: Simon and Schuster.

Nyhan, Brendan, and Jason Reifler. 2010. "When Corrections Fail: The Persistence of Public Misperceptions." *Political Behavior* 32:303–30.

Oppenheimer, Danny, and Mike Edwards. 2012. *Democracy Despite Itself: Why a System That Shouldn't Work at All Works So Well*. Cambridge, MA: MIT Press.

Page, Benjamin I., and Robert Y. Shapiro. 1992. *The Rational Public: Fifty Years of Trends in Americans' Policy Preferences*. Chicago: University of Chicago Press.

Page, Scott. 2007. *The Difference: How the Power of Diversity Creates Better Groups, Firms, Schools, and Societies*. Princeton, NJ: Princeton University Press.

———. 2012. "Microfoundations of Collective Wisdom." Lecture delivered at Collège de France, Paris. http://www.canal-u.tv/video/college_de_france/micro foundations_of_collective_wisdom.4046 (accessed January 11, 2016).

Page, Scott, and Lu Hong. 2001. "Problem Solving by Heterogeneous Agents." *Journal of Economic Theory* 97:123–63.

Page, Scott, and P. J. Lamberson. 2009. "Increasing Returns, Lock-Ins, and Early Mover Advantage." Unpublished manuscript, University of Michigan at Ann Arbor.

Palfrey, Thomas, and Keith Poole. 1987. "The Relationship between Information, Ideology, and Voting Behavior." *American Journal of Political Science* 31:510–30.

Pettit, Philip. 1996. "Freedom as Antipower." *Ethics* 106 (3): 576–604.

———. 2012. *On the People's Terms: A Republican Theory and Model of Democracy.* New York: Cambridge University Press.

Pincock, Heather. 2012. "Does Deliberation Make Better Citizens." In *Democracy in Motion: Evaluating the Practice and Impact of Deliberative Civic Engagement,* edited by Tina Nabatchi, John Gastil, G. Michael Weiksner, and Matthew Leighninger, 135–62. New York: Oxford University Press.

Ponza, Michael, Greg Duncan, Mary Corcoran, and Fred Groskind. 1988. "The Guns of Autumn? Age Differences in Support for Income Transfers to the Young and Old." *Public Opinion Quarterly* 52:441–66.

Rawls, John. 1971. *A Theory of Justice.* Cambridge, MA: Harvard University Press.

———. 1996. *Political Liberalism.* New York: Columbia University Press.

———. 2001. *Justice as Fairness: A Restatement.* Cambridge, MA: Harvard University Press.

Read, Leonard E. 1958. "I Pencil." *Freeman,* May 1. http://fee.org/the_freeman/detail /i-pencil (accessed January 11, 2016).

Rhodebeck, Laurie. 1993. "The Politics of Greed? Political Preferences among the Elderly." *Journal of Politics* 55:342–64.

Riker, William H. 1982. "The Two-Party System and Duverger's Law: An Essay on the History of Political Science." *American Political Science Review* 76:753–66.

Rockoff, Hugh. 1984. *Drastic Measures: A History of Wage and Price Controls in the United States.* New York: Cambridge University Press.

Rosato, Sebastian. 2003. "The Flawed Logic of the Democratic Peace Theory." *American Political Science Review* 97:585–603.

Rousseau, Jean-Jacques. 1997. *The Social Contract and Other Later Political Writings.* Edited by Victor Gourevitch. New York: Cambridge University Press.

Ryfe, David. 2005. "Does Deliberative Democracy Work?" *Annual Review of Political Science* 8:49–71.

Saunders, Ben. 2010. "Increasing Turnout: A Compelling Case?" *Politics* 30:70–77.

Schmidtz, David. Forthcoming. "Idealism as Solipsism." In *Oxford Handbook of Distributive Justice,* edited by Serena Olsaretti. New York: Oxford University Press.

Schmidtz, David, and Jason Brennan. 2010. *A Brief History of Liberty.* Oxford: Wiley-Blackwell.

Schmidtz, David, and Christopher Freiman. 2012. "Nozick." *Oxford Handbook of Political Philosophy,* edited by David Estlund, 411–28. New York: Oxford University Press.

Schumpeter, Joseph. 1996. *Capitalism, Socialism, and Democracy.* New York: Routledge Press.

Schwarzenbach, Sibyl A. 1996. "On Civic Friendship." *Ethics* 107:97–128.

Sears, David O., and Carolyn L. Funk. 1990. "Self-Interest in Americans' Political Opinions." In *Beyond Self-Interest,* edited by Jane Mansbridge, 147–70. Chicago: University of Chicago Press.

Sears, David, Carl Hensler, and Leslie Speer. 1979. "Whites' Opposition to 'Busing': Self-Interest or Symbolic Politics?" *American Political Science Review* 73:369–84.

Sears, David, and Richard Lau. 1983. "Inducing Apparently Self-Interested Political Preferences." *American Journal of Political Science* 27:223–52.

Sears, David, Richard Lau, Tom Tyler, and Harris Allen. 1980. "Self-Interest vs. Symbolic Politics in Policy Attitudes and Presidential Voting." *American Political Science Review* 74:670–84.

Selb, Peter, and Romain Lachat. 2007. "The More the Better: Counterfactual Evidence on the Effect of Compulsory Voting on the Consistency of Party Choice." Paper presented at the European Consortium for Political Research's Joint Sessions of Workshops, Helsinki, May 11.

Sen, Amartya. 1999. *Development as Freedom*. Norwell, MA: Anchor Press.

Shapiro, Ian. 2003. *The State of Democratic Theory*. Princeton, NJ: Princeton University Press.

Somin, Ilya. 1998. "Voter Ignorance and the Democratic Ideal." *Critical Review* 12:413–58.

———. 2004. "When Ignorance Isn't Bliss: How Political Ignorance Threatens Democracy." *Policy Analysis*, September 22. http://www.cato.org/publications /policy-analysis/when-ignorance-isnt-bliss-how-political-ignorance-threatens -democracy (accessed December 31, 2015).

———. 2013. *Democracy and Political Ignorance*. Stanford, CA: Stanford University Press.

Stanton, Elizabeth Cady. 1894. "Ethics of Suffrage." In *The World's Congress of Representative Women, Volume 2*, edited by May Wright Sewall, 482–87. New York: Rand, McNally, and Company.

Stokes, Susan C. 1988. "Pathologies of Deliberation." In *Deliberative Democracy*, edited by John Elster, 123–39. New York: Cambridge University Press.

Stratmann, Thomas. 2005. "Some Talk: Money in Politics. A (Partial) Review of the Literature." In *Policy Challenges and Political Responses*, edited by William F. Shughart II and Robert D. Tollison, 135–56. Berlin: Springer.

Sunstein, Cass R. 2002. "The Law of Group Polarization." *Journal of Political Philosophy* 10:175–95.

———. 2014. "'Partyism' Now Trumps Racism." *Bloomberg View*, September 22. http://www.bloombergview.com/articles/2014-09-22/partyism-now-trumps -racism (accessed January 21, 2016).

Taber, Charles S., and Milton R. Lodge. 2006. "Motivated Skepticism in the Evaluation of Political Beliefs." *American Journal of Political Science* 50:755–69.

Taber, Charles S., and Everett Young. 2013. "Political Information Processing." In *The Oxford Handbook of Political Psychology, 2nd Edition*, edited by Leonie Huddy, David Sears, and Jack S. Levy, 525–58. New York: Oxford University Press.

Tajfel, Henry. 1981. *Human Groups and Social Categories: Studies in Social Psychology*. New York: Cambridge University Press.

———. 1982. "Social Psychology of Intergroup Relations." *Annual Review of Psychology* 33:1–39.

Tajfel, Henry, and John Turner. 1979. "An Integrative Theory of Intergroup Conflict." In *The Social Psychology of Intergroup Relations*, edited by William G. Austin and Stephen Worchel, 33–47. Monterey, CA: Brooks-Cole.

Tetlock, Philip E. 2005. *Expert Political Judgment: How Good Is It? How Can We Know?* Princeton, NJ: Princeton University Press.

———. 2007. "Diversity Paradoxes." *Science* 316:984.

Thompson, Abigail. 2014. "Does Diversity Trump Ability? An Example of the Misuse of Mathematics in the Social Sciences." *Notices of the American Mathematical Society* 61:1024–30.

Tocqueville, Alexis de. 1969. *Democracy in America*. New York: Anchor Books.

Todorov, Alexander, Anesu N. Mandisodza, Amir Goren, and Crystal C. Hall. 2005. "Inferences of Competence from Faces Predict Election Outcomes." *Science* 308:1623–26.

Tomasi, John. 2012. *Free Market Fairness*. Princeton, NJ: Princeton University Press.

Tuck, Richard. 2008. *Free Riding*. Cambridge, MA: Harvard University Press.

Tversky, Andrew, and Daniel Kahneman. 1973. "Availability: A Heuristic for Judging Frequency and Probability." *Cognitive Psychology* 5:207–33.

Waldron, Jeremy. 2006. "The Core of the Case against Judicial Review." *Yale Law Journal* 115:1346–406.

Wall, Stephen. 2006. "Rawls and the Status of Political Liberty." *Pacific Philosophical Quarterly* 87:245–70.

Walzer, Michael. 1988. "Interpretation and Social Criticism." In *Tanner Lectures on Human Values, VIII*. Salt Lake City: University of Utah Press.

Waytz, Adam, Liane L. Young, and Jeremy Ginges. 2014. "Motive Attribution Asymmetry for Love vs. Hate Drives Intractable Conflict." *Proceedings of the National Academy of Sciences*, November 4, doi: 10.1073/pnas.1414146111.

Weiner, Greg. 2012. *Madison's Metronome: The Constitution, Majority Rule, and the Tempo of American Politics*. Lawrence: University Press of Kansas.

Wellman, Christopher Heath. 2005. *A Theory of Secession*. New York: Cambridge University Press.

Wellman, Christopher Heath, and A. John Simmons. 2005. *Is There a Duty to Obey the Law? For and Against*. New York: Cambridge University Press.

Westen, Drew. 2008. *The Political Brain: The Role of Emotion in Deciding the Fate of the Nation*. New York: Perseus Books.

Westen, Drew, Pavel S. Blagov, Keith Harenski, Clint Kilts, and Stephan Hamann. 2006. "The Neural Basis of Motivated Reasoning: An fMRI Study of Emotional Constraints on Political Judgment during the U.S. Presidential Election of 2004. *Journal of Cognitive Neuroscience* 18:1947–58.

Zaller, John. 1992. *The Nature and Origins of Mass Opinion*. New York: Cambridge University Press.

INDEX